SPECTROPOLIS

Spectropolis

THE ENCHANTMENT OF CAPITAL IN SINGAPORE

Joshua Comaroff

University of Minnesota Press

Minneapolis

London

The University of Minnesota Press gratefully acknowledges the generous assistance provided for the publication of this book by the National University of Singapore.

Published by the University of Minnesota Press
111 Third Avenue South, Suite 290
Minneapolis, MN 55401-2520
http://www.upress.umn.edu

▰ Available as a Manifold edition at manifold.umn.edu

ISBN 978-1-5179-1933-7 (hc)
ISBN 978-1-5179-1934-4 (pb)
ISBN 978-1-4529-7372-2 (Manifold)

A Cataloging-in-Publication record for this book is available
from the Library of Congress.

Printed in the United States of America on acid-free paper

The University of Minnesota is an equal-opportunity educator and employer.

Contents

Preface

Why should specters haunt Singapore's model of hyperrational, high-tech capital?

For much of the world, this tiny island represents the future. Or, perhaps, one of two: Slavoj Žižek has claimed that the world now faces a bleak choice between Western neoliberalism and a "Chinese-Singaporean capitalism" with Confucian values.[1] Once ridiculed as a pariah state, as "Asia lite" and "Disneyland with the death penalty," the so-called Lion City has now come to embody a vision of the forefront of governance and economy.[2] It is a global center of financial operations, at once technologically sophisticated and volatile, set within a bureaucratic regime designed to manage social and personal risk. An image as the "Switzerland of Asia," as a secretive haven amid the wealthy ASEAN region, complements its role as enabler of highly abstract, sometimes freewheeling commercial dealings. This is in no way hyperbolic. Singapore overtook Switzerland as the world's largest offshore wealth hub at the end of 2020. Its rise has been bolstered by an expanding market in stocks and derivatives, investment banking, and monetary products. The SGX exchange is the most internationalized of all worldwide floors, with approximately 40 percent of listed companies originating outside the country.[3] The city is a hub for currency markets and, with aggressive government support, is rapidly growing its share of an emerging reinsurance trade that covers the exposure of property assurers to disasters and climate change. The increasing reach of such markets and services has progressed to the point that one now sees entirely unironic references to the City of London as "Singapore-on-Thames."[4] The nation's offerings overwhelmingly invoke the ur-rational, futuristic, and secular frontier of administration and economy.

This is reflected in the skyline itself, which is continually recreated through the speculative processes that it houses. Its restless self-making has fueled one of the world's most profitable development sectors and propelled the island's limited land to astronomical prices.[5] The premium standard of its towers, malls, and offices contributed, in no small part, to the top spot on *The Economist*'s "world's most expensive cities" list from 2002 to 2019.[6] These have an unmistakable air of luxury, but also of the systematic and the technical. It is an architecture of silicone—of screens, large-paned glazing, and glossy spandrels seated in well-tempered tropical nature. Images circulate, in global media, of spectacular engineering in the pursuit of environmental control: indoor rainforests, waterfalls, and linear parks spanning between skyscrapers. Such monumental works have required great physical inputs. To accommodate a larger population of workers and shoppers, Singapore has doubled its preindependence coastline through land reclamation and replicated its surface area via high-rise construction. It has swallowed other islands, subsuming their sand and gravel alongside flows of stone, glass, metal, and other matter.[7] This undertaking has established the city as a center within Asian networks of materials and labor and as an exporter of strategies in economy and urban planning.

This futuristic metropolis is also increasingly cited as a paradigm of secure urbanism. Liberalized trade coexists alongside a notably illiberal microadministration of space and biological life. Citizens navigate circumscribed political and civil liberties, their agency largely exercised in spheres of economy, consumption, and family life. Cleanliness and safety are reinforced through what geographer Victor Savage has called "absolute planning," whereby "practically every tree and dustbin is in a designated public place, a product of overall design and conscious policy making."[8]

Security, here, hybridizes social and physical discipline with operational know-how. As former Foreign Minister Brigadier-General George Yeo has claimed, Singapore has "developed the most efficient logistical system in the world, for the movement of goods, people, and information."[9] He noted the "talent" of his countrymen for spatial choreography, seen in the stellar success of the city's container ports as a laboratory for the micromanagement of the nation more generally. Technologies like Electronic Road Pricing and the In-vehicle Unit, a dashboard-mounted device that dispenses road fees and identifies the owner of an automobile, allow for optimized and surveilled traffic. A network of cameras and screens reports drive times, waiting periods, parking spaces, and emergencies, should they arise. During the Covid-19 pandemic, the TraceTogether app tracked the location and vaccination status of citizens on their mobile phones as they moved in and out of protected urban perimeters. To borrow a phrase from Ian Hacking—one to which we will return—the state would appear to seek the "taming of chance," despite an increasing commitment to speculative capitalism in its manifold guises.[10]

This Singapore model would appear to pose an effective alternative to the anxieties of the democratic: an inventive, paternalistic authoritarianism. An unlikely marriage of fiat and free market, its urbanscape serves as a monument to all that is pragmatic and hyperrational in contemporary capital.

And yet, Singaporeans also—pace Max Weber—report spectral encounters, visit graveyards to divine lottery numbers, and offer food and money and proxy commodities to ancestors. Such activity reaches a peak during the lunar seventh month, the Zhong Yuan or Hungry Ghost Festival, when the Otherworld is said to open its gates and temporarily allow spirits to return to the city.[11] Chinese opera and pop performances, auctions, and feasts are held to placate spirits that may feel angry or unrequited and cause mischief or misadventure. Throughout the year, public discourse and social media relate tales of supernatural events at office blocks and civic buildings, train stations and roads, condominiums and public housing. The island's machinic Hilberseimer facades belie a world of unexpected compromises with often-unruly revenants.

There are reasons for these apparently unlikely preoccupations. As we will see, ghosts are not incidental to the Singapore model of economy; rather, they are integral to its emergent practices, spaces, and imaginings. Why this should be the case, why spectral rites and anxieties should exist amid the ostensibly "disenchanting" vectors of global finance, is the subject of this book.

I did not set out to write about ghosts. What follows is the result of a haunting. In 2005, I was three years into a (now-twenty-year) career designing buildings and landscapes in Singapore when my work on a residential tower was abruptly halted. This was a speculative development by a government-linked corporation. On the site stood a colonial "black-and-white" bungalow in the process of being dismantled. One room, empty but for a few old personal items and a photo of a young Eurasian woman, appeared to refuse demolition.[12] Bulldozer drivers were stricken with an odd malady like the effects of radiation sickness.[13] The events resulted in a standstill, with the contractors refusing to continue and a Taoist spirit medium being called in.

This may seem eerie, and unusual. But here such cases are common. They occur with regularity in the building sector and on government projects especially—to the extent that ceremonies to placate resident spirits are performed as a matter of routine. Moreover, many large state organizations, including the Singapore Police Force and the National Museum of Singapore, have "ghost-busting" teams on retainer to act quickly in case of uncanny happenings at their buildings.

It should not be a surprise, then, that similar incidents occurred during subsequent architectural projects also. These became the starting point for doctoral research in urban geography at the University of California, Los Angeles under Denis Cosgrove, John Agnew, J. Nicholas Entrikin, and Andrew Apter. Through expanding networks of association, over a slow process of more than a decade, I continued to collect ghost stories (firsthand and received) from friends, acquaintances, and a host of tertiary connections. In a profound sense, participant observation was inevitable—not something "out there" but a central aspect in the life of a tight-knit community, of which I remain an intimate. My embedded position as in-law to a family of Singaporean Chinese property developers meant that I was party to seemingly endless stories about ghostly incidents, haunted real estate, and the good or ill fortune resulting from these. As a result, I have benefited immeasurably from being halfway assimilated—and thus a rather spectral or uncanny presence myself. As I have argued elsewhere, ghosts and migrants in Southeast Asia share a known intimacy.[14]

While I pursued the subject with the traditional methods of the qualitative urban social scientist, fieldwork was increasingly an activity interpellated into professional routines and relations. I continued to practice concurrently as a designer, and colleagues and contractors approached me with other stories, feeding what was becoming a well-known fascination. At the same time, occasional incidents at construction sites provided a perfect ethnographic opening, because (as we will see in chapter 6) architects frequently become embroiled in ritual attempts to mollify hostile ghosts. A second tranche of research unfolded in a topological manner, beginning from alleged sites of spectral trouble, their specific histories and material conditions. Interviews branched outward, initially, through the organizational tissue of the building industry and its spiritual consultants: from workers to foremen to management; from architects and landscape designers to technical consultants to development staff and "C-suite" executives; from amateur practitioners of ancestral rites to priests, spirit mediums, and temple administrators. Later, as the project moved more deeply into matters of economy, the focus of engagement shifted to entrepreneurs, investors, fund managers, and merchants, to eventually encompass virtually all modes of employment, class positions, and faiths.[15]

This felt less like a cartographic process than a sounding of the depths, a slow and piecemeal charting of returning voices and signals. The spectral image that results—what has come to be *Spectropolis*—appears very little like the map that it was intended to be. It is more like a city seen at night through humid air: a vascular field that scintillates with the passage of sociable energies, essences, and interactions. This nocturnal view of Singapore's famously sun-drenched modernity reveals unexpected entanglements, historical debts, and traffic: the outlines of a "second city" that I began to sense nearly two decades ago.[16] At the very least, I hope that *Spectropolis* will offer a new glimpse of this model of aspirational futurity as alive with old spirits, coursing among the new.

Introduction

This book explores the haunted character of Singapore's speculative economy. It attempts to understand the central role of ghosts within the nation's emergent cultural logics, urban spaces, and ecologies— and their relevance, more broadly, to the experience of what has come to be known as "late" capital.

In this story, the spectral plays a number of conjoined roles.

First, the powers and proclivities of the nonliving are commonly called on to decipher the outcome of speculative processes and the occult character of risk. Cosmological assumptions of so-called Chinese religion—a syncretic accommodation of Taoism, Buddhism, Confucian philosophy, and evolving popular tradition—provide an ostensible set of natural laws to make sense of a moment in which Singaporeans are increasingly exposed to forms of "casino" capital, where speculation is the dominant mode of value-production.[1] Ghosts provide a form of popular theorization that speaks to epochal anxieties and a new regime of "crazy" money characterized by a problematic materiality, by absent presences and unseen determinations. This lends itself to explanations about who gets rich, and why.

Second, these discourses animate a world of practice: a trade in lucrative reciprocities between living and dead. Ghosts, in Singapore, are not merely agents of traumatic recollection. They are also imagined to be economic agents and partners. The condition of the Chinese afterlife is one of inherent scarcity and lack, with ever-present dangers of "hunger" and of wasting away. Ghostliness is a mode of personhood propelled by wants and needs that mirror our own and that can be satisfied only by offerings from the human world: rites and remembrances, food and prayer, paper money and commodities. Spirits, be they ancestors or ghosts or deities, are presumed to possess the power to influence matters of chance. Individuals who court their gratitude—gamblers and market punters, businesspeople, investors, and fund managers—hope to affect the outcomes of everything from national lotteries to real estate developments. This gives rise to a lucrative secondary market, channeling millions of Singapore dollars and producing tangible wealth effects.

Although this is a site of calculation, it is not a cynical one. Viewed through the lens of a phantasmic populist finance capitalism, rooted in Chinese religious and environmental ontologies, the present order contains the potentials of an immanent "market paradise," albeit one rife with hazards. Minor players can leverage flows of money, moving within numinous circuits, to realize personal prosperity and collective well-being. Spirits, both ghostly and ancestral, enable popular access to the nation's sophisticated aeries of trade. Their influence reverses economic relationships of force, means and ends, to posit a radical democratization in which "small" money can exert an irrationally powerful influence via metaphysical know-how—to wag the dog, in effect. Such a discourse sees in both cash and commodity a wildly productive and sociable magic, not just a force of abstraction. What is built upon this alternative understanding, in real terms, is a speculative shadow trade of considerable volume that is inextricable from the nation's formal businesses.

Participation in rites and spirit care, as we will see, is not simply understood as a technology to get rich. Profit, here, comes with (and is discursively inseparable from) broader notions of enhanced life, expressed in Singaporeans' talk of "luck," "prosperity," and "health." Spectro-economics imagines occult manipulations of value as a lever to influence every aspect of the human condition and to seize full ownership of the self. Via the correct ritual procedure, any unit of money can be placed into circuits of exchange that reshape fortunes to an extraordinary degree. Likewise, the humble urban flat—if its builders or owners observe ghostly etiquette—can serve as a vehicle both for profit and for limitless personal improvement that includes fertility, academic achievement, and abundant friendship. Commerce is frankly articulated as a *medium of being* in a total, qualitative sense. This is both individual and social; in the connective warp and woof of a pragmatic holism, individuals and their friends or families may benefit by association. There is an imagined benevolence, for example, in the extractive and physical violence of the construction site that claims to conjoin the fate of local property magnates to that of migrant laborers (see chapter 6). Here the concept of value is elevated to truly divine proportions. Its "proper" use, in popular accounts, serves to resolve the contradiction at the heart of the commodity, reconciling use and exchange in visions of wealth and wellness.

Third, spectral discourses are intensively caught up with questions of urban spaces, of their crucial role in value-production and civic order. Singapore's economic system, as a carefully calibrated speculative superstructure, makes explicit use of the physical city as a primary instrument. The pursuit of foreign and domestic investment has involved a sweeping reconstruction of the island's architectures and landscapes, removing informal settlements and forests and old graves to make room for modernized housing and a financialized "property state."[2] This has subjected their physical substances, processes, and long-standing sociospatial networks to unprecedented transformative violence. At the same time, such heroic travails are required for developmentalist governance, which pursues a necessarily paradoxical strategy: allowing volatility ever further into collective life, while attempting to minimize risk (broadly defined) via a securitization of the island's lived fabric.

This upheaval must be read against understandings of geomancy and ghost ecology inherent to Chinese religion: a view of the city as a congelation of flow spaces in which human disturbance (including construction, investment, and devaluation) can attract, repel, and trap spirits and wealth amid congruences of energetic currents. In the accounts of believers, ghosts have quite literally been *produced* as unintended by-products of the nation's economic ascendancy. In turn, they are thought to prey on both commercial *and* government development projects in ways that cause delay and necessitate offerings and negotiations by mediums, priests, and others. We will see how their alleged mischief, and the practices of ritual appeasement, introduce short circuits and localized breaches into what Singapore's prime minister has called "a nation by design": a spatial system of metonymic distributions, functional cells, and zones of exception, all of which work to promote investment, pacify the workforce, and reap the lucrative gains of risk without hazard.[3] The disruptive field of ghosts, the presumptive locations and motives of their visitations, must be understood as an inverted topology—as the nation's triumphalist tales and manicured districts, read from their nocturnal undersides.

But this, too, is understood to create opportunity. In the examples that follow, varied forms of traffic interact within the city's disturbed parcels. These act as nodes of attraction and pulsion, synergy and conflict, synchronous and asynchronous agencies and events, streams and reservoirs of materials and media and energies and forms, modes of life and nonlife. Spectropolitan readings of the urbanscape—performed by mediums, geomancers, and practitioners of Chinese religion—draw on established spiritual-ecological principles. This is an art and a science that allows for diagnoses of material and energetic conditions of specific plots. These also suggest entrepreneurial openings, in which proper rites and protocol addressed to the putative concerns of resident spirits court their favors (monetary and other).

It is important to make clear, at the outset, that this book is not intended as an ethnography of Chinese popular religion in Singapore, or its metaphysics. There already exists a growing interdisciplinary literature concerning death, ancestral practices, and the afterlife here. Tong Chee Kiong, Terrence Heng, Kit Ying Lye, Janice Kam, Jack Meng-Tat Chia, and others have produced expert work that addresses these subjects.[4] Nor do I offer a definitive or encyclopedic study of Singapore's ghosts. The latter would broadly exceed the present work and would need to reflect the old and ever-evolving interplay of supernatural and religious discourses among the nation's Chinese, Indians, Malays, and Eurasians, alongside its migrants and variously "blended" communities.[5] It would also necessarily engage with regional spirit culture and *hantu*.[6] As discussed later, there exists no purely "Chinese" imaginary in this diasporic context—all ghosts are, in the postcolony, intercultural beings.

Nor is the subject of what follows, qua hauntology, the spectral *for itself*. Rather, I am concerned with imaginative interventions into the life of capital. The ghosts in this work are a subpopulation that are understood to be partners in trade, entailed in matters of finance, and are imagined within a common cosmological and geomantic frame. As such, they provide an opening to another series of questions. By what means does a people at the ur-rational frontier of modern economy, so famously beholden to abstraction and fetishism, find room to reimagine their conditions? How might they construct an idea of agency within the "capitalist real"—one that imagines commodity, currency, and investment as magical means to manipulate and reconceptualize the terms of their pecuniary and political powers?[7] And we may ask, not least, how is this accomplished within the strictures of illiberal laws and spaces? This is a study of how the spectral is deployed to produce a holist, ecological, quasi-utopian "true world" (in Nietzsche's problematical sense) that is imagined not in the future—that central preoccupation of both neoliberal states and radical movements—but in an eternal, capitalist present. Ghosts, too, have their "end of history" to proclaim. This would appear to permanentize the regnant economic order, while at the same time imagining it fundamentally altered. Just as this "speaks back" to established theorizations of the social role of "specters" and "phantoms," it likewise has consequences for an array of unsettled matters, from revolutionary theory to questions of desire and the notorious reality principle.[8]

Spectropolis argues that Singapore and its ghosts are of consequence, then, for several areas of academic concern. They are relevant, certainly, for the unfinished theorization of late capital—or for several definitions thereof, as considered in the next section. I will entertain questions of how the spectral helps us come to terms with the ineffable character of risk and the changing basis by which value is "produced"—both in the cultural imagination and via forms of speculative operation. I will consider, also, how spirits connect to questions of transformation and praxis. The fundamentally optimistic, if sometimes gothic, phantasmagorias of Chinese religion also provide a non-Western instance of controversial "accelerationist" models often rejected by more traditional Marxists and the progressive left.[9] The stakes here extend beyond this particular approach to illiberal development and city making to broader questions of the life and futures of our present mode of production. In short, I argue, popular supernaturalisms help to theorize capital's strange new forms, where Marxism and other analytical frameworks have proven to be less insightful—for reasons that will soon become clear.

At the same time, this context brings to bear a different, expanded conception of the ghost for the field of spectral studies: a possibly broader vision of its social role and imaginative potentials. Certainly it continues in its august functions: dysregulating time and space, reminding of traumatic pasts and lost futures, and personifying the generational sin of dead labor.[10] But in the Singaporean collective mind, this figure breaks the narrow bounds of a Western melancholic construct—no matter how rich or troublesome. The spectral here extends to an inclusive subjectivity: economic and ecological actor, stochastic meddler, political bête noire, folder of Cartesian space. Taken seriously, its liveliness might inform new territories in the cultural life of the nonliving.

Last, I believe that what follows holds lessons for ethnographic models in which human and "other," diversely defined, touch: the living and the departed, but also othered species, materials, energies, and configurations of relationality (what might be called "society," in the broadest sense). This book directly concerns the fraught ontologies and epistemologies of intraspecies relationships and of environmental studies pursued beyond the frameworks of "science." Its second half, in particular, explores how Singaporeans imagine ghosts and money via a crypto-ecology, a matrix of interdependencies among seemingly incommensurate entities. These are not merely relational but fundamentally *social* in nature. As I hope will become clear, the evocative and explanatory power of phantasmagoric holism lies precisely in its refusal to abandon questions of contact and influence amid the creep of abstraction—just as its logic appears to reject unweighted or "flat" cybernetic models of the world.

Amid such unsettled questions, *Spectropolis* argues that the projected personhood of the homeless, entrepreneurial soul may serve, in Marx's sense, as a cipher: a guide not merely to the conditions of Singapore but to the faint outlines of a common planetary condition as well. It articulates a future that we all seem to be promised.

CITY OF RISK AND SECURITY

We must consider then, by way of introduction, this planetary condition. To do so, we should ask what is meant, here, by *late capitalism* or *late capital*? These terms are not intended in the rather Weberian manner originally deployed by the Frankfurt School theorists, under the influence of Friedrich Pollock and Henryk Grossman. Despite Singapore's muscular and assertive state, this is not meant to denote the rise of an "administered" society, an authoritarian phase of bureaucratization, or even a subtle Foucauldian penetration of power grids into the recesses of the subject.

For the purposes of what follows, late capital is understood to be a complex accommodation among modes of private enterprise, in which industry has come to stand alongside other powerfully "productive" spheres: finance, insurance, media, real estate, and tech. The prior history of this dynamic process is well-known: the rise of stocks and securities, the invention of money markets, the integration of global trading floors in 1986, wage repression, and the rise of a "shadow banking system" in the decade after 1980 stand among other watershed events in an ongoing ascendancy.[11] Herein I retain key elements of Fredric Jameson's characterization, which operates less like a finite list than as a collection of contributing factors and associated phenomena: globalization of production chains, linked markets and financial infrastructures, computation and automation, and real-time communication and logistics.[12]

Equally central for our story are questions of how value is *understood* to be produced. As David Harvey has argued, varied strains of capital now coexist. These are often in competition and disagree over motives, money, and methods, as was seen in bruited tensions between "business" and London's City over Brexit.[13] Spectral discourses respond to conditions in which the speculative mode, of finance and assumption of risk, *appears* dominant, at least to the extent to which the public mind cannot avoid the notion that this is how value is created. And, moreover, the notion that one is increasingly vulnerable to volatility produced elsewhere—via banking crises, national economic strategy, or other "macro" factors.

In Singapore, most new millionaires and billionaires are now understood to emerge through foresight and canny entrepreneurship. There are notably productive and quaintly neotraditional examples: massage chair sellers and spring roll millionaires.[14] Among the routes to "crazy rich" fortunes, these stand alongside property development, insurance, digital assets, market activity and timely trades, retail, drop shipping, and other "grinds" that exploit marginal differences in online valuation. These are, despite their differences, viewed by respondents predominantly through the lens of speculation, not industry. Some enterprises succeed, while others fail; even "real" goods, after all, are subject to uncertain futures at market. It is well-known, moreover, that physical assets are financialized: fed into a superstructure that feigns their conversion to variable, abstract values.[15]

Hence, though the average Singaporean's income is still earned as hours of work, this fact would appear to carry increasingly little weight at the level of belief and anxiety. Like elsewhere, for example, the retirement savings of today are invested predominantly in market-linked funds. The value of one's nest egg thus hangs upon the mood of the market, at the mercy of wagers by large national and corporate actors. One accumulates hours paid at a socially determined average, but when it comes time to realize this value one is back at the betting table. In this context, a typical approach combines mandatory savings (under the Central Provident Fund or CPF scheme), linked to the success of a national investment program, with the growth in market resale prices of subsidized flats.[16]

It is beyond the scope of this study to weigh in on transcendent cultural effects of late capitalism, as with postmodernism in Jameson or time-space contraction and the various "fixes" described by Harvey or Edward Soja.[17] Likewise, I won't wade into debates with Marxists who argue that financial markets do not actually produce value.[18] What is more important, here, is that we—the global we—*believe* that speculation operates increasingly as the mysterious crucible of value; that we exist in societies where those who get rich are the ones who successfully, and heroically, "stake"; and that we see our futures as increasingly "in the cards," despite the nature of our labors.

This is absolutely the case in Singapore, for reasons given later. But such precarity, I would argue, is the case in much of both North *and* South. In fact, it lies at the epicenter of late capital itself, whereby profit and value increasingly emerge from—and are quantitatively determined by—degrees of risk. Economists such as Allison Schrager have shown how this has become the primary, indeed almost exclusive, basis of the calculus of modern value.[19] The more vulnerability one assumes, the greater is the reward. By association, the yield on an investment diminishes as it gets safer. This is not merely a pricing mechanism; there is a growing literature that seeks to comprehend the far-reaching consequences of this for both macro- and micro-economies.[20] In public commentary, we see the renewal of criticisms (now centuries old) that characterize the financial world simply as gambling by another name. In the legal and institutional realms, the boundaries that would separate speculation from "gaming" continue to be redrawn in a restless history documented by Ann Fabian, Jonathan Levy, Stuart Banner, and others.[21]

In this context, the notion of "managed risk" is a chimera that promises all the rewards of taking a chance, with limited exposure to its hazards.[22] The operation of capital now hinges increasingly on courting dangers—necessary for value-production—while simultaneously attempting to diminish or mitigate them. One can always find someone to assume the potential downside of a given venture, at a price. This is securitization *stricto sensu* and in principle can be applied to any situation. It is possible to "short" future prices of stocks or commodities, insure or swap debt obligations, or defend against mortgage foreclosures (as happened prior to the 2007–8 financial crisis). The volume of such securities, derived from underlying products, now vastly exceeds the value of manufactured goods and services in the world economy.[23]

From here originates the unsettling enigma of finance. The logic of speculative markets requires risk. For these to operate, all players must assume it, or pay to pass it to others. It is clearly impossible to gamble on a phenomenon with a known outcome. At the same time, players put enormous ingenuity and effort into limiting their relative exposure. This is the case with diversification—spreading "positions" among a common market—or with hedges that offset bets against investments with noncorrelated vulnerabilities.[24] This underlies, also, the continual appeal of algorithms or complex mathematical systems that attempt to outsmart the market in one way or another. These invariably fail, as most famously happened with Ryan Kavanaugh's Monte Carlo model for foolproofing Hollywood productions against box-office flops.[25] Today, there is always a proprietary Excel spreadsheet, based on quasi-occult mathematical formulas, that purports to tame chance for its users (and not for all the others). Clearly no speculative system can tolerate zero risk. This is why systems that *do* beat the odds, like card counting or insider trading, are forbidden: determinism threatens death to the game itself. This same is true for Singaporeans who seek lotto numbers or stock tips from ghosts: they seek not an end to gambling but a magical "edge" that will diminish their own exposure.

This first contradiction gives rise to a second: as Strange observed,[26] securitization overwhelmingly appears to produce more risk and invite further security. The rise of options and second-order products, intended to offset the dangers of their underlying stocks and commodities, have introduced more volatility. Such devices are subject to increased internal complexity and a growing remove from any productive basis.[27] While primary valuations—such as stock prices—often seem unmoored from the logic of productive conditions, derivatives behave yet more loosely.[28] As one Singaporean day trader put it,

> options are pure gambling. Typically, the number of people betting on options outnumbers the buyers of the underlying stock, and this makes for crazy changes in value at crazy speeds. The value of a stock may drop 3 percent on the exchange, but a derivative based on that stock may drop 25 percent. This kind of trading is not really about the underlying business, but more about volatility itself.[29]

Famously, Warren Buffet has warned against the effect of these in fueling volatility, saying that "derivatives are financial weapons of mass destruction."[30] The essence of Strange's famous argument was that such volatility can be shown to ramify even more extensively across our economic systems. This was the same point made by former Bank of England director Mervyn King with respect to nations as "lenders of last resort."[31] As seen in the wake of the 2007–8 meltdowns, such expectations work to incentivize bigger and more reckless bets as losses are socialized—which seems inevitable, as the wagers themselves become catastrophically greater in magnitude.

A similar contradiction is also evident in practices beyond the markets. This was the case, for example, in attempts by Singapore's Ministry of National Development to secure market dominance in petrochemical facilities at its satellite Jurong Island, which now handles up to a quarter of ExxonMobil's global chemical capacity. Billions were invested in infrastructure, which has undeniably cemented the island as a key partner for major players. At the same time, it has produced increased exposure to industry-wide shocks, as in the collapse of oil prices in 2020. Ironically, state attempts to assure stability have chained the overall economy to the inherent uncertainties of specific sectors.[32] In a similar manner, the price of guaranteed participation in contemporary forms of value-production in other fields, such as finance, has been liberalization—of monetary policy, import and export restrictions, and foreign access to local markets—that produces vulnerability to capital migrations. Here, too, the higher the stakes are, the bigger is the exposure, and thus more obvious becomes the need for coverage. And this greater security would then appear to beg for greater risks to be taken in the name of "opportunity cost."

Singapore operates as a heightened example of this fraught condition—not as an exception to, but rather as an unusually advanced instance of, a global pathology. The city-state pursues the formula of speculative economy full bore, with intensity and ingenuity and without Euro-American ambivalence about the role of the state. Moreover, it embraces many key tenets of neoliberal thought, despite their apparent contradiction with statist illiberalism.[33] As such, it represents not a marginal case but an extreme, through which global tendencies can be read with unusual clarity. Among these tendencies, two are particularly notable: the embrace by the ruling People's Action Party (PAP) of speculative value-production and its insistence on the securitization of space.

The history of Singapore's development is important here. As shown by Gavin Peebles and Peter Wilson, and by Linda Low, the city-state's strategy has been built in large part upon the aggressive growth of the so-called FIRE industries: finance, insurance, and real estate.[34] This has involved chiefly the positioning of the nation's banks and investment houses as the financial center of a broader, vastly popu-lous, and resource-rich Southeast Asia: a place where the dirty and bruising extractive industries of the region can be processed.[35] Here receipts from trades like palm oil are converted into abstract invest-ments, into financial "products" and gilt-edged condominium units. The decades from the mid-1980s, in particular, marked a full-scale embrace of both free-market ideology and the concoctions of invest-ment houses, funds, currency traders, and other financial operators. A fore-tremor of this came with the spectacular case of Nick Leeson, the expat "rogue trader" who lost nearly a billion pounds for Barings Bank in the city in 1995. The full exposure of Singapore's government and people became clear in the 1997 Asian financial crisis, which dev-astated the fortunes of a public grown fond of betting on market shares and related investments. This led to a raft of protective controls—but not to a diminished commitment to the sector, which has since ex-ploded in size and diversity.

The dedication of the PAP to new, primarily financial and service-oriented trade has much to do with the timing of its transition away from light manufacturing—itself an acknowledgment of the domi-nance of China as the "world's factory." This coincided with the global emergence of new industries: IT, biotechnology, digital media, and the expanding universe of speculative property development and sales. All were pursued by national development groups, such as the Jurong Town Corporation, as possible replacements for a transient produc-tive sector.[36] Against theories of economic "take-off" popular during its independence moment, Singapore was haunted first and foremost by a sense of limited potentials, hindered by a paucity of space, citizens, and natural resources. There was no basis for a conventional industrial economy, as founding father Lee Kuan Yew was fond of reminding. Manufacturing and assembly could be, at best, a temporary stepping-stone toward reliance on more immaterial sources of revenue.

And of no small consequence to what follows, Singapore has in-creasingly bet on literal casino economics. In 2010, Marina Bay Sands was constructed on reclaimed land near the city's central business district (CBD). This was reported to be the most expensive casino property investment in the world, a joint partnership with Las Vegas Sands amounting to 8 billion Singapore dollars (S$ or SGD). At the same time, Malaysia's Genting Group built Resorts World Sentosa at the popular vacation island on Singapore's southern coast.[37] In April 2019, it was announced that the existing Marina Bay and Sentosa island "Integrated Resorts" (IRs)—the term itself is a careful avoidance of the word *casino*—would be extended to the tune of S$9 billion dollars. As Lee Kah-Wee has shown in his *Las Vegas in Singapore*, the rise of the IRs drew attention to the ambivalent view of the PAP toward gambling.[38] Singaporeans and permanent residents are allowed to visit only by paying a hefty entrance fee of S$150 per day, and the casinos themselves are buried within labyrinthine malls containing retail shops and restaurants. Ironically, the construction of these was hampered by the global financial crisis, itself a result of betting on collateralized debt obligations largely pushed by investment banks and funds. Upon completion, however, these enterprises have proven to be as staggeringly lucrative as one might expect of a gaming hub in Southeast Asia. Revenue for each of the two locations is reported to exceed S$2 billion per year.

Such transactions proceed amid a model of development that exposes citizens to varied, calculated risks. This exposure is manifested in all walks of life. Certainly it is at the heart of the nation's public housing under the Housing Development Board (HDB). This sacrament of political theology—which positions homeownership as the basis of participation in the Singaporean project—itself serves as a mode of quasi-speculative capital accumulation.[39] Young couples can purchase newly constructed flats under the "Build-to-Order" (BTO) scheme. Owing to the managed growth of the national economy and the inflationary effect of land scarcity, these rarely lose value. No aspiring bourgeois would miss the chance to purchase a unit that is sure to be valued above the offering price when resold on the open market.[40] Most rush at the opportunity, which is awarded by lottery. A BTO is a game of chance as well as a subsidized investment—putting it rather far from conventional notions of public housing anywhere else in the modern world.[41] Its sale allows movement up the property ladder. The government thus spurs participation in a white-hot housing market, allowing the use of funds from the mandatory CPF savings scheme. HDBs can be purchased using money that is otherwise limited to few investment options. Hence the general market remains flush. This can drive worrying inflationary tendencies. Ironically, the authorities often step in with stringent "cooling measures" to limit participation in the speculative frenzy that they have at least partly created. New laws have extended the mandatory ownership period before a flat can be "flipped" or have added sales duties. These policies may be prudent but are nonetheless met with displeasure by a citizenry often overly leveraged in property. This is a particularly sore point for many older adults, who invested to the detriment of their retirement annuities.[42]

In reality, Singaporeans are participating de facto in modes of sanctioned risk all the time. The selfsame CPF fund is portrayed as a safe and staid "nest egg" and has limited lending options precisely to reduce exposure to risk, or literal gambling. Hence the ambivalence that shadows the nation's casino projects, which generate vast sums and support large workforces. As noted, ministers have attempted to walk a tightrope here—expanding the presence of gaming while protecting Singaporeans from their own desire to play stakes. At the same time, CPF deposits produce sovereign wealth that is deployed in all manner of diversified speculation, without the knowledge of its contributors. Some of these positions have performed poorly in the bubbles of the "oughties."

This does not come without anxiety. The government has shown concern about citizens' exposure to the probabilistic enterprises that have made it rich. Although private investments are not regulated, the state has attempted to offset personal risk with heavy restrictions on CPF. There is clearly concern that a financial system built upon probability—as opposed to production—will eventually extend intolerable levels of volatility to the working public. The PAP's managers have sought to inhibit destabilizing factors arising from an open economy, via monetary policy fixed almost exclusively on stabilizing the exchange rate of the Singapore dollar against currency trading. Such policies are shored up by a vast and penetrating regime to ward off social disorder and other potential ills associated with Western-style free markets and democracies. This involves the design of environment, and of social life, at the micro level. Here lies the central contradiction of Singapore today: a paradoxical desire to balance risk with certainty, and probability with determinism. Having mostly given up on industry, its leadership has allied itself with chance while promulgating a nanny-state political culture that would seek to curtail destabilizing events before they arise.

In fact, the power of the Singapore model stems not merely from its wealth or logistical prowess but also from an explicit engagement with late capital *as a problem of danger and security*. The state has attempted, through a variety of means, to control risk. It has done so, first, by obliging citizens to participate in the emerging economy and to privately absorb shocks and crises through assisted personal savings. These could be used to access quality housing programs, workfare and retraining initiatives, and subsidized health care. Second, it has disciplined all behaviors seen as excessively "chancy" or destabilizing, such as addictions or gambling. Third, it has narrowed the domain of human agency to civil life. Implicit in the nation's formula is the presumption that social order helps to defray the volatility of economy. No less, it helps to maintain a flow of foreign direct investment in good times and in bad—and in the latter, through a conspicuous performance of a well-behaved polity in a tidy city.

In this way, the city's efficacy emerges from a hard-nosed rejection of the association—common in Anglo-America—between free markets and Western-style democracy. Lee protested vociferously against the idea that liberalization of markets promotes or demands a liberal society. Instead, the PAP's architects argued that the enabling of business required precisely the opposite: cooperation with an attentive, competent state. They worked to strong-arm the nascent trade unionist movement and demonstratively crushed the Singapore Airlines pilot strike, among other collective actions. At the same time, colonial-era emergency laws that curtailed speech and assembly were left intact and remain in effect today. Lee's contrarian rejection of Western models—and, with them, the positive value attributed to an open society and democracy—embodied a belief that freedom to engage in value-production could be disassociated from other kinds of public agency or civil protection. He bet (correctly, as it turns out) that most Singaporeans would be content to pursue wealth independently of political participation and that a risk-minimizing society was optimal for the pursuit of finance—and likewise, that international capital prefers places that are maximally secure.

It might be argued that the West is edging toward Lee's position.[43] A quiet march of illiberal securitization appears to be under way in those nation-states where speculation represents a large share of the economy. Beyond the clear contemporary tendency toward illiberalism and antidemocratic movements within the present economic modality, cities that have increasingly opened themselves to speculative processes appear to invest in the largest amount of surveillance and policing and in narrow restrictions of allowable behavior.[44] U.K. public order provisions, like the Criminal Justice and Public Order Act and the Serious Organised Crime and Police Act, have effectively limited rights to protest in public spaces through the legal fiction of "aggravated trespass."[45] At the same time, large cities like London have seen an unfettered proliferation of surveillance and defense technologies. Something very similar is happening—in perhaps an even more corporate modality—in the United States, where the privatization of public spaces has opened the door to a raft of new prohibitions, occurring alongside an occlusion of civil liberties and an expansion of executive powers. Much of the world *does* appear to be Singaporeanizing.

There is something inherent in the anxieties of this emergent economic mode that would bias a shift toward the authoritarian. Populism, where it joins an embrace of unfettered financialization, moves ever more in this direction. It is entirely reasonable to suggest that Singaporean statecraft anticipated a central tendency of late capital itself and responded via the medium of urban governance and environment. This remains an unsettled business—securitization merely sets the stage for newer and more creative sources of insecurity.

HAUNTOLOGY'S EXPANDED FIELD

To interrogate this insecurity, I draw on theorizations of the "spectral" as constellations of concepts and associations: absent presences, disrupted and paradoxical temporalities and spatial constructs, alternative and projected subjectivities, revisitations and recollections. It should be noted, from the outset, that words like *specter* and *phantom* are not often used in Singapore, just as they are gradually disappearing from nonacademic usage in other English-speaking contexts. Here people most commonly speak in English of the "ghost" or the Mandarin *gui.*

The Chinese-Singaporean ghost, as a variety of spirit, is a complexly projected social being, a species of *homo economicus,* and a spatial operator. Its imaginary, I believe, suggests new territories that expand on existing characterizations of spectrality within the theorizations of the 1990s' so-called spectral turn. In particular, these speak in interesting ways to the insights of Jacques Derrida's seminal *Specters of Marx* (1993). Preoccupations of this Southeast Asian context—regarding the dead, their spirits and ghosts, and the relation of these to phantasmal economies—echo many central strains and suggestive tangents of Derrida's analysis. Certainly the imaginary of Singapore's "local" specters—as historical and contemporary, nonmelancholic, *social* beings—elaborates in several respects on Derrida's and Marx's characterizations.

The first of these is an attention to space. Derrida, famously, proposes a vocabulary for the time and motion of the ghost: antecedence, generationality, fatherhood, and the repetition of exits, entrances, and reentrances.[46] The haunting, as absent presence—as an appearance of a bodiless incorporation—puts time "out of joint." It sets history, like a door, "off its hinges." Shakespeare's phrase is both spatial and temporal: a dis-placement of past and present, and of proper sequence. With the return of the exiled father-king, old crimes are restaged, and recursion dysregulates the contemporary. This necessitates a lexicon of portals, passages, and connective potentialities, folds and divergences, superpositions and juxtapositions. Derrida's approach insists on the inextricable dualism of chronology–location: the specter, as agent of "*différance,*" creates slippages as well as delays. At first, the specter is exiled within the grave and beyond the ramparts of state. Then, without notice, it is proximate: in the body and the walls, the halls of power, and Hamlet's Denmark.[47] It "spooks" with the evocative force of exteriority, before—in the very gesture that underlies the uncanny—appearing without first traversing the threshold of distance or duration.

It would be unproductive to dismiss such language as merely metaphorical. Just as Derrida's theorization conjoins space and time, it likewise refuses to divorce conceptual categories from "real" geography. For example, the "heterodidactic" complex of inside/outside alternately refers to life and death, to presence and absence, and later (via *The Communist Manifesto*) to Europe and its Others. This opposition thus structures categories of things and phenomena, as well as states of being, in terms of their abstract location in the collective mind. It also describes a relation among specific sites within an international order. I do not share Martin Jay's concern that this confuses "the metaphoric and the real, the symbolic and the literal."[48] Derrida argues, and Singapore will attest, that blurring such differences is the essence of ghostly power. In fact, the elisions of such a "hauntological" orientation would seem eminently logical to Taoists—who believe that worldly and otherworldly places, with their materials and energies, are causally linked to (and by) words and images.

These are spatial clues that, in spectral studies, have largely gone without detailed consideration. The reasons for this are unclear. It is perhaps due to a Western preoccupation with the temporality of recall and repetition and with the ghost's communicative function. Or it may arise from a psychoanalytic preoccupation with tragic recollection (see later). This chronotrope appears inescapable once the ghost is understood primarily as the messenger of past event and collective memory. And to be fair, recurrence is central not only to the oft-referenced writings of Freud but to contemporary clinical literature as well.[49] Regardless, when the ghost is assumed to be an agent of repressed history, the spatial imperatives of Derrida's theorization seem destined to fade into the background.

Other authors have taken notice, however. Achille Mbembe and Ruthmarie Mitsch, for example, deploy ghostliness to explore migratory circuits of laborers and refugees.[50] The netherworld of these devalued and necrotized humans is understood as another intimate "outside," a global slipstream that at once underpins, and is exiled from, the ostensibly safe spaces of a liberal order. This "nocturnal" conduit is further elaborated in Mbembe's *Necropolitics* as both proximate and marginalized—whereby death increasingly forms both a site of production and a political limit-condition.[51] This argument channels the critical spirit of Frantz Fanon, who situated the ghost in the anxious Manicheanism of the colony, a schizophrenic condition held together by a quotidian brutality.[52] For Arjun Appadurai, it is the emergent megacity that is the locus of spectrality. As in Singapore, real estate provides for Mumbai a discursive channel that relates physical properties and phantasmal exchange-values.[53] It is interesting that many such suggestive attempts at spatialization emerge from "southern" authors and subjects. These attempt to find a proper place for the spectral within analytical frames of society and politics.[54] A similar focus on the "lived" discourse of the ghost, amid Singapore's Western-Asian culture, likewise aligns what follows with ethnographic studies by Aihwa Ong, Erik Mueggler, Joseph Bosco, Julie Chu, Tine Gammeltoft, and Kenneth Dean, among others.[55]

In a sense, such an approach signals the timely recurrence of older ethnological literature on death, spirits, and religion. The "revenant" here may be Émile Durkheim, whose own treatment of ghosts and spirits was heavily topological—and, like Derrida's, spoke of space in a register that was at once conceptual and literal. In many of the world's religions, he noted, the departed are "separated and live in a world apart." This delineation, which echoes observations by Victor Turner of Ndembu cosmology, operates as but one form, among many, of locational distinction among sacred and profane.[56] In what follows, however, I attempt to illustrate how the peripatetic movements and materializations of the Singaporean ghost inhabit not merely a settled order in the social imagination but also an anticartography of the portalized and the un-hinged—of apertures and of disruptive byways that resist Cartesian demarcations and smack of deconstructive affinities.

Such is the case, for example, with the burning of offerings at urban sites (chapter 5), intended to draw ghosts to the flames and to "feed" and enrich them. This popular practice temporarily converts unremarkable spaces into sacred ones. Smoke and flame are thought to create a point of interchange between human and spectral worlds and to render this site visible within the crepuscular and confused perceptual domain of ghost-life. At the same time, the nonliving possess an independent ability to dis-locate and transport themselves instantaneously among noncontiguous loci: among urban locales, across cosmological planes, and into the hearts of securitized sites and protected areas. Discourses of trespass and transgression are animated by a metaphysics that casts space itself as an energetic medium that structures and regulates spectral activity. This medium is defined not by metric quantities such as distance but rather via qualitative properties and transmissions. Places are defined by a fluid logic of currents and pools, in which manifold forms of qi—as well as modes of value—come to be located and conducted. These share a fundamental substance with a spectrum of beings ranging from hungry ghosts to ancestral spirits to wealthy and powerful gods.

Here, too, the disruptive is connective. While disjoining the intended order of Singaporean state space, ghosts link points that were disconnected by design. They reconfigure "metonymic" state space, making unexpected circuits that defy the adjacencies and cataracts of the planner and the civil servant.[57] At the same time, nature and city are possessed of energetic qualities that conduct and induce flows, force events, articulate pasts with possible futures, and produce wealth or ruin. Such spatiotemporal effects will be integral to an expanded theorization of the specter, across its variously imagined powers.

Derrida offers, also, a second theoretical opening—one equally suggestive. This concerns the relationship of ghosts to money and value. In a final chapter, he expands on Marx's famous image of the "turning" table:

> The form of wood . . . is altered if a table is made out of it. Nevertheless the table continues to be wood, an ordinary sensuous thing. But as soon as it emerges as a commodity, it changes into a thing which transcends sensuousness. It not only stands with its feet on the ground, but, in relation to all other commodities, it stands on its head, and evolves out of its wooden brain grotesque ideas, far more wonderful than if it were to begin dancing of its own free will.

This excitation references a European craze of the 1850s, séances, during which tables would appear to rotate under ghostly locomotion. This was the stock-in-trade of somnambulists and spiritualists and was adopted by Marx to illustrate the deceptive "necromancy" of the commodity. Derrida goes a step further: this nexus of modern production contains, within itself, a ghost. As a technology for the extraction of abstract labor—whence the mysterious substance of exchange-value arises—the metamorphosis of an object into a thing-for-sale represents, in *Capital,* the very "phantomalization of property."[58] The "phantom" here refers to not generic ghostliness but a specific type: a deceitful false substance or impostor that possesses the humble piece of furniture and hijacks its concrete function. Derrida seizes on this lively image of the wooden automaton as the clear hauntological (that is, antiontological) entity. It is haunted by a stubborn irresolution, arising from the internal contradiction of the factory product—a struggle between the abstract and the concrete that has been further elucidated by Bill Brown, Bruno Latour, and others.[59]

The Marxian discourse of the commodity-as-possession, as ghost-vehicle, can be understood in at least two principal ways. As earlier, when the table gets ideas in its "brain," and dances and spins, it has been converted from a useful thing to a phantom. This is the spectral understood as abstraction and false appearance. A second, related process of "hauntification" concerns the object's newfound *objectivity.*[60]

Under the regime of exchange-value and the sway of a generalized fetishism, these appear—like the table—to have qualities that are independent of their collective human origins. Marx uses the religious metaphor of the fetish and that of the specter interchangeably, to evoke the uncanny autonomy of the thing given false appearance of life through the ventriloquism of capitalism's productive magic.

Derrida observes that, for Marx, this ghostliness of the commodity—its animating or possessing spirit—is only exacerbated in the question of money. Money yet further abstracts the commodity-form, and, through spectral equivalence,

> the metamorphosis of commodities . . . was already a process of transfiguring idealization that one may legitimately call spectropoetic. When the State emits paper money at a fixed rate, its intervention is compared to "magic" (magie) that transmutes paper into gold. . . . This magic always busies itself with ghosts, it does business with them.[61]

This Faustian conception of currency, its haunted aspect, has everything to do with this same fictional character of value, now purified in the bill of tender.[62] Because the origin of this value remains concealed behind the false front of fetishism, its very Durkheimian power source—the mana of society itself—is misrecognized. Clearly this is the same "*spuk*" that dwells inside all the tat of a market economy. But in the monetary form, the final remnant of use-value, that last shred of concrete specificity, is relegated to pure fungibility. Metals and cash contain already, within their logic, the dangerous and self-propagating sorcery of financialization and fictive economy. Gold is "at once ghost and idol."[63] Liberation from even *this* substance, however, results in the "apparition of the bodiless body of money: not the lifeless body of the cadaver, but a life without personal life or individual property." The material substrates were dangerously agnostic, but the unrestricted traffic between paper, gold, and goods is yet more so. We are left merely with "appearance or simulacrum," which for Marx is the wondrous and fearsome essence of one spectral modality.[64]

How is this relevant for the next chapters? In the Singaporean case, Marx's logic of ghostly goods is absolutely taken for granted—if, in moral terms, also stood on its head. We will see commodities that are quite literally ghost-possessions and -vehicles: economic instruments that are intended for use by the dead.[65] The already-haunted nature of the commodity is clarified and instrumentalized in the invention of the spectro-commodity (see chapter 3). The latter rearranges the relationship between use-values and exchange-values by imagining these (contra Marx) as thoroughly interdependent. Typically, these are representations of "pure" value that become nonfungible use-values in the afterlife. This is the case with the purchase of a paper house, whereby money is exchanged for a form—effectively a bill of house-money—that is then presumed to give shelter in the nether-world.[66] Alternately, overpaying for a cheap calculator or backpack, and attracting ghosts into them, radically "amplifies" their use-value and creates a method for controlling the vicissitudes of risk. In both cases, it is a disproportion or surplus of value itself that provides the magical efficacy.

Such practices engage the logic of evolving commodity forms, while yoking the spectral "problem" of the commodity to supernat-urally enhanced modes of personal agency. At the same time, these serve to make meaning of incomprehensible relationships between objects and values. Through the commodity, ghosts generate value, just as value attracts ghosts. The spectral figure embodies the "prob-lem" of valorization—as well as a resolution that is enacted through the dramaturgy of ritual exchange. As we will see, Singaporeans opera-tionalize this connection as a lever for the holistic betterment of an existence made increasingly precarious by economies of probability. This is perhaps most clearly embodied in the contradictions of archi-tecture, which in Singapore plays a heightened double role: both a primary form of capital accumulation and an aspirational domestic lifeworld. The spirits in a block of flats, drawn and placated through the channeling of value-as-money, are expected to engender further "prosperity" in all aspects of life (see chapter 6).

Spectral play becomes yet more literal in the case of money. Here the conception of the ghost passes beyond any Marxian conception of death-magic to a rather remarkable extent. Ghosts and value are, quite literally, seen to be forms of a common interacting energy. They are one and the same. Granted, these same qualities underpin everything in the cosmos, to some degree. But as the components of spirit are lib-erated from corporeality and matter, they are transformed into some-thing of almost identical character and (in a heavily analogical view of the universe) can influence the fluid dynamics of capital's "religious" substance to a hyperbolic degree. These relations are causal and direct. Here the spectral is not imagined under the signs of simulation, deception, or inversion; instead, the kinship of ghost and currency is explained as entirely authentic and "scientific" in nature.

Not only are the dead beyond the reach of probability in Chinese cosmology; they are also able—in fact, they are compelled—to interact amid the energetic flux of spaces and physical landscapes. The "push" and "pull" of an urban parcel arises from monetary inflows, quantities of material (which contain, also, their own varieties of qi), and the consequences of histories of trauma and transformation. In such a conception, the relation between ghosts and money is metaphorical *and* metaphysical; virtually any investment in a site will directly affect its underlying and invisible supernatural landscape. Engagement with local spirits, as in the work of mediumship described in chapter 6, must thus occur via physical substances qua substance, as well as through their function as substrates of social history.[67]

Derrida's two theoretical trajectories—space and capital, in the form of goods and money—are deeply intertwined in the conceptions of Singaporean Chinese ghosts and ghost-practices. As I have mentioned, the flows of spirits and value are related via a highly precise, geomantic ecology that casts space as a medium where materials, histories, and energies are subject to a calculus of mutual force. It is largely impossible to speak, in this context, of the spectral *without* the spatial or the monetary; these are considered not via separate discourses but as components of a common epistemological tradition. These threads of spatiality and value are similarly enmeshed in the physical spaces of architecture and in the constructed urban landscape, as these underlie the Singapore state *as a project*. The complex discourses of ghost-topology—in rupturing and reconfiguring the dispensations of metonymic national construction, whereby the models of ideology and physical planning are analogous—cannot be meaningfully separated from the urban order of a regime of capital. I argue that "making place" for speculation entails both the physical production of the city as a site of speculative activity *and* its ongoing financialization. And, as we will soon discover, these processes animate the spectral phantasmagoria of this society to a remarkable degree.

What follows remains attentive to these theoretical precedents but differs, in other respects, from common tropes in spectral studies. I do not believe that the "s-word" can simply be applied to anything that is periodic, incompletely known, suppressed, Othered, multiple, provisional or conjectural, weird or eerie, melancholic-historical, or characterized by a problematic materiality or visuality. We should be careful with reified claims, for example, that modernity "is" ghostly[68] or that modern media—film, digital media, literature, and music—are equally so. Instead of claiming that our present is spectral, we might do better to ask how spectrality is used to make sense of an increasingly alienating (but affectively urgent) array of structures and experiences: phantasmal equivalences, cyclical inequities, and "slow" violences.

To this end, I return to those practices (signifying and other) through which the ghost is "lived." This presumes no simple or empirically given reality and in no way disparages or devalues the necessity of theory for the spectral. As we shall see, the ghost is itself a medium of theorization for Singaporean respondents, while remaining experientially real. They contemplate, make sense of things, and engage in symbolic labor. They are also conjured for their peculiar social gravity, albeit in ways that sometimes smack of confusion, negativity, or reactionary populism. As such, the spirits of Derrida's heterogeneous inquiry must be called upon in their various guises as we consider the praxis by which the spectral returns to productive life.

To this end, this book is divided into two parts. The first, titled "Spectro-Capital," explores in detail the history and financialized contemporaneity of ritual transactions, involving transfers of value and risk, between the human and spirit worlds. These chapters attend to the roles of money and commodities in the relations between ghosts and the living—as well as, in the case of auctions and burnings, moments of spectacular exchange that perform and concretize the liturgical rationality of sacred speculation. Chapter 1 introduces first and foremost the figure of the Singaporean Chinese ghost itself, the cultural conventions of spirit and afterlife that underlie its imaginary, and the logic that animates reciprocal exchange with the dead. Chapter 2 describes the use of so-called hell money and other forms of paper currency considered to be fungible in the afterlife and the circuits of reciprocity arising from their use. Chapter 3 shifts focus to the spectral commodity-world: the modern proliferation of paper goods used in burnt offerings and their own complex, postconsumer existences. I demonstrate how the procedures for such commerce follow conceptions of value as a cosmological energy, cycling among forms and materials and modes of signification. Such conceptions make legible, and provide agentive inroads into, the often ineffable nature of Singapore's speculative doings and famous wealth.

Part II, "The City and Ghostly Ecology," links spectral economy with the economies of the urban environment. It is in the latter that discourses of value encounter the crypto-ecologies of geomancy and the "reading" of the city's spaces as both material and haunted. These qualities are not opposed but radically interdependent—and implicated in the trauma of the national project. Ghosts play havoc and "assert," through mediums and other interpreters, alternative regimes of ownership and social power. Their observance, moreover, would seem to reorder space as planned and designed. In this view of things, the architecture of the city may be spooked and reterritorialized, but it is not alienated. Chapter 4 briefly relates the story of the island's sweeping re-creation and examines how ghosts are understood to be "born" from the project of national modernization. Chapter 5 deals specifically with the spatial effects of ancestral practices and how ritual manipulation of value at particular sites is thought to "rewire" the urbanscape, crosscutting its metonymic ordering with unexpected gateways and cataracts. Last, chapter 6 brings the book's subjects together in an analysis of the most profitable and freighted local enterprise, real estate development. In this business, allegations of spectral violence exist alongside visions of a utopian, populist capitalism, entangling local and foreign agents within shared fates and fortunes.

By way of closure, the conclusion briefly considers consequences. One must ask what to make of the spectropolitan imaginary that underlies accounts of homeless, entrepreneurial souls—a redemptive populist ecology, its energies pulsing within the "real" city. How might we interpret its reversed lines of force, its stubborn holism, and its exorcism of the future? What might this mean for theorizations of capitalism *and* of the ghost?

PART I

Spectro-Capital

1

Specters and Spectral Economy

> Dead men are at work. Their cause is not lost. They labor on,
> screened from us by smoke.
> —Hilary Mantel, *The Mirror and the Light*

We should begin, no doubt, by introducing the two primary subjects of this book: the figure of the ghost and the reciprocal circuits of exchange—whether for care, or profit, or both—that are constructed in its name. These must be set within two historical frames. The first concerns the beliefs of diasporic populations who migrated to Southeast Asia from southern China. These are traditions of ancestral veneration and funerary rites, for tending to the dead in the netherworld. The second is more recent and concerns the reimagination of these practices within a speculative logic.

Singaporean Chinese are a migrant population, now just over 76 percent of the citizenry. Their ancestral lands are found in southern provinces of Guangdong (particularly Chaoshan in the east), Fujian, and Hainan. This is a diverse population that today includes communities from all regions of the People's Republic of China (PRC) and from other points across the diaspora of so-called *hua ren,* Nanyang (literally, "Southern Ocean"), or "overseas Chinese."[1] The nation's recognized dialect groups include Hokkien, Teo Chew, Hainanese, Cantonese, and Hakka.

Many cosmological assumptions of Chinese religion emerge from the common practice of religious Taoism and Buddhism, with other "folk" conventions. This remains an identifiable, though flexible, amalgam of ritual forms in prayer, geomancy, and mediumship. The form of Buddhism–Taoism practiced in peninsular Malaysia has also been called *Shenism* (deriving from *shen,* "god/s" in Mandarin), which connotes the worship of numerous deities. Early twentieth-century scholars also used the term *Tankism*—putting emphasis on the figure of the *tang-ki,* or spirit medium.[2] The variant that is observed by Nanyang throughout Southeast Asia is thought to have begun as a hybrid of Hokkien and Cantonese folk traditions with Taoism during the Qin and Han dynasties, in a moment of absorption into the broader Chinese empire.

Formal Taoism is traced to Lao Zi (born 1301 B.C.) and his writing of the *Tao Te Ching* during the Shang dynasty (1751–1152 B.C.). Many of the deities that survive to the present are thought to be of even older provenance, having merged into mainstream Taoist practice from strains of agrarian animism.[3] Gods have been transported across provinces, also, through labor migration and trade. There remains a very strong influence of Confucian thought in the particular admixture practiced throughout Southeast Asia. Buddhism–Taoism in Singapore can be traced to the earliest days of Cantonese and Hokkien settlement. The stamp of these regions can be seen in the deities who are worshipped, as well as in the liturgical forms—and, centrally, nuances of funerary practice—that continue into the present.

Taoism, in its religious aspect, centrally involves offerings made to a pantheon of gods, spirits, and lesser deities. These number several thousand, and a neotraditional Chinese altar can appear rather populous. A temple dais often includes figures such as the nine Emperor Gods, the child deity Ne-Zha, Guan Yin, and the infamous monkey god Qi Tian Da Sheng (Great Sage, Equal to Heaven)—he who features in Wu Cheng'En's famous sixteenth-century novel *Journey to the West.* The cast also includes patrons of very specific professions, including the Goddess of Prostitutes and of Night Entertainers. Dedicated "homes" exist in Singapore for specific deities and their mediums, such as that for the popular Sun God in the western Bukit Batok neighborhood.

Taoist worship takes place in temples and small shrines (*sin tua*) throughout the island. The location of these is not legislated, and the separation of the sacred and the profane—to follow Durkheim's famous analysis—often takes place at a microspatial scale, if at all.[4] Small altars are found at niches in hotel basements, at the service entrances to shopping centers, in living rooms and doorways, welded to security gates, in the spiral ramps of parking garages, or on the fore-columns of traditional Singaporean shop-houses.[5] Taoist prayer, for the most part, is integrated flexibly into the course of daily life. There are also significant periods set by the lunar calendar, such as the first and fifteenth days of the month—as well as annual sacred dates—on which particular rites are observed.[6]

Extent of participation in Chinese religion on the island is unclear, as there is officially no such category; the government acknowledges only singular faiths. "Taoist" may be the closest proxy. In the 2010 Singapore Population Census, members numbered 339,149 out of 3,105,748, or just under 11 percent—and appeared to decline to 8.8 percent in 2020.[7] However, such figures fail to account for syncretism in popular worship. Many among the nation's Buddhists, more than one million, take part in rites honoring ghosts and deities.[8] It is impossible to determine how such individuals are classified, as the census format does not allow one to claim multiple affiliations. Many Taoists also visit Buddhist temples, which may include altars to *shen*. For the same reason, there is no way to account for those who pray at both the Sri Krishnan Hindu temple and the adjacent Kwan Im Buddhist temple in Waterloo Street, for example—a well-known local practice.[9] This makes for a rather unsatisfactory picture, as nonexclusivity appears to be common; Victor Yue, a prominent commentator on local Taoist matters, has noted the joint appearance of Hindu and Taoist deities on daises.[10]

There is an acute awareness, among Singaporean respondents, of this polyglot nature. For example, Mrs. Tan—an elderly landscape gardener "auntie"—noted that she and her coreligionists were "not *really* Buddhist. Buddhist pray Buddha only. But Singaporeans are all mostly mixed."[11] Likewise, Harry, a Christian property developer, described local religion as

a *rojak*. A salad. It's so much of a mix inside that even a lot of the worshippers confused. Taoism has been mixed up in Buddhism. Buddhism has to do only with Buddha. Not with all these gods— Sun God, and so forth. You find that Taoism is more animistic. . . . These two have illegally married together, so to speak, and now nobody knows what is the bottom line.[12]

Beliefs regarding the character of ghosts mirror the diversity *within* Chinese religion. Here, too, there is notable variety. In interviews, those who considered themselves "more Buddhist" often emphasized a soul's unhappy attachment to worldly things and resistance to reincarnation.

Others, of a more Taoist bent, focused on the presumed character of yin and yang energies and their relationships to the built and natural environments.[13] In certain depictions, the netherworld is tightly bound, with visitations occurring primarily during the seventh month; in others, nonancestral spirits haunt Singapore year-round. Likewise, their manifestations seem to vary. In some tales, they speak and act, assume the forms of people, and pursue specific ends (see later). In other cases, their being is characterized by a certain generality, a social "type" described via norms of motivation that are largely assumed.[14]

Moreover, diasporic diversity has produced a certain novelty in beliefs about cosmology, energies and geomancy, the spirit, the soul, ghosts and deities, life and death, and the nature of the afterlife. These often appear to conform less to "traditional" discourses, such as those described in studies of Fujian and other regions of China.[15] Even more, these have rubbed shoulders with Indian, Malay, Javanese, and Western concepts for more than two centuries. There are continual rapprochements and compromises, which in my own experience have occurred most anxiously between folk traditions and new forms of charismatic, evangelical Protestantism.[16] Such accommodations become yet more heterodox when one factors in the undeniable influence of local and foreign cultural production: films, books, comics, and the like. What follows represents the accounts shared by an array of respondents that varied along lines of dialect group and language, class, age and generation, faith (or lack thereof), education, and profession. We must proceed with the awareness that there can be no "single" account of the Singaporean ghost, nor even of the ethnic Chinese ghost. Rather, this polyvocalism gives rise to great interpretive and practical creativity, as well as to some confusion. Modern spirits are constantly subject to conjecture, rationalization, and reimagination.

Broadly speaking, however, most nonliving entities are thought to fall within a spectrum denoted by the Mandarin compound term *gui-shen*. *Gui* means "ghost(s)," while *shen* refers to "spirit(s)." *Shen* is a term also used to refer to deities and other celestial beings, as Chinese cosmology does not differentiate "gods" in a Judeo-Christian sense of sui generis, all-powerful creators. All disembodied souls exist as formations of energy *(qi)* of yin (female, dark) and yang (male, light) varieties. As a rule, *gui* are more dominantly associated with *yin qi* and *shen* with *yang qi*. Properly speaking, *shen* might refer to a well-tended ancestral spirit, while *gui* carries the impoverished, submissive/recessive, damp and dark associations of the spectral—of true ghostliness. In short, while ghosts are a subset of spirits, only unlucky and forgotten spirits become ghosts.

Explanations of ghosthood within Chinese medicine are complex and involve the five modalities of *shen,* which dwell in different organs of the body of the living. After death, two—*hun* and *po*—linger. *Hun* is primarily of *yang qi* and upon death rises upward, like warm air, into the spiritual planes. *Po,* by contrast, is cold and sinks to remain entangled with the corpse and grave. By consequence, the "soul" of the departed can be multiply located. *Hun* is often thought to return to be reincarnated, to join the ancestors, or to be situated near the deceased's plaque in the temple. *Po,* by contrast, will often roam the earthly plane as lost souls. In mainland Chinese traditions, *hun* and *po* hauntings differ in character and intent. By contrast, Singaporeans often truncate this complex relation in speaking of *gui,* and aspects of both infiltrate the modern imaginary.

Such assumptions engage more social-behavioral ones, arising from modernized folk conceptions of a Chinese "hell," a somewhat confusing term that refers both to the spirit world and its spaces of punishment (from the Mandarin *di yu,* "earth prison"; both words appear in respondent accounts and are used herein). Chinese popular understandings depict *di yu* as striated—comprising tiers that increase in discomfort and misery as one descends.[17] The world of the living sits (like Singapore) near the equator. This relates to older historical notions of China as the Middle Kingdom and is thought to explain why "both good and bad things are happening" on earth.[18] Hell has ten courts of judgment, and the assignment of the deceased among the levels of torment or comfort depends on their actions in life.[19] As designer Arthur noted,

> you can move up to hell and heaven at any time, depending on your credits. So, feeding a ghost and burning paper money is giving them credit, so they can move up. [*laughs*] So, it's totally commercial. Somehow you can buy your way; the living can help the spirits. That's why people feed ghosts, to allow them to better themselves.

"Credit," variously imagined, is the factor that moves individual spirits along the axis from ghosts to gods; even the gods are themselves of variable standing and rely on human action (such as mediumship) to elevate their own positions.

Hell, like Singapore, is a very expensive place. It is also similarly bureaucratic. There are precise roles in the work of godly administration, an expansive collection of offices including, among others, judges, assistants to the chief justice of the Court of Hell, judges of the infernal courts, and seemingly endless aides and functionaries. Costs incurred in this sphere have to do, perhaps, with the Taoist idea that we incur debts in life that must be paid in the netherworld.[20] Other explanations characterize *di yu* as a venal entrepôt, where officials and guards can be bribed for better conditions and accommodations (unlike in Singapore, rent-seeking behaviors are said to be rife).

The ghost's condition is perpetual lack: it is, to various degrees, in need of status elevation and fungible goods. Our reciprocal relationship with the spirits consists of helping them to be elevated through the levels but also to *not be forgotten.* For this reason, Taoist practice—and Chinese religion more widely—centrally involves ancestral observances. As with all folk religion, this, too, is a hybrid form with a rich and varied repertoire of rites, rules, and representations. There are numerous essential features, however. Strict Taoists will keep tablets in home shrines, inscribed with the names of predecessors. These may be accompanied by photographs or personal effects. Beyond special moments in the lunar calendar, such as Hungry Ghost Month (Zhong Yuan) and Qing Ming festivals, offerings of food and joss paper are made to the spirits of immediate family in a loosely regular way.

In a common version recounted by Tong Chee Kiong,[21] the ancestral dead become "hungry" ghosts in the absence of care: when their descendants do not tend to them via rites and offerings, when there are no descendants, or when the spirit was flung from existence by a violent event. When untended, even beloved ancestors may undergo a frightening process of wasting; they become disoriented, forgetful, angry, and vindictive. Prior to this, they are "bright spirits." But hunger is a fact of afterlife just as it is of life. The experience of the netherworld is not composed primarily of penury and bitterness but becomes so if one is neglected. There might be a literal pain caused by such deprivation or—as described of the Ndembu by Turner—the indignity of diminished social status and respect. In this vein, Hui Ping, who joins her mother in making offerings annually during Zhong Yuan, notes that "Chinese just feel that the ancestors will get upset" if

FIGURE 1. During specific days of the lunar seventh month, it is common to see multiple offerings taking place along a street. *Top,* A modest one is conducted using a cooking oil can as a brazier. *Bottom,* An expedient offering is made, here, directly on the ground; no officially provided brazier is used, resulting in a cloud of "contaminated" ash drifting along the street.

you don't make sacrifices to reaffirm remembrance and care.[22] Here, as in many of the religious questions that follow, Singaporeans appear divided between abstract discourses of remembrance and literal, rationalized and monetized understandings of metaphysical conditions.

A spirit can become a ghost through starvation—but also, more rapidly, via trauma. The speed and violence of road accidents, suicides, and murders leaves the soul stranded and wracked with pain and are said to produce ghosts instantaneously, even if proper funeral rites are administered. These tortured souls are said to haunt the sites of their misfortune. The result, as in so many other global contexts, is that *gui* serve to draw attention to specific historical tragedies and their sites. In an analysis of popular discourse and among my respondents, such recollections overwhelmingly concerned atrocities committed by Japanese occupiers from 1942 to 1945. (This is discussed in detail in chapter 5.) This mode of explanation quickly returns to the economic dimension: the role of the ghost as a victim of trauma ostensibly makes it yet more powerful as a potential business partner, and sites of tragic events are (by the same logic) rife with opportunities as well as dangers.

However, everyday Singaporean haunting narratives are often surprising for their *lack* of emphasis on trauma or historical evil.[23] Visitations do concern past injustices. Just as often, however, the ghost emerges to demand a glass of brandy, suggest a course of action, or protest some trespass by the living. *Gui* are presumed to exist in an alternate present, in a space outside of time, rather than in some repressed past. They visit, rather than return—and as such are often concerned with immediate needs or wants. Discourses surrounding Singapore's spirits are frequently not nostalgic or backward looking, for the simple reason that they are assumed to remain, in the contemporary, as a form of lingering personhood. As we will see, trauma and memory sit amid a cacophony of other cultural preoccupations: desired commodities, money, filial obligation, climate and landscape, political and social power. Ghosts have something to "say" about practically everything in Singaporean life.

Because spirits are understood to be social beings and not representations, death provides a projective zone in which all the concerns of the living are often contemplated via inversion, mimesis, and disproportion. This, combined with the popular assumption of the Chinese *di yu* as a condition of privation, can result in spectral obsessions that seem oddly prosaic.[24] As Singaporean gravedigger Wong Shun Feng pointed out in 2009, "ghosts are the same as human beings. . . . They have feelings and emotions as well."[25]

This opens a broad series of potentials for the dead to speak and to behave, many times in a way that is poignantly human. In this respect, the ghost is pictured very differently from Western analogues. By contrast, this is a man or a woman: rebellious, hungry, and angry or kindly, curious, generous, *ham sup* (Cantonese for "perverted," "horny"), or playful and mischievous. These ghosts do not merely *haunt,* in the sense of "remind." In fact, their motivations, as assumed by those who speak of them, are purposive and familiar. They are often driven by the same consumerist desires as typical Singaporeans. Or, like their living relatives, they are compelled by bureaucratic rules and legalities, a notable characteristic of hell. They must file petitions and occasionally pay an infernal civil servant.[26] As perfectly summed up by gravedigger Wong, ghosts are people (albeit dead ones) and share our foibles.

GHOSTLY ENCOUNTERS

The "spectral" refers to a problematic mode of being and of perception. The etymology of the word, which is tied to visibility, is troubling because the visuality of the ghost is fugitive. It exists on a *spectrum,* accessible to human sight to varying degrees: haunting narratives describe presences that can be seen, that can barely be seen, or that can only be grasped via other senses or through logical deduction—or, as in the case of Derrida's "visor effect," not at all.[27] Detecting a specter may require conjecture, or intuition, in the absence of empirical evidence. It is, in this way, also intimately related to the act of speculation.[28]

Singaporeans often spoke of "seeing" ghosts, but this phrase was shorthand for a wide array of actual experiences. Often, they saw a normal person whose true nature was revealed only by odd behaviors or through questioning or interaction. Others materialized in unreal ways or were clearly out of place: walking through walls or suddenly standing in the corners of rooms in private homes or hotels. Many descriptions shared the association, in modern media, of ghostliness with transparency. The body may look incorporeal or empty or may lack clarity or detail. Here Singapore resembles other societies with highly developed filmic and telepictorial sensibilities.[29] In a frequent trope, the dead were said to present themselves with traumatic injuries or in the form of monsters or animals. An example is Jean, a doctor in her sixties, who was repeatedly visited by a departed relative in the guise of a partially simian creature.[30] Such transfigurations might clarify, or confuse, the meaning of the visitation.

Respondents also frequently shared the notion that ghosts can be viewed only obliquely or peripherally, in the corner of a space or on a tree branch above. It is common to hear the leitmotif that a haunting "happened right next to me." Terrence, a young architect, experienced this on a march in the night during his army days. He felt a vague presence, following just out of sight on his left. A friend and fellow soldier, walking on this same side, was suddenly abducted when his gaze was briefly averted.[31] Likewise, investor Mr. Ang recounted numerous incidents of mischief, in the form of stolen and broken objects, that occurred "very close to me, at the moment I looked away."[32] The living are often said to be surveilled or approached from behind, especially during the seventh month, when one is cautioned not to suddenly turn around.

As David Toop has argued, however, vision is not the sole mode of apprehending the spectral.[33] Often, this takes place via other senses.[34] In Southeast Asian lore, supernatural presences are associated with odors. This is most famously so with the Pontianak, a vampiric female spirit of Malay-Indonesian origin who is attended by a heady scent of frangipani (a traditional funeral flower). Respondents enumerated other aromas for Chinese ghosts, from bodily musk to perfumes and colognes to specific foods or liquors favored by the deceased. Inexplicable smells underscore the disquieting character of invisible presence and the sense of being watched. A similar unease arises with auditory phenomena, with the creaking of footsteps on floorboards and the eerie suggestion of weight exerted by incorporeal visitors. One common phenomenon, in this context, is tactile: an inexplicable microclimatic effect, described as an unnatural chill within Singapore's hot, humid air. This is said to be cooling by yin energy, associated with death and the grave. The sensation is compared, unnervingly, to the hypercooled currents of air conditioning.

Spectral atmospheres are also often affective. Witnesses describe waves of feeling that arise with a ghostly presence. These can be associated with the terrifying, as in cases described elsewhere by Tom Gunning.[35] But also common is a sense of the ineffable, of a mood that evades classification. Such narratives articulate what Edgar Allan Poe called "a feeling for which I have no name" and "a sensation that will admit of no analysis."[36] There are echoes here of Brian Massumi and others, who place certain affective states beyond the assimilating effects of emotive categories.[37] In this aspect, Singaporean ghost stories recall tropes of nineteenth-century "eerie" fiction, of works such as Henry James's *Turn of the Screw*, Rudyard Kipling's "They," or Poe's

"Fall of the House of Usher" and "Ligeia."[38] Herein ghosts present as "a sentiment ineffable": a bafflement or unease, characterized by what Mark Fisher defines as "something present where there should be nothing, or nothing present where there should be something."[39] This is sometimes followed by "dread" or "horror."[40] There is often, also, an unexpected sense of power and possibility. Witnesses frequently had difficulty putting such multivalence, and discord, into language.

Charles, an oral surgeon in his fifties, expressed a common position. "I've sensed them before," he said. When looking to rent a flat on Balmoral Road, Charles felt something deeply amiss. When he entered the unit, he sensed "something heavy or oppressive." This was followed by sadness and a yearning without a clear object. Charles told me, "When I left, the realtor said, 'OK, I'll tell you because you're not interested in renting, but the owner died on the stairs.'"[41] Mei Zhen Jie, a retired domestic helper, told me that she feels "confused" and saddened when ghosts are nearby. She clarifies, "They are wherever we are, like our shadow. I've never seen them, but I feel their presence."[42]

Experiences of sense and affect often exacerbate problems of articulation—of decoding what a ghost "wants." Literary specters have commonly been cast as bearers of comprehensible, if untimely, messages. In Singaporean narratives, however, their statements are often described as mixed and opaque. Certainly some are straightforward: a plea, a corrective, a want in need of satisfaction. As often, however, the ghost seems to be attempting to impart multiple meanings or significations that go beyond language.[43] This may be evidence of mixed feelings or the confusion of hunger and anger. As such, the *gui* is depicted in many accounts as an unreliable procurator of its own desires. For this reason, one experienced in such matters—a medium—cautioned me not to take the messages of the spirit world at face value.[44] Rather, he suggested, we should place the stated intentions of the ghost (when one is able to speak) within a pattern of phenomena: shifted objects, aggressive acts, and affective atmospheres. Spectral events, moreover, typically take place against a complex backdrop of social circumstance: a family disturbance, a ritual occasion, tragedy, or a streak of bad luck. These are themselves open to an array of competing decryptions. Such factors may be complicated yet furthered by the copresence of other spirits with conflicting or competing wants. The dead themselves exist in a condition of social relatedness, with balances of power, objectives, and reciprocities of their own. The inference of these constitutes a sort of popular detective work, one of the skills that distinguishes an effective medium or geomancer.

But the ghost is still, for all this, a ghost. Although it is often depicted in familiar, all-too-human terms, it nonetheless remains a source of very real fear: a powerful, incorporeal subjectivity. The confused condition of the hungry spirit gives rise to unpredictability and disproportionate violence. Incidents at construction sites and army camps, among other locales, describe an astonishing brutality—a sort of performative excess that is in blatant disproportion to the triviality of its wants (we will see this in chapter 5, in the evisceration or displacement of bodies, of soldiers or builders, over minor infractions).[45] Their abuse is often presaged by moments of corporeal strangeness; the possessed are forced to express nonrational motions, like dancing or convulsion, or the characteristic stagger-step of the *tang-ki* in trance.

Events of this kind wreak havoc upon plans. The fear of violence serves, almost without fail, to disrupt an operation or venture: the military exercise, the scheduled construction or development timeline, or the functions of a bureau. In a moment of "weak" messianism, the ghost steps in to alter the course of scheduled events.[46] *Gui* would appear to militate against knowable futures, producing a rule of the unplanned, to which humans must react rather than assert projective agency. The result of such happenings—to the chagrin of all concerned—is to pause the flow of time, to prolong the present moment and obstruct (if temporarily) the passage into the new realities touted by government and speculative actors.[47] This serves to emphasize the present as an ambiguous locus within which divergent objectives, subjectivities and legalities, and sources of power are suddenly corelated. The actions of the ghost emphasize the present above the historicity of pasts and the determinacy of designed outcomes. This stands in direct contrast to state discourse that presents its urban utopianism via a regime of inevitability: photorealistic imagery and unwavering timelines. Such disruptions should not be subjected to the "romance of resistance"—often, the ghosts merely want to be paid.[48] But the outcomes of haunting nonetheless contrast the linear projections of the PAP, with its forward rhetoric of "paths" and "laps." The ghost thus stands as an inversion of that ur-Singaporean figure, the planner.

Hence one more key quality of the ghost should be considered for what follows—its power as a socially projected subject. Just as death places the soul beyond the reach of probability and risk, it is allowed to "act" beyond the spatial-legal boundaries of the living agent. The spectral performs, via a kind of collective ventriloquism, a potency that is seen by civil society as originating outside itself. This is not conventional political agency. It does not follow a coherent or consistent program and often is involved only in the work of negation. But the hauntings are understood to cause genuine trouble where contestation rarely occurs and to assert alternative modes of control. *Gui* assume the character of "concrete abstractions," acquiring inexorable force even within an avowedly secular regime.[49] They are deeply feared by believers, and the intensity of this fear is respected (as we will see) even by those who doubt.

Allegations of visitation thus create a sticky issue for governance; the dead heckle the state in ways that fall outside of its carefully structured limitations on speech and political demonstration. The ghost is a Singaporean, but not a "citizen." Its actions are not easily framed as subversive in any of the registers in which the PAP defines this term. As I have argued, elsewhere, the ghost's disembodiment creates difficulty for an authority that is based on the disciplinary and biopolitical.[50] These are persons without flesh; they have nothing against which "law-preserving" violence can be threatened. Public order is famously associated, here, with forms of corporal and capital punishment, with hanging and caning (the latter being very much the icon of the nation's discipline in the global imagination).[51] The spirit's immunity to such treatment is dramatized in the practices of local *tang-ki,* who are publicly whipped by their disciples during possession states and show no outward signs of suffering.[52] Ghosts are, equally, beyond the state's provision of the stuff of life: housing, jobs, health and social services. In terms of formal governance, then, they are characterized chiefly by a fearsome independence.

SPECTRO-ECONOMY: AN INTRODUCTION

Ghosts are not, however, beyond the regime of the economic. Quite the contrary: Singaporean Chinese spectral culture presumes an uncommon intimacy between ghosts and matters of value, money, and speculation.

This should not be viewed as exceptional or exotic. In fact, the spectral has long been associated with forms of risk-based capitalism—both at its putative "centers" and in colonial peripheries—and has fueled schemes of prognostication and manipulation. The Clafin sisters, a duo of clairvoyants who conducted séances to pick stocks, were the doyennes of London's exchanges as early as 1870 (their role appears to have narrowly preceded the various "magic formulas" and secret algorithms that now pervade finance culture). In England and New England, women were frequently accused of witchcraft, in cahoots with the dead, when their gambles paid out.[53] Tabitha Stanmore has shown that, while women were being persecuted for a range of allegedly "satanic" practices, enterprising Englishmen *and* -women were plying the trade of "service magic" to hedge private bets.[54] Transnational organizations of churches preaching the prosperity gospel must be considered as, likewise, a medium for the seemingly endless expansion of charismatic discourses that exchange spirits (plural) for *the* Holy Spirit. Economic enchantments, past and present, now constitute their own interdisciplinary research network, with a growing roster of publications, meetings, and podcasts.[55] Not least for our purposes are Derrida's painstaking attentions to Marx's use of ghostly analogy—in the famous opening to *The Communist Manifesto*, in *The Eighteenth Brumaire of Louis Bonaparte*, and in *Capital, Volume 1*—which have provided the basis of the field of hauntology.[56]

Ghosts in Singapore, while generally feared and avoided, are also assumed to exert a determining effect on the efficacy of capital. This occurs in their mastery of risk, in the production of good and bad luck, and in their ability to direct flows of value. Power over speculative ventures is derived from their nature as beings of powerful yin (dark, female) energy. While often lost and confused, spirits exist outside of human time and thus can see transparently through probabilistic phenomena. They are thought to know, for example, whether the values of stocks will rise or fall and which lottery numbers will be drawn. The more powerful among them—such as those who die in tragic circumstances (see earlier)—are also thought to alter the outcomes of deterministic phenomena at will.

What I call the *spectro-economy*, the sum of ritual transactions among the living and the dead, is built around a vocabulary of sacrificial conventions to transmit wealth and nourishment to the afterlife. While the living care for the spirits out of a broader sense of filial responsibility and religious obligation, it is presumed that the latter may return the favor with improved fortune in business or gambling, health, and happiness. Offerings of food and drink may be consumed when placed upon altars with lit incense. Myriad forms of joss paper "spirit money" *(yin zhi)* and so-called hell notes are also burned, remitting their vast denominations beyond the mortal plane (see the next chapter). These are purchased at local shops and markets, and their value is thought to pass to a specific ancestor or nearby ghost. Elaborate paper architectures, palatial homes, and office buildings—and, more recently, banks, fast-food outlets, and cinemas—are likewise set ablaze to provide the dead with shelter and entertainment. There is a whole proxy commodity-world on offer: computers, smartphones and tablets, designer shirts, credit cards, unusual pets, and domestic workers that exist as paper simulacra. When reduced to ash, these objects reappear in the netherworld.

In a related practice, ordinary commodities and ornamental objects are auctioned for exorbitant prices at public events during the Ghost Month festival. As Tong Chee Kiong describes,

> a schoolbag, which normally costs less than ten dollars, may be sold for two to three hundred dollars. A rice-cooker, sold in the

FIGURE 2. A typical offering consisting of varied joss paper *(at right)* and foods. The three central candles determine the duration of the period during which the spirits "consume" these goods. When these burn near to the base, a coin toss or other method will be used to determine whether the rite is concluded.

stores for less than fifty dollars, can fetch up to five hundred dollars. Lottery tickets, which cost a dollar each, can command prices of up to one hundred dollars.[57]

These items are considered to be unusually lucky and effective because they have been invested with spiritual power and will assist the owners in meeting life's challenges. The schoolbag, for one, is a hotly contested item, as it is believed to assist the winning bidder's child in the merciless competition of the Singaporean education system. Proceeds of these sales fund large pyres of paper cash and goods for dispossessed spirits.

Reciprocal circuits leading through the afterlife operate year-round, reaching considerable volume during festivals. It is impossible to estimate the total value of goods and services involved, as the spectro-economy is cash dominant, and much takes place off the books.[58] However, some figures are indicative. We may consider the cost of Ghost Month hampers: boxes containing an assortment of *yin zhi*, hell money, paper coins or ingots, joss paper clothing, and other popular items. These are standard purchases of individuals and companies, to be set alight at the beginning, middle, and end of the festivals. They range from a low of S$60 to a high of S$888 for those who court greater protection and profit in the following year.[59] Such packages are often bought in multiple. They are stacked high in the specialist shops during run-ups to significant dates and are offered with an ever-diversifying range of contents available online—especially given the vast inventories of contemporary e-tailers, such as Lazada.[60] There is no bad year for burnt offerings. Lean times and crises sharpen the need for protection by spirits, and bullish economies are seen as opportunities for growth. Likewise, orders for the conventional large-scale bamboo-and-joss-paper effigies are fulfilled during this period. These still represent the pinnacle of postmortem luxury, likely due to their intimidating prices and traditional prestige. Artisans make them by hand in a process that is bespoke and punishingly labor intensive. Lai Yew Onn, a well-known fabricator, sells increasingly personalized homes, vehicles, and pets for S$30,000 or more.[61]

Forms of wealth burned for the dead are understood literally as remittances, not as metaphors for filial piety or respect for lineage. Tong clarifies that they are "perceived by informants to be real," rather than representations.[62] The bills are considered legal tender between the human and spirit worlds. Importantly, these offerings open reciprocal exchanges that are expected to benefit the living in turn. While understood as a form of care and benevolence, burning is also the original moment of a cycle of wealth production, whereby the ghosts return the favor in the form of windfalls or improved luck. The effect of this trade is seen as self-evidently positive, as a win-win that profits everyone involved.

Value here is imagined as a cosmological essence—an energetic flow, capable of "feeding" spirits. It multiplies via intercourse between the markets of Singapore and *di yu*. These bounded territories are open to the traffic of the universal energies that animate objects and phenomena. As one such force, value is not delimited by the partition between life and death. Earthly money and goods provide only temporary reservoirs for it; when these are destroyed, it is again free to migrate across the mortal horizon—and, in so doing, multiply exponentially. Passage of value among media and across the borders of the ghost-world is assumed to generate dramatic leaps in value—bypassing conventional economic rationality. Spectacular gains occur through transfers from "real" dollars to spectral currency, from paper to ash, from this world to the other, from yin energy to lucky numbers and winning outcomes. A hell note costing ten cents is assumed to become millions in the netherworld. It is the hyperbolic nature of this mysterious currency to be, at the instance of purchase, worth more than it costs. A paper house or office block may command anywhere from a few Singapore dollars to a few thousand but materializes in the beyond as an asset worth vast amounts. In this way, as we will see also, the ghost-economy elides currencies and commodities, in a play on dominant investment logics. In the spirit world, everything is rendered speculative, as inputs to reciprocal exchanges are thought to bring unlimited returns.

The nation's popular 4D lottery system is also centrally associated with the logic of spectro-economic practices. Lucky combinations are frequently selected with the aid of hungry ghosts or cooperative ancestors. Alongside stacks of hell notes, chits of paper containing numbers are set alight at graves or accident sites, and the last to burn are used to configure four-digit sequences. Alternately, selection is performed by shaking dice in a cup or using wooden sticks.[63] These are particularly popular among "uncles and aunties" in their fifties and sixties. There is even a shrine in the famous Maxwell Market, an open-air

FIGURE 3. Hell notes may be burned individually or in stacks or fans. This contrasts with more traditional joss money, which is typically opened into circular spirals or individually folded.

food court, that dispenses 4D numbers during the seventh month on an LED screen.[64] Contemporary practices grow here, also, from Chinese popular traditions in which the dead have been thought to speak to the living via numerical sequences.[65] This is a brisk trade during the seventh month; dispossessed or "hungry" ghosts are considered to be particularly solicitous when it comes to dispensing tips, as they long most acutely for wealth, food, and attention. Those who die by unnatural causes are even more so.[66]

Interestingly, however, the ghost is assumed to wield power even when outcomes are *not* subject to pure luck. The clearest example is in real estate and property. Development and construction are predominant foci of haunting narratives, and deals with ghosts are known to have great impact on value. This may have to do with costly delays in construction, as mentioned earlier, or with depressed sales prices, or with resident *gui* ruining the fortunes of occupants or causing sickness.[67] In many cases, though, as we will see, spectral intervention is assumed to exert a contrary, *positive* effect. Architecture provides a conduit for their agency in numerous ways: as the home of people at the mercy of life's uncertainties, or as a speculative commodity. These powers are understood to be at work wherever value is at stake—which is everywhere. In this view, increasingly, all matters are matters of risk.

THE REGIME OF CHANCE

This, in summary, describes the broad assumptions of the ghost and its own economic circuitry. The following chapters delve into this in all its evocative detail, with special attention to questions of money and financialization, commodities, and real estate. Before moving forward, however—and by way of some conclusion—we should address an immediate question that arises with Singapore's *gui* and their dealings. Why should a well-informed public resort to ghosts as a medium to explain, and participate in, economy? Why should the link between specters and speculation exist at all?

Peter Geschiere and Jean and John L. Comaroff have theorized similar phenomena of "occult" economies in South Africa and Cameroon, in which the accumulation of ineffable wealth in the age of deregulation and financialization is explained as the work of dark, supernatural forces—particularly by those living at the remote margins of a new economic dispensation.[68] No doubt, we might find similar explanations in Singapore. Mysterious sources of disproportionate wealth are accounted for by the mechanism of spiritual intervention. It is perhaps not surprising that Singapore's own numinous discourses should mimic those forms of finance that are least understood—or seen as most able to produce wild disparities of income that exponentially outpace labor.

But the citizenry of Singapore is not, as in the examples of Cameroon and South Africa, a rural population at a remove from the sites where contemporary value is created. This is a public that is relatively well-versed in business. Awareness of, and participation in, the world of speculative economic practices is widespread. The expansion of Singapore's economy into operations based on risk has not been limited to business elites—quite the contrary. There is a generalized interest in abstract financial and monetary instruments, and investment activity remains high among the public, despite often painful memories of the 1997 and 2008 crashes. Moreover, the nation's businesspeople—entrepreneurs, investors, fund managers, and cryptocurrency "bros"—are often those participating in ghostly exchanges and (as we will see) spending baffling sums on offerings and Ghost Month auctions. The hundreds of thousands of Singapore dollars for haunted commodities and amulets are, after all, not paid by low-wage workers. I have spoken to geomantic experts who make and sell charms for bankers, fund managers, and venture capital executives. Likewise, property developers with publicly listed companies employ mediums to purify and align the spiritual forces on their building sites. This might be initially surprising, and it may be unclear why those with privileged access to capital should want in.

In what follows, then, we must answer a more difficult question: why a population of relative cognoscenti should resort to ghostly understandings of economy. They do so, I argue, because spectral and speculative economics today share common anxieties regarding the fundamental ineffability of risk. Unlike industry—in which profits can, at least in theory, be estimated via inputs and normative pricing—there is an irreducible mystery at the center of late capital. Value here is ultimately beholden to the outcome of unknown events, which, despite sophisticated modes of statistical divination, ultimately *resist* calculable certainty.[69] In this strange condition, as willing or unwilling participants in this game, we are all at the mercy of a metaphysics of value that can be only dimly understood by proxy. This proxy might be the algorithm or unproven formula in the office of a hedge fund (see the introduction to this volume)—or, as in the case of *gui* or London's Clafin sisters, it may be the ghost.

Respondents' discourses about ghosts, as we will see, address concerns about life's risks, broadly imagined. In turn, their religious practices purport to offer practical means for *managing* these risks. Chinese religion allows for an understanding of probability as embedded in the totality of our conduct and spatial location: as beholden to a calculus of "luck" and "prosperity" that arises from our actions and personal energies, ritual practices, and the spaces in which we live (at scales from the domestic to the notional and beyond). Financial success cannot be separated here from the broader conditions of being. Singaporeans frequently make sense of inchoate patterns of good and bad events, unexpected occurrences and coincidences, through an interplay of spirit, geomancy, energy, and value, often alongside modes of statistical estimation. Those entrepreneurs who bet on ghost-trades still obsess over business plans, projected costs, and prices—in short, their odds. It is worth noting, however—as have Hacking, Gingerenzer and colleagues, King and Kay, and Taleb—that such calculations provide reliable predictions only when phenomena are isolated from broader causal networks, which is never the case. They cannot handle the widespread, wicked problem of "radical uncertainty."[70] There remains a mystical irreducibility to matters in the real world, because our commitment to the stochastic does not do away with interventions by complex determinate phenomena, or what insurers call "acts of god." There is likewise the hard nut of theodicy; probability may suggest the likelihood of an outcome but not an explanation for its causes.

At the same time, other problems of knowability arise from the emergent legal-technical conditions of finance as practiced, which create problems that are not reducible to economic literacy. After all, many financial instruments exist within "black boxes" of proprietary code or in the form of experimental scripts and functional code that are not fully comprehended even by their inventors—who often adapt other formulas experimentally using market simulations. In effect, no one knows, the buyers or even the banks and funds themselves, precisely how these come to be effective or if they might suddenly and disastrously fail. As a former analyst at JPMorgan Chase in Singapore admitted, "they work, but we don't exactly know *how* they work."[71] This logic is replicated in those practices and "products" directed to ghosts. Many who offer food or joss paper money admit that they do not understand precisely how value or substance is transferred to hell or why *yin zhi* should experience wild fluctuations of value. They employ these rituals simply because they are known to be efficacious and because they can be *simply explained* by the gratitude or disfavor of the spirits.

Ghosts, in sum, appear to solve the problem of risk. This is what gives them their social power, alongside their presumed capacity to cause harm and create disorder. The spectral world provides straightforward rules of conduct and protocol. These concepts are conceived not as probabilistic but rather as areas in which determination is invisible and unknowable and available to divine intervention.

This, of course, speaks primarily to epistemological concerns. But we should not dismiss the glamour of a participatory economy that would purport to offer unfettered access to circuits of capital, that democratizes modes of investment and promises potential returns far beyond inputs of labor. We will see actual wealth effects that are based on the social logic structuring ghostly reciprocity. Within communities of belief, haunted objects do generate actual value in ways akin to the charismatic megachurches that are also popular in Singapore. They dramatize a kind of efficacy as "evidence" that they work. The attraction of this is not hard to see. Singapore is a predominantly lower-middle-class society in which more than 80 percent of the public lives in subsidized housing.[72] The rise to extreme wealth has overwhelmingly enriched a small business elite and left many behind. Although it is true that the nation offers greater chances of upward mobility than elsewhere, much accrues to those who already benefit from the advantages of embourgeoisement: inheritance, educational capital, or work ethic. No less significant is the depression of wages as a key aspect of the government's strategy for attracting multinational corporations since independence. This means that many have not seen significant growth in spending power, while others in rarefied sectors have gotten ahead. One can imagine, in this context, the appeal of the radical freedoms and rewards promised by the spirit world.

The ghost, as a source of fear *and* comfort, is blissfully unaffected by that stubborn mystery that underlies the human predicament. While the dead continue to suffer deterministic privations, and behave quixotically, they have been placed beyond the influence of that which is both Singapore's shared terror and its dream: the dictatorship of the unknown outcome. In an economy and society largely premised on the quixotic control of volatility—speculative construction, securitized transactions, the inflation and marketing of tourist spectacles, logistics, and naked betting—such power is nothing short of godly.

2

Hell Money

VALUE ACROSS THE PAPER HORIZON

> A descriptive analysis of bank notes is needed . . . for nowhere more naively than in these documents does capitalism display itself in solemn earnest . . . ornamenting the façade of hell.
>
> —Walter Benjamin, *One-Way Street*

> It is said that in antiquity when the sage Cang Jie invented writing, "all the ghosts wailed in the night."
>
> —Wu Hung, "A Ghost Rebellion: Notes on Xu Bing's Nonsense Writing and Other Works," *Public Culture*

We have now seen, in outline, the potential of ghosts to liberate speculative practices—as partners in the realm of freewheeling exchange. This gives rise to a space of radical possibility, freed from the strictures of formal economy. The wildness of such spectral traffic is expressed, in no small part, through the imaginary of money—itself a near-magical medium with an unruly and proliferating aspect. Spirit-bills, of varying kinds, give rise to transactions that inhabit the monetary as an imaginative space: novel modes of currency manipulation, investment, and hedging. In these, value is dramatized as a cosmological essence. It is a coursing stream of energy, channeled by faith and technique, no longer yoked to labor and production. Given care for protocol and the correct environmental setting, its flows are subject to spectacular increase.

While ghost-bills might seem to be purely fictitious repositories of value, their invented status differs very little from accounts of money by theorists, historians, and critics of speculation over the ages.[1] The connective, proliferating character of hell notes mirrors long-standing, general perceptions of paper currency as dangerous, artificial, and promiscuous. As Jack Weatherford has noted, each variety of money gives rise to its own "culture" of practices, its own value-logic, modes of use and circulation, and even metaphysics.[2] Bills and notes represent a young and unruly strain, as mutable as paper itself—and, unsurprisingly, have conjured unseemly and infernal associations.[3] Satanic origins were most explicitly articulated in Goethe's second *Faust,* in which Mephistopheles offers a fictional emperor the alchemist's formula for turning paper into gold.[4] The latter is merely a guarantor's scrip for a thousand crowns, signed by the ruler himself. This "great secret" allows the note in the present to represent future gold not yet mined; it was, in effect, a futures product.[5] The production of bills has also been viewed as hazardously democratic—in a sense, anyone can conjure them out of thin air. Prior to nationalization, in most places, this process was largely decentralized. In the United States, for example, there have been more than eight thousand varieties of tender in circulation in a single year. Such tendencies fueled the perception of currencies as instruments of speculation—"impossible conjunctions of disparate parts, monstrosities of human thought."[6] These were able to draw incommensurate objects together and make equivalences among them, compounding the unnatural associativity of exchange-value observed by Marx. In spectro-economy, this worrisome vision is taken yet further. Spirit money is money with an almost unimaginable degree of combinatorial power.

Chinese have long offered proto-monetary "gifts" to the afterlife. These *yin zhi* were made from joss paper of various colors, sometimes printed with the image of the object(s) to be transferred in the offering—for example, cloth and clothing or medicinal plants and foodstuffs. Here the paper itself served as the medium, and the gift was captured through representations. These should be understood as abstract material qualities and affordances, not as amounts. Among these, money is a subset, appearing as rectangular sheets with printed rectangles of red or circles of gold foil. The foil region grows larger and thicker as the earthly cost of the bills increases, and the papers are of heavier grammage. This is said by many to be most valued by ghosts and thus most efficacious. High-end variants come in smaller stacks and may fetch as much as a dollar apiece. Unlike more recent forms of spirit currency, older *yin zhi* are not typically printed with a specific face value. A wide variety of these are still in common use. In the market stalls near hawker centers and housing estates, there are multiple versions to choose from, and those in the know offered many "rules of thumb" regarding which to purchase.

I was told, for example, that the purchase price of *yin zhi* money, alongside the heft of the paper and the amount of foil, was a deciding factor. Those that are evidently of better make and cost more are assumed to remit more in the afterlife. Mei Zhen Jie claimed that "so long as there's more 'gold' on the paper, then it will be more expensive. Also, if the paper is better quality, it would be more expensive."

I asked, "Does this mean that it's up to you to judge the quality of the paper money?"

"Yes," she replied. "You look at the paper and decide. If it's good, then you spend $2.50, or $3. If it's not so good, you spend about $1.20."

"What about fake versus real paper money?"

"There's no such thing as fake, lah; it's really just a question of quality of the money. The quality of the paper."

Similarly, others noted that there is no counterfeit *yin zhi*—simply shoddy goods that the buyer can freely assess. If the product is of good make, it will be in demand; if evidently poor, it will not. It is a relatively straightforward calculus: the spectral power of the bills arises at the moment of purchase, from their exchange for Singapore dollars. It had been my assumption that some appropriate authority, most likely a Taoist priest or medium, would be responsible for blessing the notes and making them legal tender. In fact, informants were quick to clarify that there is none. They are simply made in a factory and shipped to the point of sale. And like most unregulated goods, their value is set in the market. For example, they are marginally more expensive in the seventh month, when demand is at a peak. Their quality is evident to the canny consumer; there is simply higher- and lower-quality merchandise. In this sense, I was told, buying ghost-money is like shopping for produce. One has to "squeeze the vegetables" and buy observantly.[7]

However, Singaporeans also increasingly enrich the dead with another type of printed bills: hell money or hell bank notes. As the name suggests, these are a form of tender for the netherworld. In contrast to the calm abstractions of older *yin zhi*, they are covered, on both sides, with a riot of graphics and color. Many bear the endorsement of the "Central Bank of Hell." This formidable institution is depicted as a gigantic and somewhat nondescript pagoda or, in some designs, as an American Federal-style megalith.[8] This is interesting in light of Benjamin's characterization of the design of paper money as ornament on the "façades of hell"—in fact, most of these notes literally depict the frontages of *di yu,* to which they are thought to be able to open a portal.[9] There is quite a bit of imaginative leeway here; for example, I have seen a version emblazoned with "Federaerreserve [*sic*] Bank of Philadelphia, Pennsylvania" (apparently the location of the infernal mint). These bills come in staggering denominations, with eight figures being the norm.

Singaporean conceptions of hell money, its production and the source of its value, vary greatly. It was a common assumption that none of the forms of paper ghost-money are printed in Singapore for the local market. Some items were said to be imported from Hong Kong, Taiwan, and Malaysia, but the vast proportion is thought to hail from the PRC.[10] Mrs. Tan, who frequently uses hell money during Zhong Yuan, noted, "All this paper comes from China. But last time when Mao Zedong time, they banned. Banned people from praying. But still they pray. Quietly. The ancestor's anniversary, they also burn. Close the door and burn." Other informants, including Chee Wai, Harry, and Mei Zhen Jie, also believed China to be the largest source of the bills, "as it is with everything else."[11] A few cited Taiwan as another origin, as many of Singapore's ghost-practices are thought to have originated at least partly in Fujian Province.

Unlike the older *yin zhi,* hell money is a rapidly evolving aesthetic medium. A few tropes have become established in recent years. For example, many copy the iconography and visual language of U.S. dol-

FIGURE 4. Hell note depicting the Central Bank of Hell. This is a common motif and appears typically in traditional Chinese architecture or American Federal style.

FIGURE 5. Hell notes that mimic U.S. dollars are of the most common, and least expensive, varieties.

lars, as a kind of universal tender.[12] These include serial numbers and signatories—often none other than Yan Luo, the chief magistrate of the netherworld's courts, or the Emperor of Heaven Yu Di—as well as the familiar matrix of curved lines seen on the greenback. The protean character of paper and print allows for endless addition and recombination of forms. New bills are printed with whimsical flourishes and expensive associations: logos of famous fashion brands and cars, images of Singapore's tourist attractions, hybrid orchids, and "iconic" birds. Benjamin's sinister description perhaps fails to capture the explosion of pictorial imagination on the faces of this phantasmal currency or the ludic aspects of its theater of inventive capital.

Notes that mimic familiar national currencies are relatively cheap. A thick stack, wrapped in a rubber band or plastic sleeve, can be had for a few Singapore dollars. This stands in contrast to more traditional spirit money, which is typically more expensive and uses joss paper of different weights. The role of pricing here is similar to that of *yin zhi* and ghost-auction items (discussed in the next chapter). Value is not understood to originate in an officiating body but from the market itself. In this way, it appears to be rather demotic. Hell money, like anything else, exchanges for whatever we are willing to pay for it. This commodity logic struck most informants as self-evident, and there was some amusement at my assumption that legitimacy would need to be vested by any official party—an idea that smacked, perhaps, of more hierarchically institutionalized religions. The same logic goes for the notes' production. Office worker Nelson noted, for example, that homemade ones from an inkjet printer would likely have little worth, as they would be cheap to make and (probably) shoddy looking.[13] Ghosts might see this and refuse the offering. On the other hand, if one were to pay for materials and perform the labor necessary to create beautiful hell notes, these would have automatic value due to the time and cost sunk into their production.

IRRATIONAL MONEY AND FLUID VALUE

As with all speculative instruments, hell notes contribute to flows of increasing value, in this case via passage to hell and back to Singapore. As we will see later, surplus—in the form of overpayment, gift, or unproductive expenditure—is seen to solicit ghostly attentions and favors. This power to instigate a quid pro quo lies here and hence is at the core of all local spectro-economics. Symbolism of excess is a recurrent motif.

The actual value of a bill of hell money as an input to reciprocal exchange, however, remains ambiguous. There is the problem of denomination: those huge numbers printed on the front and rear, which ostensibly connote its worth. This is hard to understand in rationalist economic terms. Clearly it goes against any logic of currency; one could vastly increase the value of a bill simply by stamping a larger figure on it, leading to immediate hyperinflation as sellers pump up their face values. Certainly this fact is met with skepticism in some quarters. As Harry complained,

> you find that a lot of [burnt offerings] are very commercialized. So commercialized that . . . it's exploited by people. They go and burn money, hell bank note. And all have so much zeros! Inflation so high. Hell is worse than Zimbabwe now.

Certainly the zeros appear to have been increasing annually, although not to the degree of the "Zim dollar" or the pengö.

Interestingly, this does not mean that paltry hundred- or thousand-dollar notes go unsold. I was told repeatedly that the power of a burnt

FIGURE 6. Joss paper money, of a more traditional design, is sorted before burning. The spiral is created by gently kneading a stack of sheets with the thumb and three fingers.

offering to please the spirits ultimately derives from the Singaporean currency spent on it. Here, as in other modes of ghostly exchange, value and power arise from "real" expenditure (especially on items with no apparent use-value). Regardless of what may be printed on one's hell notes, a sacrifice worth S$500 is considered more efficacious than one of S$50. This is why bills marked with six zeros may cost the same in the market as those with ten. Some of the most sought-after and prestigious *yin zhi* notes have no denomination whatsoever.

If this is indeed the "true" value, then the utility of the huge numbers must be explained. Several accounts make sense of this phenomenon. The simplest, and by far the most common, is that large figures simply signal largesse: a spirit of *dafang* (generous) intention is thought to add efficacy to the rites and to the social relationships that they would augment.[14] The dominant logic, in this version, is addition: *more,* of both quantity and kind. When asked about the most powerful of hell notes, office manager Huey Ling replied that she would "burn *all* the denominations, from two to a trillion, and many different

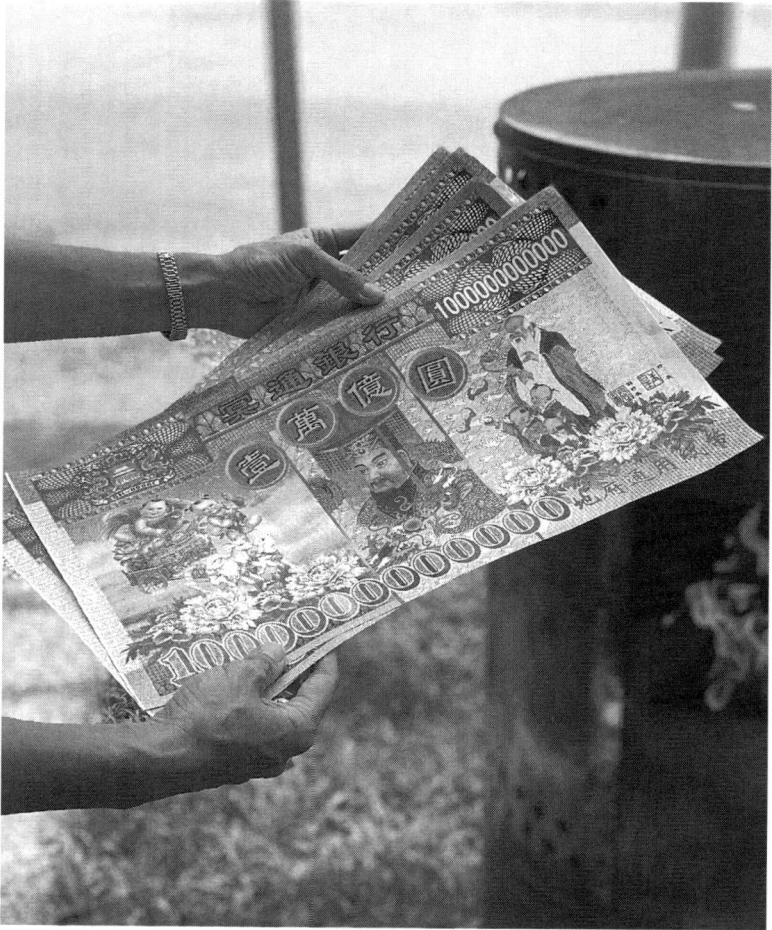

FIGURE 7. A larger, more extravagant and expensive version of hell money, printed in color and with even greater denominations.

designs . . . better to have all." In spectro-economic bricolage, value is always additive and prone to multiplication—a logical extension of its underlying cosmic energetics.

A differing (although not contradictory) account, offered by banker Edmund, is that paper bills embody speculative values that are real but unknown. Although their exact denominations may be understood by believers to be symbolic—or as stand-ins for flows that cannot quite be quantified—the *fact* of their value is not. The outré figures may thus serve to underscore the magical character of this trade: as surplus that is produced in a manner not limited to worldly economic rationality. The phrase "one billion dollars" suggests disproportionate returns available not from a given note but from commerce with the spirit world in general. The ostensible values thus lend the rite a recursive aspect: the single act of burning is an individual investment that dramatizes the power of investment itself.

The nonquantification of such exchanges, importantly, deemphasizes the individual ritual instance. Burning is understood not as an intercourse among sums but as the originating moment of a social relationship or channel. The dead are not obliged to return donations immediately or equally. Tradition simply holds that a happy ghost is a generous one. Believers certainly expect their remittances to be rewarded—often disproportionately—but only through sustained engagement, at unexpected times, in unpredictable ways, and with unspecified interest. These rewards are likewise not "in kind": a spirit does not directly refund but rather works to improve luck in business or games of chance. Payback is thus highly variable. Offerors may ask for more specific favors, like lottery numbers, or they might court particular kinds of success at a Zhong Yuan auction. Here, also, however, the focus is not on precise returns but on the *modification of futures* (see my discussion about luck, later).

Hell money thus connotes not specific values but rather value in motion; in essence, its use signals the intention of the offering, at least in part, as capital. The logic of this is the opposite of sacrifice or potlatch, in which excess value is alienated.[15] Rather, its burning provides an opening into circuits in which value is imagined as increasing through a variable sequence of mediated and unmediated instances, embodied and "free" forms. Fiat currency is exchanged for spirit money and (via offering) for credit in hell.[16] The favor of ghosts causes these to yield, in futurity, manifold lucky returns: more Singapore dollars, or success in career or schooling. Remission to *di yu* works like currency trading or financial arbitrage—the transfer of an object across two markets through simultaneous purchase and sale—in which value increases by instantaneous movement across space.[17] The return loop is likewise polymorphic, typically involving not sums or substances but a manipulation of events and outcomes.

As a result, the use of given types of spirit money will reflect upon nuances of social relation and familiarity. Like many exchanges of value within kinship networks, the offeror walks a fine line. Gains from ancestors are acceptable if approached first and foremost as filial duty. But the use of hell notes would be considered highly inappropriate, crass even, in this context. These are associated with nakedly transactional intent and thus the financialization of family relations. Unfettered speculation is seen as less problematic when it involves unrelated ghosts. As a result, these two engagements are approached differently. Those who burn for recent ancestors will opt for their preferred foods, liquor, and goods. In the case of the more remote dead—those Mrs. Tan refers to as "passed away long already"—typical items are tea, brandy, rice, and fruit or the diverse colored joss papers that translate to specific materials, like cloth. By contrast, denominated bills and likenesses of ingots and coins are offered mostly to unknown and homeless *gui*. *Yin zhi,* as a relatively abstract form, could be used in both. In contrast to the recently departed, other dead have unknown preferences, and consequently the gifts become increasingly fungible and anonymous. This reaches an apex in the impersonality of cash. Attention to such nuances is important, as inappropriate offerings can easily cause umbrage for the would-be recipient.

FREE VALUE AND ASSOCIATIVE MAGIC

The horizon for all types of spirit money, however, is the act of burning. This is the moment in which value is released into its free-flowing phase and assumes a sudden power to bring things, even the most distant and numinous, into direct contact. Spatially, this causes a localized collapse in which Singapore and hell are brought to one another. A ghost is "present" at the burning, as the destruction of the medium draws them to the site and transfers the monetary essence into them.[18] Informal tender thus mimics the ability of capital flows to alter the nature of space and time, to bring the remote near and transact among the incommensurable. In accounts of this moment, the stream of revenue is like unchanneled electricity: connective, generative, and dangerously fluid. Infection by death and the netherworld is possible in this process—hence the chalk outlines drawn around sacrifices, as well as the strict rules about the positioning of ritual paraphernalia and the presumed secondary contagion of ash and other detritus (see chapter 5).

As with Huey Ling's statement about denominations, the logic here likewise emphasizes addition and association. We might think, for example, of Singapore dollars exchanged for a Chinese-made paper note depicting a Louis Vuitton boutique that is burned in exchange for lucky lottery numbers. These in turn generate winnings that help to pay for a real "LV" purse, which is then used to hold Singapore dollars (an actual case).[19] The hell note is a microcosm of the process itself: its stolen luxury iconography is understood to literally and figuratively combine disparate objects—money and branded consumables—which are conjoined in a common circuit when its value is unleashed. The moment of immolation also puts the power of selected representations (the fetishistic character of the notes and their ornament) into play.

For value to be "healthy," for productive associations to occur, it must cycle with regularity through phases of freedom and incarnation. This includes occasional instantiation, but it will become stagnant if imprisoned for too long in a single form. Destruction must also occur for the process to continue. The materiality of sacred value is continually being written and reversed: meaning reduced to ash and reinscribed. As in the history of money more broadly, practitioners of these rites express a clear discomfort with hoarding, with value that is kept out of the stir of motion. This aligns neatly with aspects of capital aesthetics as demonstrated by Elizabeth Helsinger and others.[20]

As described to me by neigong Master Timothy, the logic of this system mirrors geomantic notions of flow in air, water, and temperature, and of *qi* and blood in Chinese medicine. In these fluid models, energies must move. *Qi* can flow through the body and interact with other beings through expanding social and natural conduits. Trapped or impeded flux lies at the root of most pathology. Illness or ill luck, in this system, is often a symptom of a common abnormal etiology. The movement of value through channels and instantiations is similar. This passage is akin to *jing* in the body or language in calligraphy and publishing. These currents are not the same as their embodiments: the written word is not language, in the sense that a dollar is not, by itself, value. Each of these is merely a temporary reservoir, imbricated within ever-larger circulatory systems.

In this respect, value also resembles language, which courses through speech in a manner unlike the written word. Understandably, there is great concern regarding entrapment or ownership. Meaning become disproportionately textual is degenerate and deathly. Ideas demand a certain freedom and are prostituted by being held to ransom for money. For this reason, neo-Confucian thinkers have condemned Western notions of intellectual property as "whorish."[21] The wise ghosts of Wu Hung's epigram, as beings of peripatetic energy, bemoan the technology that would force discourse into fixity or exclusive possession. Wealth, likewise, must be predominantly in motion, and joss paper notes or hell bills stored at length without burning are said to be unlucky. They represent an unwillingness to put value in motion, to reciprocate with ghosts and ancestors, and may even cause financial loss.

The process of embodiment and disembodiment, of capture and release through forms, allows money to operate as the associative medium par excellence. Paper untethers its infernal magic. As *yin zhi* and hell notes are "money to burn"—that is, simply a vehicle that enables value to be sent across the spectral frontier—they are also, inherently, speculative technologies. The unit of currency thus serves as both temporary holder of abstract value and a vehicle by which this value itself may increase, through destruction. We see here the appearance of a paradoxical union between cash and abstract modes of investment—which most commonly occur in computerized ledgers. Through the common medium of paper, there is a kind of playful equivalence, in spectro-economy, between bills of tender and other specie, such as gold bars, ingots, and silver and gold pieces. Because today's thin card can be both planar and volumetric, it can be a surface for symbolic projection or a cunning three-dimensional approximation of objecthood. This playfully bridges traditionally opposed economic realms: where finance is money that is elite and rarefied, notes and coins are typically associated with trade at its poorest and most informal, those "cash ghettoes" of political-economic theory. Recent years have also seen the incursion of other monetary instruments, resembling credit cards from local banks, which ostensibly allow ghosts to charge indefinitely. This is a chain of association seemingly without limit; in the next chapter, we will see cash merge with the commodity via this same associative logic.

MAKING LUCK

Despite the dramatic elevation of value within spectro-economy, it is a subject that, perhaps oddly, goes unmentioned when one asks Singaporeans about their exchanges with ghosts. Many will first emphasize the moral aspect: intentions to be filial or to continue long-standing cultural traditions. Many, of course, *do* describe desires for compensation, but they do so in nonmonetary terms. "Prosperity" is one—a concept that connotes a general well-being extending beyond the financial (explored in chapters 5 and 6). Even more common is the invocation of *luck* or that which is *huat* (lucky).[22] Luck must be understood as the return flow of value, as that which "comes back" from the spirit realm. This implies a kind of convertibility, but not one that is subject to notions of strict quantification.

Others underlined this same idea. *Gui* may command the currents of earthly fortune—they can give us winning numbers and improved rates and margins. They do not write checks or provide direct windfalls. Ghostly deals thus centralize luck in facilitating returns; it is the spectral medium par excellence. In many walks of Singaporean society, this is perceived merely as a form of nicety or "doublespeak." Jean spoke of luck in rather skeptical terms, noting,

> Chinese will always pay homage to anything that gives them money. They are not talking about spirituality or eternal life. They are very temporal. As long as you allow them to "touch" 4D already they will pray to *anyone*.

Such a view perhaps simplifies the degree to which exchanges like auctions (see the next chapter) and the burning of hell money create moral forms of speculation in which luck puts the pecuniary at a distance. Of course, Chinese religion does not strictly prohibit monetary dealings in social life or even within the family. This reflects the significant admixture of Confucianism in Chinese popular religion—as well as in Singapore law, under which older adults can demand maintenance payments from grown children.[23] Regardless, the numinous mode of speculation is one in which participants are careful to maintain respectable social and spiritual motives, and avoid the stigma that lingers over high-risk "quick money" schemes at the margins of business practice.

Here, too, however, there is significant polyvocality: while respondents were quick to emphasize the importance of protocol, each seemed to have a different account of the "correct" procedure. Many were quick to warn, for example, that reciprocal divination practices—those that involve the possibility of creating luck—could not be attempted with just any ghost or deity. Rather, specific conventions dictate which may be approached. I asked a number of regular lottery players if they felt able to pray to Buddha for luck; all of them answered that this would be a shameful practice. This did not rule out Singaporeans going to Thailand to pray to Buddha for luck, which they would not do "at home." Harry pointed out,

> You find a lot of [Singaporeans] go to Bangkok, they do this in Bangkok year after year. They pray to the Four Faced Buddha, pray that OK, if you give me a good life and so on. And I will come back a year later and make offer. Same thing. Next year, somehow you must return the favor.

Gardener Mrs. Tan had undertaken this trip herself. When asked why Thailand was preferred, she cited its heightened state of paranormal activity. Thai temples are considered places of uncommon mystery and power, where occult dealings produce both wealth and misery. It is assumed to be a place where anything is available, at a cost. For Mrs. Tan, this was true in the search for luck, as well as for health and healing. She noted of a Thai temple near the Malaysian border,

> That's why we go! We thought this type of thing, movie only got. . . . Yeah I go there, there were every time those people I was, "Eh, ask one, ask for luck! Can you give me luck?" He said, "Money, ah? 4D, is it? No, now you got sick, we are curing your sickness first. After, when you cure ah, you sure have one." Really! After I cure, I come back, I strike twenty-five thousand dollars. [*Laughs*] Really. But true, lah, I believe in all this. Really have one. Every time we go, ah.[24]

Closer to home, Harry noted that specifically Taoist shrines and temples (*sin tua*) as well as some Buddhist organizations within Singapore will make small loans in the belief that this produces luck. These nominal amounts serve as a form of speculation similar to the use of spirit money. He notes that "they even have these temples where you can borrow money." This is not large sums but token amounts "for good luck only, [like] a couple of dollars, ten dollars or so." The following year, the borrower will return double the amount. Like bank loans, he says, this convention is "generating money!" Overhearing the latter, another contractor was quick to describe this practice in less venal terms, noting that "[whatever luck or profit you receive] is for thanks. It's a token of appreciation" for the spirit of charity.

In response, Johnny pointed out that if "you want number, you must go to Toa Pek Kong; that's the one in charge of wealth, 4D number, and all that."[25] Construction sites make use of a rather strict division of labor of different kinds of luck among various ghosts and deities. Toa Pek Kong ("Grand Uncle," or the god of prosperity) is responsible for wealth generation, whereas Tu Di Kong (the earth god) is in charge of accident prevention.[26] Hungry ghosts and resident spirits are the "gatekeepers" who must be appeased to avoid bad luck and negative energies. Many stories of such exchanges have nothing to do with the lottery, and many individuals evidently feel some discomfort in admitting to gambling. Other iterations of this trope involve different conceptions of luck: promotion at work, an ability to find lost items, aversion of accidents, and the like.

While luck serves well to explain the backflow of value, it does nonetheless raise some thorny questions of evidence. Nonbelievers would naturally assume that the outcomes of national lotteries still obey typical probabilistic distributions. For this reason, a person who enlists the aid of gods or ghosts may very well continue to lose. Business ventures, likewise, fail as well as succeed. How, then, is stubborn reality of bad luck accounted for? If someone engages the spirits with the correct protocol and does so unsuccessfully, how do they justify continued belief?

I encountered several modes of explanation when things do not go as expected. The first arises from the fact that the faithful appear to dismiss isolated events in light of larger beliefs. They maintain confidence that, sooner or later, the ghost will get around to making good on their reciprocity. This is consistent with the nature of spectral economics writ large—that is, as a faith-based practice, and not an immediate transaction. Here the logic does not differ dramatically from the prosperity gospel preached in many of Singapore's megachurches: the higher power's doings are mysterious, and the greater plan is beyond human understanding. This is reinforced by discursive characterizations of ghosts themselves, who are thought of like irascible, willful older relatives. Their behaviors are not expected to be rational or systematic—and this is part and parcel of the danger in courting them. They will improve one's luck when they are good and ready, and sometimes not at all. The consequence is that gifts may be late arriving. This is seen, simply, as a cosmic fact that requires patience and undiminished conviction.[27]

A second mode of explanation arises from the nature of betting systems. Punters do not play a chosen number once. They do so multiple times, often until it comes up in some form, either in whole or in part. Almost all gamblers have lucky or favored combinations, and a common local saying when something unusual happens is "buy 4D!"—meaning, play the current date as a number, as divine forces are clearly at work. Important, in this regard, is the fact that 4D also pays out smaller stakes for partial combinations. The game is structured such that many winners get smaller amounts. Regular bettors commonly have stories of winning a few hundred or a few thousand. Interestingly, this system designed to keep punters "on the hook" also keeps them engaged with spirit practices. A divined number serves not as a single test of faith but as a prolonged, sustained commitment. When eventually a combo does win, it is understood as spectral reward.

Anecdotally, there also appears to be a great deal of confirmation bias at work. Those who followed these practices emphasized successes and dismissed failures. Fortunate attempts were understood as proof of faith, but no one seemed to believe that ghost-reciprocities guaranteed success at every offing. Rather, the expectation was that luck would be generally more in their favor, and that sooner or later their practices may be rewarded with a big payout. As with gardener Mrs. Tan and husband, Tony, many attributed gambling wins (for themselves or acquaintances) to sacrifices long past as well as recent. Contractor Mr. Ong claimed that one divined lottery number failed, but his firm was awarded a sizable commission on the next day.

Last, as we will see in the case of ghost-auctions (in the next chapter), there also appear to be self-fulfilling wealth effects at work here. Those who dutifully perform rites are presumed, in this climate of faith, to be prone to better luck and more successful outcomes. They are thus thought to be more reliable partners in trade and are sought after and trusted in business dealings. It is thus not hard to see how offerings can produce luck, also, via explicable processes that are beyond their immediate explanatory frameworks of cause and effect.

GHOST-MONEY AND THE FINANCIAL IMAGINARY

For participants, the exchange of spirit money is no less genuine that the other "immaterial" economies that have made Singapore a locus for abstract forms of multinational finance—and in which many, themselves, participate. It is thus perhaps unsurprising that exchanges based on spirit currencies appear to mimic the logic of many forms of capital so central to the island's wealth. These draw on a complex and sophisticated understanding of money in which cash is but one form. In the realm of *gui,* however, such operations are democratized and liberated from regulators and larger institutional players. Government and brokerages, managers, and funds—and even religious authorities—are largely eliminated. Spectro-economies imagine speculative finance from the standpoint of the individual punter; the majority of transactions occur directly between the citizenry and the ghost-world. While they embody actual economic activities, the practices described earlier have the quality of market ethnography—authored via the circulating narratives of those who are deeply affected by a world in which sources of wealth become increasingly remote and removed from deterministic factors. In its double role as economy and contemplative mechanism, ghost-worship is not unlike the tradition of American "bucket shops," where the working class made bets on the rise and fall of stocks that they could not afford.

In conclusion, then, we might ask, how do the economic presumptions of hell money and other paper offerings mimic, invert, or distort this world of speculative practices? Where are the parallels and analogisms?

Monetary ghost-economics, what we might think of as spectral finance, does not traffic in the arcane detail of equations or operations but exists in the slipstream of the imaginary: via symbolic, systematic relations of risk and value, security and surplus, futures and presents. The burning of money adopts the operational forms of Wall Street (or, more locally, Shenton Way), albeit combining their tricks in ingenious and unorthodox ways. It is possible herein to identify certain tropes of the speculative that recur across the field of ghostly monetary practice.

Most clearly, spectro-capital resembles the cyclical process of investment. The believer who exchanges her "real" currency for hell notes and burns them sees this as (among other things) the opening of a sequence that can realize more money over and above her initial input.

This act takes a given amount of value and puts it in motion. It is not important what the exact nature or quality of the investment might be; the medium of spirit agency can turn bad debt into good—as ostensibly could subprime collateralized debt obligations. Spectral investment is determined by expectation and not by effectiveness, and it is the nature of markets that some deals will be more efficacious than others. As noted, ancestral observance constitutes a special case in that it is understood as ethical finance, tied to filial piety, as well as a circuit of exchange.

Here, as noted earlier, investment achieves a kind of exaggerated freedom. It is liberated from association with any specific venture or event and rather becomes a wager on one's *financial futures in general* via the medium of "luck." Investment is made not in a given "vehicle" but *in the person of the investor*—a kind of individual magic or mana thus arises as the effect of social magic.

A second parallel is with insurance. Reciprocal deals to get hold of winning numbers, like uncannily effective commodities (see the next chapter), clearly attempt to realize a degree of added certainty. They are instruments to intervene in the normal working of chance: to alter the flow of luck in favor of the offerer and hedge against the normal course of enterprise. Many who utilize these have "skin in the game"; that is, they are tradespeople, of various kinds, with capital at stake.

The *huat* potentials offered by spirits are expected to act upon luck generally and not upon a given venture—the negative potentials of life are *generally* "covered" (one hopes) by a deal with ghosts or ancestors. This is an attempt to protect against specific as well as abstract threats, not least from the vengeful acts of wrathful ghosts. Burning remains a propitiating act, and hopes for improved fortunes stand alongside obviating setbacks or disasters. Like insurance, increasingly, this is seen by believers as an obligatory social responsibility. Life's risks are not necessarily financial, but are offset by financial means—that is, by the conversion of Singapore's "real" dollars to spirit money.

This imaginary of cover is most clear in the construction and development sector, which is the subject of chapter 6. Here it is common to hear of a kind of Pascal's wager among nonbelievers. It is better to make offerings out of respect—for cultural tradition, for others' beliefs, for the unknown in general as a catch-all category. Building sites are often the locations of violent accidents, and spirits are understood to make these more or less likely to occur. Different deities are solicited for different types of protection, but ghosts remain the wild cards; those who "receive" sacrifices on sites may be the nomadic and the hungry or historical residents who are assumed to take a dim view of the arrogance of changes made to their property. The insurance offered on-site thus melds the idea of coverage with a kind of protection racketeering; ghosts may stop normally occurring construction injuries as well as those potentially inflicted by the ghosts themselves.

Last, the potentials of spirit tender replicate monetary play: financial operations that would appear to make money from money, without engaging in either production or the buying and selling of physical things—for example, through the conversion of "forex," or complex traffic among bank and money market accounts with differing rates and conditions. Herein, value seems to arise through the inherent properties of money itself. Such activity is very common in the higher echelons of "personal" retail banking as an incentive to high-net-worth customers. Such clients typically reap lucrative rates and amenities for providing liquidity to banks, which draw upon their retail arms to buy investment products, currencies, and corporate debt.[28] Private subsets of banks that offer such deals, alongside luxurious consultation rooms and concierge services, have made themselves visible as aspirational spaces in the nation's upmarket malls and hotels.

Here hell money merges largely abstract and digitized modes of exchange with cash—both of which have a reputation for replicating dangerously, for enriching and destabilizing by turns. Age-old associations with devilry and alchemy tap into a vein of (largely antispeculative) cultural paranoia in which bills, notes of credit, stocks, and debt are all related forms of unholy and unreliable wealth. In fact, corporate debt is still called "corporate paper," though it now exists mostly as blips in digital ledgers. Here, also, the postcolony's shared Anglo-Chinese visions of paper as a powerful but unstable medium of transformation echo monetary history: from the earliest days of Chinese mulberry money under Kublai Khan to letters of exchange and bills, paper money was seen as an instrument of speculation. In reality, both paper money and coins, for most of economic history, have traded for amounts different than their face values.[29] Here, as in many other aspects, the phantasmal properties of hell money seem more like hyperbole than pure invention.

Not least, the playful freedoms of spirit money must be read against conservative Singaporean policy positions that maintain a dogged focus on the stabilization of the SGD's exchange rate—even to the exclusion of conventional Keynesian monetary strategy.[30] The PAP, from the days of its early financial architect, Goh Keng Swee, worked primarily to secure the purchasing power of the public and against the threat of currency traders. While the nation offers a staid and technocratic vision of currency, the ghost-world tantalizes with ineffable gains and "notes" that grow in value at the moment of their purchase.

How might this be understood as a "social fact" of the spectropolis? Neither the use of spirit money nor the idea that gods and ghosts exert numinous powers over wealth is new—in fact, these predate the rise of modern speculative financial practices, in Singapore and elsewhere. However, the rites and their paraphernalia have clearly kept pace with the times. *Yin zhi,* which has been used among southern Chinese for centuries in one form or another, is notably more abstract than hell notes, which are a relatively recent innovation. The current versions, with their vibrant graphics, have emerged only with the rise of cheap, high-resolution digital color printing and are even newer than many of the monetary products that they have come to mimic. Where *yin zhi* creates a diffuse reciprocity of unquantified value for unspecified prosperity, hell money has introduced a symbolism of dollar amounts. As we have seen, a radical elasticity and unpredictability still permeates the conventions of its use. Chinese spectro-economies have long replicated investment; it is only recently that explicit mentions of "venture capital," "funds," and "money markets" have entered the discourse.

This financialization is influenced, also, by changed understandings of volatility. Older respondents in particular noted a marked shift in discourse, in which *luck* serves as a hedge against economic downsides in particular. This stands in opposition to more generalized notions of one's life faring well or poorly, which might encompass considerations like health and social standing or a negative logic of narrowly missed accidents or setbacks. Here ghost-practices may be following a broader drift toward the ascendance of a commercialized cultural sphere. At the same time, such a preoccupation may represent increased unpredictability in Singaporeans' personal wealth. As economists Tan Kim Song and Manu Bhaskaran have noted, the public has recently begun to experience more frequent downturns, and the high capital investment in specific sectors has exposed the national economy to more volatility in general.[31]

Not least, the last few decades have seen a relative stagnation of economic advancement for many Singaporeans, in particular those in the middle and lower tiers of the class system. Overall wealth inequity has skyrocketed. Government-sanctioned expenditure on housing, a relative lag in the expansion of "adequate social security against the volatility of an open global economy," and the depressive effect of foreign labor on wages relative to gross domestic product have all been cited as contributing factors.[32] Concerns about the CPF model have caused a number of older adults to return to work in low-end service positions. In the shadow of the Singapore miracle, macroeconomic forces become more mercurial and individual futures more precarious. Perhaps unsurprisingly, the notions of prosperity imagined in ghost-exchanges reflect this larger financial fate, in which individuals have increasingly been subject to diminishing returns on labor and to the ups and downs of remote forces. Hell money represents, centrally, an opportunity to bypass earthly titans and appeal directly to spirits who are far older, and far more accessible.

3

Spectro-Commodities

Singapore is often depicted as existing in unchecked thrall to retail, to branded goods, and to the power of the fetish. Cherian George, for one, has lamented a social compact whereby the loftier aims of civic discourse and self-rule are routinely sacrificed in an officially endorsed pursuit of the tangible—where one is encouraged to "pursue prosaic material comforts, rather than live up to high-minded political principles for their own sake."[1]

C. J. Wan-Ling Wee, an astute cultural critic, has likewise observed that "the state's petit bourgeois, philistine modernity" has often been concerned primarily with accumulation.[2] The phrase "delivering the goods," with its air of vulgarity, has often been used to describe this feature of PAP politics.[3] An emphasis on aspirational consumption has engendered a particular type of urban culture in which gazing upon luxury items—alongside eating—is thought to dominate an anemic public sphere. This society boasts one of the highest rates of shopping per capita in Asia, giving rise to a city that, as described by sociologist Chua Beng Huat, "often appears as one continuous shopping center to foreign visitors."[4]

Such concerns are undoubtedly well founded. At the same time, more can be said for Singaporean consumption.[5] At the very least, its practices include unexpected notions of property that extend far beyond the realm of the tangible. There are possessions, in local shops, that the living cannot own or must share with numinous others. These include paper simulacra of smartphones and tablets, designer shirts, credit cards, unusual pets, and cars—even syringes full of an infallible Covid-19 vaccine.[6] One can find, here, an entire commodity-world by proxy. At the same time, there are earthly goods, owned by humans, that gain superhuman efficacy in being "inhabited" by ghosts. In their complex rules of purchase and use, such spectro-commodities hold magical potentials and powers: an order of possessions that appear to possess themselves (in whole or in part) or respond to the prerogatives of an unseen and increasingly illegible new regime of ownership.

The objectivity of the object assumes, in both, an ever more supra-human aspect: a transfer of emphasis in which agency is seized by the inanimate and familiar rules of property stand inverted. As with spirit money, formal economic categories of commodities and currency, alongside vehicles of investment and securitization, are scrambled and imaginatively recombined.

Whence comes this imagined affinity between ghosts and goods? Like speculation, the commodity has often been described in spectral terms. Arguments by Derrida, Žižek, and Diefenbach, among others, echo such language from older passages in the first chapter of *Capital,* which explain the cultic effects of exchange.[7] In this venerable formu-lation, the commodity-form gains a phantasmal autonomy, an illu-sion of life, through the coexistence of two modes of value. The social character of production, a determinate engagement between laboring bodies, becomes obscured by a conjuring act: the "necromancy" of an apparent transaction between commodities themselves. In per-fectly ghostly fashion, these appear to act by their own volition and are possessed of objective qualities. Marx invoked a language of spir-its to describe this collective self-delusion, "a definite social relation between men, that assumes, in their eyes, the fantastic form of a rela-tion between things."[8] This can only be explained by recourse to "the mist-enveloped regions of the religious world." Via a perverse magical inversion, we are ruled by a regime of valorization that appears to be exterior to ourselves and running amok.[9]

The commodity is where Marx's notion of the fetish intersects with that of Sigmund Freud's *unheimlich*: a creeping unease that arises when the foreign is detected within the familiar. The capitalist "alienation" of the object is not merely the seizure, removal, or abstraction of the social and the "homely"; it also necessarily entails reencountering the expropriated as a sinister and autonomous entity. The artificial invest-ment of an inanimate thing with living (if borrowed) social force is perhaps the *most* uncanny of possible conditions, hearkening back to the murderous wagon wheels and farming tools put on trial through-out "prehumanist" European history.[10] This grows yet more alarming in the broader Marxian critical theory as not merely a category of malevolent object but as that which determines the entire logic of a socioeconomic regime and a phenomenal lifeworld.

Some recent commodity types would appear yet more spectral. For the theoretical arc from Georg Lukács to the Frankfurt School and Guy Debord, the ghostliest of goods is the "cultural product": film, music, popular literature, horoscopes, and magazine features. For Theodor Adorno, societal belief in ghosts reflected the occult mystification of this new world of consumption, an animistic throwback that served to sublimate the effects of alienation through irrationalism.[11] The specter and the spectacle act in concert to promote quiescent consumption. In this formulation, ghostliness is but one guise of the fetish—a component of its social regime. Quite literal assumptions of haunting have characterized "pop" products in the collective imagination as well. As Jonathan Sterne and Neil Kirk have shown, this is particularly true in the case of audio and visual recording, which have long been thought to have an otherworldly affinity. Gammeltoft has documented a similar phenomenon with prenatal ultrasound.[12] Assumptions of kinship between technical and spiritual frequencies go back to the invention of the microphone and gramophone, which were assumed (even by their inventors) to be able to pick up voices of the dead.[13] More recently, similar claims have been made about digital media as well. As we will see, many of these are now considered to be preferred by *gui*.[14]

In this chapter, I introduce the categories of Singaporean commodities that are explicitly spectral—their uses, protocols, and trade. More generally, I attempt to demonstrate how these embody an imaginative popular ontology that contemplates the power of things and their regime of value. Central among its concerns are the boundaries between objects and value-generating processes and novel, emergent regimes of fetishism and ownership in the era of the digital. As we shall see, phantasmal goods also underscore emergent qualities of Marx's recondite and "necromantic" formation that appear to signal a world-historical shift in the constitutive relations between human beings and their property. Last, we will explore the status of obsolete or "dead" commodities, their afterlives as imagined in tales of haunting.

KIMZUA AND EMPTY THINGS

Mr. Tan, age fifty-six, describes seeing a suckling pig that has been offered in sacrifice to the Otherworld. It looks "the same but not the same." Somehow, he puzzles, "you can tell that there is nothing behind the skin." Such gifts of food and liquor are not touched while the joss sticks burn. When the flame sputters out, these are considered to have been consumed by the spirits, their flavor and nutritional value exhausted. They may be eaten afterward, but with the proviso that they are "empty" of the qualities of food, and they are often given to construction workers or domestic helpers. You may eat them, but you cannot consume them; a respondent warned me that they are tasteless and that "you will be hungry almost immediately after." The object, now, has a purely formal existence. Value is considered to be emptied on the altar, awaiting a reciprocal investment of favor and luck from the spirits.

What Mr. Tan describes in the pig recalls a pair of *kimzua* (joss paper) shoes or a shirt—the proxy paper commodities that have evolved from large, hollow-framed effigies to a sophisticated market (online and offline) for printed objects. There is a thinness at the surface that one cannot quite place, the suggestion of missing internal substance. It is the visual hallmark of an object that is presumed to have entered the ghost-economy. This notion of commodity emptiness is a dominant trope of sacrificial items: ritual can imbue hollow forms with power or value or create them by taking away the substance of that which is materially present.

Kimzua are visually riotous and wildly diverse and sold throughout the island in specialist shops and market kiosks. One can purchase houses that often combine (in one exquisite corpse-like object) the homely Southeast Asian bungalow with a bank, an ATM, a KFC franchise, or a corporate office tower—or a French Hermès shirt in the pattern of a regional *batik*. These are burned alongside effigies of everything from perfume and shaving kits to nannies and maids to family dogs, aircraft, credit cards, bottles of liquor, and mahjong sets. Presumptions of the ghost's desires typically involve bricolage: assemblages of seemingly irreconcilable objects, valuations, and ideas.

Kimzua is a variant of the Mandarin *zhiza*, a craft tradition that has served both funerary and celebratory purposes. The cremation of effigies is said to date back thousands of years, to strategies in the Northern Song dynasty for foiling grave robbers—and, perhaps apocryphally, to human sacrifice of retainers by wealthy nobles. Bamboo and joss paper are three-dimensionalized using methods similar to the construction of lanterns for seasonal festivals. This is laborious work, requiring the artisan to split stalks with a blunt, welded metal blade. These are combined into frames lashed with rattan and clad with colorful patterned sheets that represent, in various degrees of abstraction,

FIGURE 8. Screen capture from Kimzua.com.sg, one of many online sources for ritual items and paper goods. Items available to be gifted to the dead include a "mansion," an office tower with luxury retail at base, a petrol station, a Mercedes G-Wagon, and a Louis Vuitton set.

materials and ornaments. Papers are also printed with numerological and geometrical symbols to increase the efficacy of the overall object in its journey to the ghost-world.

Kimzua includes structures for the dead and for funerary rituals that assist the passage to ancestral status: bridges and vehicles, as well as mansions that resemble fifteen- and twenty-story versions of traditional Chinese architecture.[15] These cater for the journey to *di yu*, as well as an eternity (mostly) spent there. There remains, however, a very broad array of other comforts and necessities that has expanded continually in the last century—especially in the context of Singapore, Hong Kong, and Taiwan. As noted in chapter 1, these are painstakingly constructed and built to order; their associations of spectral power have much to do with fearsome price tags in the tens of thousands. Historically, such costs were subsumed into large funerary budgets and often paid for with insurance and savings schemes.

More recently, however, the range of conventional *kimzua* has been complemented by cheaper, factory-printed paper goods. These are almost entirely China-made and shed the abstractions and traditional materials of the older artisanal process. These make use of high-resolution, large-format reproduction and easy access to online stock imagery. When they first entered the local markets, the majority mimicked small-scale consumables, and this remains the bulk of the product. Online sites list packages by type: necessities (like toiletries), staple and luxury-branded clothes, "sinful" sets of liquor and cigarettes, electronics, check books and debit cards, and Mitsubishi air-conditioning units. There are even cards and gambling items, which are perhaps less useful to *gui-shen,* who can predict and alter the future.

The past two decades have also seen a proliferation of miniaturized buildings and vehicles. These are far cheaper than the traditional items and thus can be burned more frequently and in greater profusion. Access to Adobe Photoshop has also, apparently, led to some experimentation in architectural design—the conventional Chinese design of *zhiza* has given way to a postmodern orgy that combines corporate modernism with a range of building styles and vernaculars. These also meld virtually any thinkable combination of functions. Banks and shops are particularly prevalent, as these can serve the dead in perpetuity. Cheap *kimzua* has mostly put the artisanal building trade out of business. One of the last producers in the grand style told me that he only supplies directly to temples and has closed his shop front to make a few items a year out of his flat.

The technological shift in paper goods has been closely attended by a transformation in their nature and aesthetic logic. Traditionally, specific joss papers were thought to have unique capacities to transfer materials and substances to the afterlife, depending on their color. Green paper, for example, was used to send cloth. *Zhiza* thus had a certain conventional materiality, and the mimetic character of effigies existed alongside a certain abstraction. That is, the logic of these objects was not entirely pictorial, depending also upon color, writing, and symbology. Zhong Yuan offering "packages" still contain these older items, which are more expensive due to the inherent cost of the joss material. The rise of printed Chinese simulacra, however, has introduced a very strong countercurrent of pure visuality. Ghost-objects now compete for verisimilitude, and photorealistic surfaces take the place of simple approximations and volumetric forms. In this transition, there has emerged an increasing association of the ghost with photographic resemblances.

This is demonstrated in what have become among the most popular of all ritual gifts: smartphones and tablets, such as Apple's iPad. The iPhone for ghosts is a cardboard box with the familiar touch screen printed on front and metallic texture on its back and sides. While this is adapted from a product photograph on the company's site, it has a model number far higher than those presently on the market—at the time of writing, the iPhone 25 was available. This follows the inflationary logic of ghost-offering, in which all numbers tend to increase. It likewise reflects the belief that those in hell are atemporal and thus exist, at least in part, in the future. The ghost-phone is thought to allow the ancestor or *gui* a means of communication within and beyond the spirit world (to haunt, in effect). In fact, the paper object is doubly effective: by virtue of its being set alight, it is already considered a mode of communication between worlds.

I have been given logical explanations for the appeal of such objects. In an echo of late Victorian beliefs, respondents described ghosts as existing "like waves," oscillating in nonvisible parts of the spectrum. As such, they are attracted to technologies that radiate similarly, and in particular to artificial light and video screens. I have also heard a more pedestrian version: that the dead, like everyone else in Singapore and the modern world, seem to love novelties. In other accounts, this

FIGURE 9. A "technology" set of ancestral gifts. Despite their apparent realism, all are made of printed card and will be burned in offering.

affinity appears more complex and evocative. The preferred iPhones and iPads are conduits, and ambivalently so: on one hand, they appeal to the consumer as an ostensibly unmediated connection to a world of images, spectacles, and experiences; on the other, the medium itself remains an object of desire. *Gui* are thought to prefer things that have this "empty" or referential quality. Tech devices present a world that, like the ghost's, is reduced to a shadow play of appearances without substance. The hollow paper smartphone dramatizes this insubstantiality, just as it underscores the divorce of the ur-modern commodity's form from its contents.

Affordable Chinese *kimzua, like tech devices,* draw their power from resemblance—from the traffic of pictures and desires. They reproduce a spectral "attitude" toward consumption: an endless parade of approximations. The ghost and the ghostly commodity, in their mirroring of each other and of advanced economy, gesture back to the logic of fetishism—not to Marx's vision of occult obfuscation but to a phantasmagoria of longing, self-making, and ownership endlessly deferred. Interestingly, however, the dominance of these items has come up against a limit: the problem of value itself. The affordable house/bank/boutique has not entirely replaced the *zhiza* palace, owing to an effect that we will see in the next section. This is the role of expense itself in the remission of value to the dead. As discussed with respect to ghost-money, many still consider the worth and efficacy of burnt offerings to be derived from Singapore dollars paid and not from the appearance of the proxy itself. Thus promises of "proper" bamboo and joss paper houses are still made to ghosts who deliver on reciprocal exchanges. And these are still seen by many as the most effective bait for ghostly payouts.

Harry noted this practice with divination at the sites of road accidents in particular. A modest burning is made in situ, with promises of a larger gift if the divination proves correct (a performance bonus for the ghost, in effect). The former is used to divine the numbers, which are immediately put into circulation. However, "people do say, 'OK, if I [win], I will come back with lots of offering, even a paper house.'" Owing to its careful construction and price, such a house is still seen as the most reliable protection in the netherworld—and the Singaporean emphasis on homeownership, as the baseline of personal success and security, is likely a contributing factor as well.

Believers related numerous versions of this exchange of a ghost-home for forms of luck. Mrs. Tan, for example, described purchasing both a *zhiza* house and altar space in the temple for her in-laws. Her husband's brother and sister-in-law were not well loved in life, and proper observances had not been made on Qing Ming or death anniversaries. As a consequence, they had been seen haunting the outside of Mrs. Tan's house. A friend had suggested burning a house and placing plaques for them in the temple, where further observances could be made. Mrs. Tan recalls,

> We said we have no money. If you give us strike—4D, lah—then we'll put you to the temple. And really, we struck! That day when [my husband] Tony buy for me my IC [identity card] number, then I have to go and buy. Then he said, "Hey I go and buy for you your IC number." Then I go and buy, then two persons struck.[16]
>
> *Both of you struck?*
> Ah, second prize. Each person three thousand dollars. So, we put them into the temple.
>
> *How do you move them into the temple? You move them, you move the plaque?*
> Ask people to make [plaques], then put them [in the temple]. Then they've got a place to stay already. They won't come and disturb you.

They also spent a thousand dollars on a modest, three-story paper-and-bamboo building. This decision grew from concerns about the separation of the *shen* after death, and an anxiety to provide multiple "places" for the dead, to cover all the bases. On a similar occasion, Mrs. Tan and her husband proposed a reciprocal exchange with her husband's grandparents. She told them that if they struck 4D, they would buy a large paper house for them to use. She recalls, "Then on seventh month, first day, we strike!" Her husband won S$13,000, and they sacrificed a paper house costing S$5,600.[17] In this narrative, it is important to note two things. First, the 4D payout was ostensibly achieved relatively soon after the offer of reciprocity was made. Second, the winning event occurred on the first day of the seventh month, or Ghost Month. This was thus understood by Mrs. Tan to confirm her actions as having been the right thing to do—bringing comfort to her dead relative while making some money in a moral way.

What emerges here is an unsettled tension between two under-standings. In more traditional accounts, as we have seen, numinous power still derives at least partially from real-world value. Though inputs of Singapore dollars may be irrationally amplified, they are still considered crucial to the production of surplus. This is being increasingly challenged by a new, predominantly representational logic whereby value originates in resemblance. This recalls the analogical structures of what Marcel Mauss termed "sympathetic" magic, in which objects that look similar are assumed to be causally linked.[18] This emergent approach has obvious advantages, as the ratio of expenditure to profit is far lower. It also aligns neatly with a growing emphasis on the visual in the production of wealth, via digital products and spectacular commodities.

At the same time, there are familiar factors of social distinction that influence these trends. As described by Pierre Bourdieu—and as reflected in Singaporean (and global) consumption more generally— kimzua purchases increasingly signal choices of identity among increasingly variegated and specialized proto-commodities.[19] The fact that the dead may have "lifestyles" simply underscores their being imagined as social beings. Among paper houses, there are "traditional," "postindustrial," and "minimal" versions for sale. These can be assembled a la carte, with choices of furniture, art, and carpets (mid-century modern furniture, such as Eames recliners, has a clear fan base). Taipei and Hong Kong, in particular, are sources for "hipster" kimzua items available from e-shops, including sleek, minimalist paper homes and modern cheongsams like those worn by actress Maggie Cheung in Wong Kar-Wai's In the Mood for Love (2000). Expensive, imported paper goods are often justified by the good taste of departed "haute" consumers. Numerous respondents, at least, expressed discomfort with off-the-shelf objects in "cheena" ("crass Chinese") style.[20]

We see here revived tensions between standardization and bespoke design, where mass goods have been increasingly replaced (as elsewhere in Singapore) by an ethic of niche marketing. Xuan, a university student who worked as an apprentice to one of the nation's last remaining zhiza craftsmen, noted that her employer became tired of constant requests for customization. He complained that "everyone wants a paper house like their actual home, or their dog, or their helper."[21] Though tailored forms eased the "boredom" of churning out standardized houses and cars, the master quickly realized that his eco-

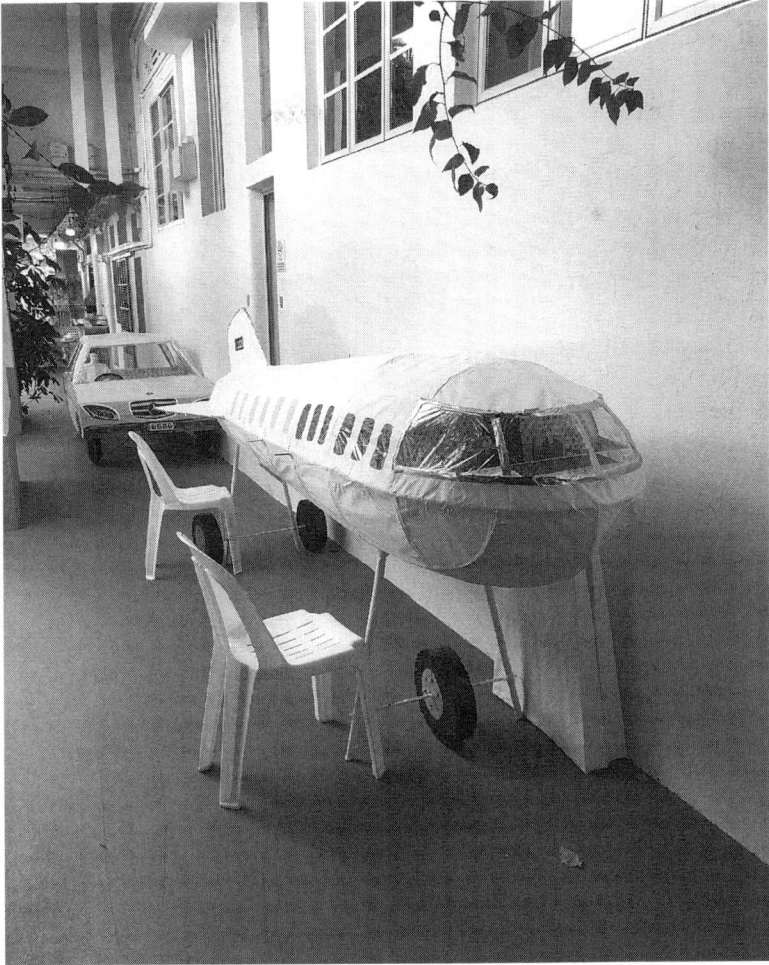

FIGURE 10. Expensive, large-scale bamboo-and-joss-paper items, built traditionally and by hand, stand next to a tent where a wake is in progress. These are still considered to be the most efficacious of ancestral gifts.

nomic survival depended on repetition. This change in tastes contributed, in part, to his eventual decision to retire.

This transformative tendency exists alongside another. As shown in the previous chapter, the medium of paper allows for contradictory aspects of cash and commodity to converge, and to assume characteristics of speculative finance. In the newer Chinese *kimzua* items, everyday architectures merge with sites of production and value-creation—hence the allure of paper condo buildings that contain their own offices, ATMs, and luxury boutiques. Or of paper banks, which in theory allow the dead to continually draw on funds. While the single printed object is finite, the open-ended pictorial nature of the ghost-economy implies that printing a Visa or Mastercard may multiply the worth of the offering indefinitely. These are a sort of meta-money; like Mephistopheles's mint, they push into the realm of the infinite. By the same token, this fundamentally alters the traditional temporal character of gift exchange from an isolated instance to a kind of perpetually generating mechanism. The ghost continues to receive and to give. This has the flavor of venture capital, of credit, of "passive" income. At the same time, it recalls observations by Fei Xiaotong about concerns, within Chinese cultures, to avoid closing reciprocal cycles.[22] Being "even" results in the closure of social obligations and, with it, the withering of circuits for value's unquiet motion.

GHOST-AUCTIONS: HAUNTED INVESTMENT AND BLESSED SURPLUS

The Zhong Yuan auction dramatizes a process that is nearly perfectly opposed to *kimzua* and food sacrifices. Here we find a logic more akin to the haunted bric-a-brac that is discovered at the outset of many ghost stories or construction "incidents." Where burnt offerings are characterized by an emptiness—a formalism that is recuperated by usefulness in *di yu*—Singaporean conventions also allow for spiritual investment into prosaic things, and the elevation of these to a condition of supernal "fullness."

As Tong notes, these popular events offer inexpensive commodities to eager bidders, fetching far more than their typical market prices. The surplus is due to the belief that these have been "blessed by the spirits and are thus more efficacious in fulfilling their functions."[23] Schoolbags and exercise books are believed to help the buyer's child with the Primary School Leaving Examination and other stressful challenges.[24] Culinary items bring satiety and health. Business paraphernalia, like calculators and stationery, supercharge one's commercial enterprises. A variety of toys offer protection and well-being to children of various ages and serve in effect as numinous minders.

FIGURE 11. Lee Yuan Xing, an auctioneer at a seventh month dinner event, stands in front of an evening's lots. This includes alcohol, Louis Vuitton handbags, urns and statuary, kitchen appliances, a Rolex, and a mahjong set, among other items. All are considered *huat* (lucky) when purchased in this context. Auctioneers like Lee may conduct as many as twenty such events over the course of the month. Still taken from an interview by Our Grandfather Story, a Singaporean online media group, posted September 2017.

More recently, lower-end phones from Huawei and Samsung allow a teen user to cultivate online status as a social media "influencer" and to ward against cyberbullying. Here, as ever, the spirits' gifts are imagined in terms of exponential potency and variations on the theme of "luck" and "prosperity."

Rather spectacularly, total proceeds on items at a single event regularly surpass S$100,000 and often climb into the millions. While the effectiveness of the goods is clearly a draw, larger auctions also provide a highly conspicuous venue to associate oneself with otherworldly prosperity through generous bidding. These occur across the lunar month, at banquets to which important members of the community, including local business leaders and members of parliament, are invited. They form a major revenue stream of the ghost-economy, as a complement to *yin zhi* and *kimzua*.

Renee, a young architect, noted that enthusiasm for these auctions still runs high among the "boomer" generation. Each year, her father and his friends "will bid for this ornament at auction, that's supposed to bring you good luck." She understood that the money goes to the

FIGURE 12. Packs of lottery tickets are popular auction items. Still taken from an interview with Lee Yuan Xing by Ou⸍ Grandfather Story.

temple but was surprised that older folks were *most* covetous of objects that have no apparent use. In fact, many of the expensive lots are mere trinkets and ornaments, and prices appear to increase in inverse proportion to functionality. High rollers are known to pay hundreds of thousands for an urn or figurine that is cheaply made and chiefly ornamental.[25] Renee noted that her father often bought "an amulet, or a small statue." This isn't owned so much as rented; he buys the right to put it in the family home or office for a year before donating it back to the temple, along with his bid in cash. The most prized lot, a *hei jin* (literally, "black gold"), has no material worth at all. It is an ornamented lump of coal, said by some to contain trapped spirits, which bring unspecified wealth to its owner. It is purchased for six figures and is burned one year later so that "the ghosts may be released."[26] By this account, the *hei jin* traps spiritual flows; it is a perfect congealment that is nothing other than value itself.

The organizing of an auction need not be overseen by a temple, a medium, or some other religious authority—although, by convention, it will form part of a larger sequence of activities involving burning, as well as the offering of food and joss sticks. It is expected that part of the proceeds will go to some religious cause. Johnny pointed out that "the temple can organize it, or a hawker center, or a whole neighborhood can organize it."

It can be any bunch of people?
Yes. A few of them get together, set up a lot of tables . . . . They
have a committee among themselves. And these are not official
committees, not registered and that. So every day, they collect fifty
cents, a dollar. Collect, collect, so just before the seventh month
they pool together money. And they use the money, they go buy
offerings. And then, they have dinner as well. And during the
dinner, they auction off all those. At the auction they say hundred
dollars or so, next year they have to return the hundred dollars.
The higher bid, got to return the money. The money goes in the
pool again, must pay again before the seventh month.

As Johnny noted, the amounts wagered by the bidder are not immediately due. Rather, any tender for a given item is a form of credit that
must be paid just prior to the next year's Ghost Month, when the next
auction is to be held. In the meantime, however, the commodity is
allowed to produce prosperity for the buyer. It is, in effect, a form of
credit within the ghost-economy, as well as a bond of reciprocity between the lender and the temple. This does not need any underlying
security; it is assumed that any smart buyer will be too afraid to de-
fault. The auctions are known to be highly profitable. Harry explained,

They will do them at carparks, then they have dinner outside.
Some, not all. When they pray, that's when they auction things.
Whoever has donated will be invited. There are members, members of the group, in addition to committee members. So, every
month they will collect some money [similar to a subscription].
Thirty dollars a month, and that. That's why a lot of people are involved. A lot of charity organizations—National Kidney Foundation and all want in. For example, even these [community centers
(CCs)], before the dinner, they have to apply for a permit from
the MPs. So the CCs, some of the money goes to them. That's why
the national charities get involved.

So the charities and community centers will offer something?
Yeah, they will say, "I will issue a permit for you, to hold the
dinner." They say, then, please, auction this among the members.
And the money goes straight away to the organization—National
Kidney Foundation, or whatever it is. It's not small money. You

know how many sites there are? Even if it's a few thousand dollars from one side, it's a lot of money, you know. The Buddhist free clinics, community building fund, other building funds. There's money, everyone jumps in.

The ghost-auction thus creates an intersection between ghost-economies, charities, and state institutions like the CCs—those hubs of activity in public housing estates. In the arrangement described by Johnny and Harry, the CCs will host the event, together with a nonprofit group or local fund. It will begin with lavish burnings, followed by a banquet and auction. One portion of the proceeds benefits the operating budgets of the participating institutions, and another will serve as seed money for the following year.

The auctioned items are known to be blessed by the spirits at the moment a successful bid is recognized.[27] But, as with hell notes and other sacrificial paper, this investiture does not occur through the mediation of a religious authority. Instead, it is the mere act of purchasing the item at an inflated price, and thus providing for charities and Zhong Yuan activities, that is assumed to be the origin of its power. Participants plainly stated that there is nothing special about the goods themselves. Their utter ordinariness is an open fact. This is even true of that seemingly mysterious congealment, the *hei jin*. Many dismissed as metaphor the idea that it "contains" ghosts, saying that it is simply what it appears to be: a decorated briquette. As Harry observed, "it's charcoal. Just a normal piece."

"The temple doesn't do anything to it at all?" I asked.

"No, that one you can buy anywhere. I mean, they decorate it to look nice. You can buy it yourself at the temple at Waterloo Street. Can find in a lot of shops there. Maybe it cost a hundred dollars. But the person bids a thousand dollars. That's how they generate money and luck."

In fact, the banality of the object is indispensable to the ritual. It is this, set against the power to command large sums, that is expressed in the *hei jin*.[28] In this alchemy of the ghost-economy, coal is turned into "gold." But, as with *yin zhi* and luck, this is not seen as a symbolic act; participants are very clear about the real-world efficacy of such objects. Mr. Seng, highest bidder at a ghost-auction in 2008, laughed when he explained that many people wanted to deal with his import business because they knew that a haunted object was in his possession. Its positive influence, as with good and ill luck more generally, is assumed to be socially contagious. At the same time, accounts sometimes involve a logic of negation, to the effect that "things could have been much worse" *without* the ghostly commodity. Like the proverbial stick that repels tigers, the schoolbag or amulet is seen as having saved one from unhappy events that did not occur. The simple fact that such assumptions are unprovable appears, in practice, to close off a certain amount of doubt; good things are credited to the sacred purchase, while bad ones are dismissed as facts of life.

The logic of value-magic asserts itself repeatedly as the auction proceeds, and appraisal of the merchandise veers increasingly upward. Participants gazump one another with ever-larger tenders, beyond all proportion.[29] By all accounts, however, this mode of consumption is itself considered generative for buyer, seller, and ghosts alike—like the burning of *yin zhi* or a paper iPhone, it sets in play a sequence of compounding gains for all involved. This is because surplus, in the guise of overpayment, is understood as the motivating essence of reciprocal spectro-exchange. For this reason, the bid itself is the sacred act.

The commodity is central to such traffic; as with hell notes, it serves as an interchange where multiple forms of value are arbitrated: credit, state tender, ghost-money, and luck. These are serially vested in its "empty" interior, and a specific understanding of their intercourse is socially cemented at the fall of the gavel. It is an almost bewilderingly complex and indirect transaction that begins when the buyer offers to pay an irrational amount for a given lot. This is merely promised and is not understood as an outright exchange of dollars for merchandise. Rather, these funds—to be paid one year hence—are seen to reimburse a part of the previous seasons' earnings, which have already been spent on a sacrifice of *yin zhi* and hell notes to lure spirits to the present event and to transfer value to them. This influx empowers hungry *gui* nearby, who express appreciation by returning some of their renewed vigor into the commodity. Depending on the price, this will provide varying degrees of prosperity and security for its possessor for the next twelve months. In this convolution, the backpack or calculator is not merely a pretext. It is an indispensable conduit without which the *fort-da* of speculation would be impossible. Its ascension from ordinariness to spectral efficacy is instant but relies on a recursive temporality of credit that enfolds past and future revenue into a common moment, a time "out of joint."

In the auction, the old formula of fetishism—with which we began—would appear to be absolutely exposed, via a ritual exaggeration. The otherworldly powers of those worldly goods seem quite literally "theological" in character, and they are priced accordingly. By convention, they are presented upon a dais swathed in red fabric, in the grand manner of Taoist gods. To see this event as merely an outsize performance of the glamour of the commodity, however, would be to fundamentally misread it. The objects here are understood by all to be empty, or nearly so. They are merely temporary repositories, their powers on loan. Their overt paltriness is, as noted, essential to the dramaturgy. Rather, what is deified on the altar is *value itself*, as a cosmic force of enormous potentiality.

This understanding, shared by all present, reflects the specific vision of value-dynamics encountered in the previous chapter. What is temporarily invested in the commodity, that curious substance, does not originate in the exertion of human labor; rather, it is an inherent property of the universe. It is metaphysical. Humans cannot make it, but we may amplify it through monetary operations—through buying and selling, in secular and ritual modes. It is an independently real, capillary force that does not "begin" but circulates endlessly and may be channeled to any destination. Living people and ghosts serve merely as signalmen on its tracks, assisting the passage among beings, inanimate things, and environments. For this reason, Bataille's "accursed share" is neither destroyed nor truly alienated here. While some redistribution does occur via auctions—notably in their charitable function—it does so within a capitalist imaginary of limitless enrichment. The conception of a positive-sum economy implies that these can be both religious events and sites of nakedly pecuniary interest, without contradiction. Large bids, like large denominations, represent a faith in the tendency of wealth to expand, which here also assumes deeply religious connotations.

This strange mediumship of the commodity—its role as an interchange for real and numinous monetary flux—exerts some unexpected effects. First, as we have seen from the preceding examples, haunted things are not typically subject to devaluation. On the contrary, they *retain* value, and even produce it, after their sale. So long as they are inveigled by *gui*—or by ancestors or gods—possessions can continue to realize surplus, and enable *huat* life, until they are finally discarded or complete their contractual term. The key innovation here is that the product itself becomes an ongoing site of production. Its role is consummated not in the moment of purchase but in a lively and ongoing agency. The spectral commodity produces profit for the seller and also for the buyer, who becomes, by virtue of the sale, a "lucky partner." Importantly, the worth of the haunted merchandise is not inherent but is derived from the ghost and the real-world assets that it protects. The coal briquette defends the buyer's capital. The "magical" schoolbag is not dear of its own accord (it is an often shoddy mass product) but rather because of its ability to safeguard the enormous potential of educational capital in the school system. As noted, the poverty of the object is essential to its spiritual power.

Second, as mentioned earlier, spectro-commodities operate in a manner that opposes the hoary Marxian model of fetishism. The "occult" object is, paradoxically, characterized by social transparency: its value arises from the *relations* of humans and ghosts, not from any "objective" characteristic of its own, real or imagined. As such, it fails the test of concealment. Ghost-economies are structured around gift and obligation between people, living and dead. At no point do they appear as traffic among things themselves; in this sense, the auction plays a role quite contrary to the ahistorical, anonymizing market.[30] Commercial wares act as mere circuitry—rather than embodying an uncanny "fullness," it is their emptiness that is operative.

Last, we can see in the auction how the influence of the ghost collapses the typical relation between the twin aspects of the commodity, use-value and exchange-value. In the conventional formulation, these are independent and measured by different criteria.[31] Utility is a qualitative affordance, whereas market rates are quantitative. Although any salable item must satisfy some desire or need, function remains only as a kind of tenuous thread. There is no such schism within the spectral commodity. The more one pays, the more extraordinarily effective the object is thought to become. And the reverse is likewise true: the uncommonly powerful object is nearly always a source of enrichment. As use-values become magically augmented, even "useless" things perform uncommon practical service—not least in the further production of wealth. This explains the logic behind paying nearly S$100,000 for an urn that is ugly, poorly made, and purely ornamental. This is not Adornian irrationalism. What we see here is a recuperation of that most *unheimlich* aspect of the material world under capital: the divorce of two modes of valuation and the alienation that results. The discourse of haunted goods returns to a form of holism. Given the extraordinary emphasis on property and possession—in Singapore as elsewhere—it seems altogether fitting that everyday consumables would be reenvisioned as the vehicles of a phantasmagoric reconciliation. Through the ghost, Marx's weary "hieroglyph" is cast as something redemptive, promiscuously generative, and consequential to a cosmic degree.

Ghostly possessions, like spirit money, serve to imagine economy as a medium of agency, social relation, and betterment. In the theater of offerings and auctions, the commodity runs wild. Freed from the shackles of earthly rationality, it assumes the hybrid and hyperbolic forms of *kimzua* and—as with hell notes—merges with the speculative processes that, within Singapore's spectral practices, often stand for capital in toto. Mere paper can initiate flows of enormous value and utility, while cheap tat, sold at a premium, promises passive wealth. Here, also, Chinese religion offers a vision of agency that extends beyond the circumscriptions of the subject. As we will see with housing and development, also, its practitioners go to work on the world *through* the commodity as a lever—domesticating chance, shaping futures, directing unseen currents of health, safety, and prosperity. In this conception, anything that can be owned can provide access to the material-energetic substance of life in full.

But this is not the only possible account of ghosts and goods. In passing, and by way of closure, we may note another discursive mode in which the spectral plays a rather different—far more traditionally melancholic—role. This provides a complement to the gleeful embrace of commodity culture and perhaps gives voice to an ambivalence about the role of objects at the center of Singapore's contemporary.

As described in the preface, uncanny events are often reported to begin with the discovery of a lost or discarded memento, some rusted bauble found in a drawer or amid the rubble of a construction site. This is unearthed, touched, or removed, instigating a series of unsettling or violent manifestations. Retroactively, often via the deduction of a medium or Malay *bomoh*, the ghost is said to have been upset by contact of the living with its "property." The often-trivial concerns of *gui* frequently fix upon a world of social detritus—a devalued reflection, à la Marx's camera obscura of the glamorous objects and fantasies that populate consumer culture. Old watches, broken cameras, and tortoiseshell combs encrypt within themselves the failed utopian aspirations that are the essence of the commodity as hieroglyph: the "trash" at the heart of Walter Benjamin's writing that, in the words of Max Pensky, serves "as markers for a continuum of unfulfilled utopian expectation."[32] It is precisely such everyday social and physical detritus that, like the corpse of the commodity, is frequently reanimated in the haunting. As Benjamin predicted, the return of such objects holds the potential to trouble the regime of the new—to pull back the curtain and reveal the infernal stagecraft of capital's "creative" destruction.

To this end, the ghost appears to be beholden to the commodity in a kind of fraught double relation. Certainly there is the delirium and liberation of alternate economies, of the kind that we have just seen. But this figure is associated *also* with another netherworld, of social and commercial debris lost to the phantasmagoria of novelty: an archive of dead things. Such objects are not remembered in a properly historical sense; they are perhaps too mundane. But the ghost insists that they are still property. While enraptured with novelties, the ghost acts, perhaps paradoxically, to defy obsolescence: old ejecta of the market are re-presented in novel, mysterious, and dangerous guises. In a clearly different register, the Benjaminian jetsam of hauntings may offer a contemplative or heuristic mechanism, a kind of cry made without clear or satisfying explanation. In both registers, the spectral commodity would open a different window onto a mad and "mist-enveloped" situation.

PART II

The City and Ghostly Ecology

4

Ghosts in the Garden

> Singapore is a nation by design. Nothing we have today is natural, or happened by itself. Somebody thought about it, made it happen. Not our economic growth, not our international standing, not our multiracial harmony, not even our nationhood. *Nothing was by chance.*
>
> —Prime Minister Lee Hsien Loong, April 5, 2008

> Might the old ghosts become part of the new ecological balance?
>
> —Jonathan Lim, *Between Gods and Ghosts: Our Supernatural Skyline*

Perhaps more than anywhere else, the rise of Singapore has been engineered via the medium of the physical environment. The young country's striking successes were harried by Lee Kuan Yew's oft-repeated worry that limited land and resources would inevitably lead to underdevelopment.[1] From the moment of rupture with the Federation of Malaya, the PAP articulated a politics of scarcity-as-emergency that depicted the city-state as a "fishing village" enervated by "soporific" tropical air.[2] A presumed hostility of the equatorial climate to modernity—and the rhetorical association of islands with isolation and finitude—justified the making available of everything, all material substance and forms of life, to the cause of capital accumulation. In this, the state would act as both enabler and enforcer.

The mass razing and re-creation of the nation as a designed and securitized object has created room for radical experimentation in managed risk. In this process, the nascent government replaced a sprawling fabric of informal urban villages with an array of tower hamlets imagined as microcosms of the new state—as Singapore-in-miniature. At the same time, this monumental labor cleared the ground for an essential reterritorialization: a new geographical division of labor between housing and finance. This novel order has been realized, unified, and made operational via the medium of nature in Lee's Garden City model: a performative landscape that provides a principal medium for the partitioning of the nation, its zones and its activities. This chapter recounts the story of Singapore reborn as a safe space for speculation and, in no small irony, how the production of an investor's idyll was also understood to generate ghosts at an unprecedented scale.

To "read" Singapore's particular hauntedness, we must consider the anxieties of a nation as an intentional spatial construct. For this reason, the second half of our study entails making explicit connections between questions of spectral economy and those of urban geography, landscape, and architecture. It is here that the ghost's alleged behaviors become meaningful and agentive. The abstractions of this spectropolis require the exploitation of a physical substrate and cannot be delinked, in their reality, from the muscular violence of the island's ecological and material histories. It is precisely this turn of events—the sweeping, strategic reconstruction of the postcolony into a designed haven of financialization *and* illiberal legalism—that informs the contemporary. Allegations of uncanny spaces and visitations acquire legibility, as we will see, from the underlying environmental logic of economies that engage the spirit world. In narrating the physical landscape, spectral discourses invert official ones. The island's body is not merely a neutral container; rather, it serves as the primary substance of statecraft, economy, and social order. Read through the religious lens, it is a field of ecological spheres where materiality and spiritual energies come to be linked. This has, in no small part, to do with the principal role that architecture and nature play both in its entrepreneurialism and in the intensive management of everyday life.

Herein the figure of the ghost troubles the microadministration of national space. It haunts roads and subway lines, as well as the protected territories of military encampments, land reserves, and bureaucratic offices. Most dramatically, as shown in chapter 6, it causes problems at the sites of speculative properties in process. It flaunts borders and boundaries and so insists on the precedence of other spatial contiguities and proscriptions.[3] Last, as we shall see, it posits alternative rules of landownership and occupation as part of complex environments that determine fluctuations of value and the quality of human life in all aspects.

To explain why this should be—and to provide an opening to

the local significance of such discourse—I will attempt to introduce Singapore's self-fashioning as, in the words of Prime Minister Lee Hsien Loong, a "nation by design":[4] first, through the rollout of modern towers and superblocks by the young HDB—producing, in effect, a condensed public committed to formalized economy;[5] second, in the removal of graves and clan-owned lands that operated (alongside the spatial contraction of high-rise architecture) to clear the island's center for speculative property; and third, in the construction of a landscape viewed both as aesthetic performance and as administrative mechanism. Last, I explore how the effects of these processes come to be understood, in turn, as spectro-genetic.

THE DESIGNED NATION AND THE MICROPOLITICS OF ENVIRONMENT

For those accustomed to Euro-American democracies, the micropolitical attentions of Singapore's administrators might come as a surprise. Journalist Cherian George recounts one example, personally witnessed. While attending Tree Planting Day in Esplanade Park in 1990, then prime minister Lee Kuan Yew was seen to kneel to the pavement and, with some dissatisfaction, extend his hand. George recounts that Lee "looked increasingly agitated":

> It was the park's microclimate that he was most concerned about. Unceremoniously taking leave of the parks officials, he and Mrs. Lee took an unscheduled walk along the Esplanade, with security officers and reporters hovering. . . . He noted that although the sun had nearly set, one could feel the heat through the soles of one's shoes. He squatted suddenly and placed a palm inches off the ground. He could sense the heat radiating from the pavement, he said.[6]

It is uncommon that warm concrete, a few degrees of ambient temperature, would be considered the stuff of state. Lee himself has noted this as a peculiarity of his leadership. The maintenance of each plant on the island was considered an important task, and he wanted investors and foreign leaders to "see well-maintained lawns and shrubs" when they "visited him in the Istana." Lee noted in a late interview that the landscape was a "secret weapon" for Singapore and that its design was central to the nation's transition "from third world to first."[7] For this reason, National Park chief executive Tan Wee Kiat joked (perhaps nervously) that he was "the only gardener in the world to report directly to the prime minister's office." This echoes the assertion of Victor Savage (cited in the preface) that Singapore's landscape is the product of planning at the level of the individual shrub and dustbin.[8]

Nothing seems too tiny to escape the notice of the party. In fact, its discourse of stern care often has to do with demonstrable attention to detail. Islands in the geographical imaginary have a unique status, as zones in which life can be subjected to the fullest intensity of social power at a granular scale.[9] In an era when most states appear committed to abdicating matters to private caretakers—or to ignoring them completely—the political culture of Singapore as island laboratory often appears obsessed with minute considerations.

This makes more sense when we consider the lasting influence of environmental determinism at the heart of its ideology. Indeed, much of the nation's planning strategy has been informed by a Fabian belief in physical spaces as constitutive of the human character and its potentialities.[10] Savage has chronicled the "belief in environmentalistic influences" among Lee's lieutenants and has shown that this rather unfashionable idea continues to permeate the Singaporean project. As we will see, apparently insignificant or subpolitical elements gain importance by being linked across scales, in the metonymies of PAP thought, to larger spatial and social orders and their objectives.

This is not interpretive guesswork; the actions and statements of government render explicit its concerns with space making as a transformative social influence. Moreover, the clarity of state intentions is visible in the form of the landscape itself. In a few decades, Singapore has been quite literally reshaped: flattened, extended, sutured, and compartmentalized.[11] Its knotted topography, an involution of knolls and *longkang* (drainage rivulets), was regraded into a flatland of engineered surfaces and infrastructural channels. As numerous commentators have noted, a sense of indeterminacy lingers. Cherian George has observed a phenomenon of Singaporeans feeling "lost at home," disoriented by a lack of long-standing landmarks.[12] Most strikingly, perhaps, the perimeter of the island—what geographer Thongchai Winichakul might call its "geo-body"—has been doubled since independence due to coastal reclamation.[13] It is not uncommon to find that a road like Telok Ayer, which sits more than a kilometer inland, was once a towpath along the docks.

In true determinist fashion, the imposition of a modernized urban matrix has been understood by the PAP as a lever to galvanize labor practices and discipline and to control birthrates.[14] While other nations were beating a market-led retreat, Singapore doubled down. As Lee (the younger) noted, "public housing was much more than an urban planning exercise, or an engineering and construction project. It was a social, economic and political endeavor."[15] And while Singapore is known for policies and campaigns aimed at creating a globally competitive workforce, these are not merely reinforced or transmitted—as in Foucault's theorization—by the configuration of "*dispositifs*." Rather, the production of architecture and landscape is where the very substance of the political is devised. Where the modern state considers its work via a governmentality, we might say that Singapore does so through what Arun Agrawal has called an "environmentality": an iterative entanglement with actual lives, in situ.[16]

ENVIRONMENTALITY, OR STATECRAFT AS SPACECRAFT

The government's approach to spatialization (if we can forgive the clunky term) has been a mix of strategy and improvisation.[17] It has occurred amid what urban economist Cedric Pugh calls "the most sensitive of interfaces": a modernization of the built landscape via resettlement, in a context of heightened attention to the politics of housing.[18] The efficient provision of subsidized flats, which today accommodate more than 80 percent of the population, remains a pillar of the PAP's claim to legitimacy. For our purposes, it is crucial to understand three of its effects as a successful medium of embourgeoisement: in creating an ordered, legible national space; in producing a citizenry wedded to formal labor and invested in the national property market; and in effecting a total redistribution of built fabric across the island. Together, these laid the groundwork for a new, speculative city.

This uneasy venture was begun by the HDB shortly before independence. The PAP began its rule after the bruising 1959 general election, as a coalition between Lee Kuan Yew and fellow "first generation" leaders, including Goh Keng Swee, Toh Chin Chye, and Lim Kim San.[19] After an early flirtation with socialism, the party pursued an increasingly capitalist-corporatist approach to national development and household capital accumulation.[20]

Prior to the PAP's rise, the responsibility of housing the populace fell to the colonial Singapore Improvement Trust (SIT). Colonial authorities had repeatedly voiced concerns about overcrowding and "slum" conditions prevailing in much of the island for the first half of the twentieth century.[21] Despite a chronic shortage of space, however, the SIT did little to increase the number of dwellings available to non-expatriates. British authorities had maintained a mostly Malthusian policy; an invisible hand was expected to provide, and the administration "did not consider housing as part of the responsibilities of government."[22] The SIT's principal tasks were regulating sanitary conditions, rationalizing roads, and drawing up plans for acquiring new land.[23] Despite the creation of Tiong Bahru, an art deco *Siedlung,* the general record of the colonial administration was poor. By 1941, with conflict coming to the region, the SIT had managed to complete only twenty-one hundred low-cost units island-wide.[24]

The war and occupation by Japanese forces served to worsen the shortage. This was yet further strained by a peacetime baby boom and an influx of female laborers from southern China.[25] A committee convened in 1947 estimated that "a quarter million persons or more than 25 per cent of the population already required immediate housing while the total was increasing at an estimated rate of 30,000 people per year."[26] The situation became even more dire. From the year of the report to the time of Lee's government taking office in 1959, the number of residents swelled by another 641,000. Goh Keng Swee, in a similar study, used methods employed by Booth and Rowntree in Britain to calculate that 25 percent of the public lived below the estimated poverty line and some 73 percent in severely cramped conditions.[27]

Ideas about housing, both before and after independence, were heavily colored by the imaginary of a sprawling, unhealthy, and unruly social body and the dominance of informal trade. In 1965, much of Singapore lived in kampungs: informal urban villages of mostly self-built housing in Malay style, roofed with corrugated zinc or *attap* (palm thatch). These were understood by the young PAP, as by colonial authorities before them, as dangerously ungoverned places. This was especially acute because of undocumented labor migration in the postwar years. As historian Loh Kah Seng has observed, these ramshackle quarters were assumed to be home to a general promiscuity, a mixing of elements that were better kept apart. A variety of ethnic groups (all immigrants to some degree) coexisted cheek by jowl, as did unmarried men and women, humans and animals, and individuals plying all manner of legitimate and marginal trade.[28] Immigration from China raised the specter of Communist agitation on one hand and "secret societies" on the other. To make matters worse, many of the kampungs shared their grounds with sprawling Chinese, Indian, and Malay cemeteries.[29] This was a landscape where the "living eked out an existence in close juxtaposition with the dead, and typically, graves spaced between one to nine meters apart covered the hilly portion of the land while squatters lived in the foothills."[30] A deploring study of the location and condition of burial grounds, conducted in 1952, shows two large informal cemeteries in Tiong Bahru—SIT's erstwhile showpiece—alone.[31] The life of the kampung continued to be administered by a range of quasi-formalized political bodies left over from early in the colonial period: trades, language groups, and (perhaps most vexingly) the *hui guan* or clan organizations that had provided a paternalistic framework for community functions like mutual aid, burial, education, and temporary housing.[32] The mobility and impermanence of this informal urbanism, as well as its role in keeping the public out of the formal labor economy, were dominant motifs of official consternation.[33]

The kampungs, unsurprisingly, offered a ready symbol of the "old Singapore" that the PAP hoped to eradicate.[34] Owing to a series of relocations, negotiations, and "fires of convenience," Lee's party began the process of rebuilding.[35] And they made no small plans. At inception, the board was charged with producing 150,000 new "emergency" units of housing.[36] It bore the mandate to prepare and execute proposals for new structures, to continue the ongoing project of land acclamation and "slum clearance," develop heretofore "rural" areas on the island's periphery, manage all new state properties, and—perhaps most importantly—provide loans at an established rate of interest. In a style that mixed socialism with petit bourgeois aspiration, the HDB expanded homeownership over a series of rolling five-year plans. Apart from a brief downturn in the late 1970s, their targets were realized without fail.[37]

This was solved through a cellular approach to national space, in the design of "New Town" estates—a leap, in effect, from buildings to urbanism. In these, the PAP's micromanagerial governance devolved to local "grassroots" offices, where it was expanded and intensified.[38] The first was Toa Payoh, begun in 1965—conceived in Robert Owen style with a fixed population, light industrial facilities, and a pedestrianized high street at its center.[39] At the outset, these new urban villages were projected to house 245,000 people in 49,500 dwelling units— clustered, according to the voguish cybernetic planning theories of the time, around nodes of facilities: banks, post offices, cinemas and department stores, schools, CCs, child health and maternity clinics, playgrounds and open spaces—and, later, large shopping malls.[40] The HDB initially managed all affairs associated with the grand Singapore housing experiment, a task of staggering administrative scope and complexity. The Board did not merely oversee cleaning, gardening, repairs, and upgrades. As an independent statutory organ, its responsibilities also included administering social campaigns, enforcing strict guidelines for the use of private and public space, "community relations" among families of different ethnicities and religions, and referring individuals to counseling in the case of deviant behaviors.[41]

Here, micromanagerial concern with physical detail was moored to a larger system of political significance: the government worked to install a version of itself at every scale. PAP order commonly nests the small with the large, in a total hierarchical chain. The desired effect was not merely that the New Towns resemble one another. More important, perhaps, was the process by which each estate, indeed, each HDB tower block, was explicitly designed to replicate the nation as a whole. As Siddique and colleagues and Kong and Yeoh have explained, it is stated policy to control the racial and economic mix of each of HDB's buildings such that these mirror the national average.[42] Having learned from the painful history of unrest among ethnicities—in intercommunal violence during the years 1950 and 1963–65—it became an official policy of HDB to forbid ethnic "enclaving."[43] The PAP developed an acute awareness of these "islands of settlement," as well as a worry that the lives and labors of Indians, Malays, and Chinese dialect groups would be organized according to the protocols of clan associations and ethnic interest groups rather than by those of central government—hence the emphasis on the location of individuals from the nation's ethnic constituencies.

The cellular replication of the overall nation directly affects the physical landscape, giving it an oddly reiterative character—as pointed out by many of those who have objected to its environmental homogeneity. Critics like Pasi Falk and Colin Campbell have characterized the national landscape as "a set of city centers writ small." Benedict Anderson simply described it as "incredibly boring."[44] This is, in part, exacerbated by the pastel-painted schematism of the New Town architecture. Built chiefly from concrete and homogenous pavers and kept rigorously clean, these cannot escape the impression of being diagrammatic versions of something larger, messier, and more materially and socially sedimentary.

Regardless, the intended effects of this program are clearly manifested today. Eight out of ten Singaporeans live in HDB flats, servicing their home loans through formal employment.[45] There is only one remaining kampung on the island, which is now visited as a "heritage" tourist attraction.[46] Not least, the population now occupies a tiny footprint, leading to one of the world's highest densities: around seventy-nine hundred persons per square kilometer.[47]

THE STATE AS SPECULATOR

The re-creation of Singapore as an array of microstates ("estates," as they are known) was not an isolated project. Rather, it was part of a long-range plan to clear land and reconstruct the nation's physical and economic landscape around a zone of speculation, or, in the words of the Urban Redevelopment Authority (URA), to "remake the Central Area into a vibrant and modern commercial center."[48] Whereas the residential "heartlands" were to remain an amalgam of systematic architecture, this commercial core is spectacular and malleable.

Singapore's postindependence strategy—one might even argue, its "pragmatist" ideology—has rested largely on twin pillars of stability and capital accumulation. While this "hegemony of the economic" initially began as a Keynesian model of productive industries, managed markets, and monetary policy, it quickly evolved into a new animal.[49] This transition occurred in the late 1970s, fueled by a powerfully emergent, late modern view of government and economy—a mode of capital based in rising service and finance sectors. National organization was coming to be seen less in terms of an equitable distribution of social goods, and more entrepreneurially: as a source of partnerships between public resources and private money. In this moment lay the beginnings of a reaccommodation between the technocratic state and the circuits of ascendant Southeast Asian "tiger" wealth.

A fitting spatial division of labor was suggested by the United Nations. In November 1963, an "international" planning study was issued, authored by the team of Harvard professor Charles Abrams, Susumu Kobe of the UN, and Otto Königsberger—an émigré from Nazi Germany and head of the Department of Development and Tropical Studies at the Architectural Association in London.[50] Their "Ring Plan" proposed an arc of dormitory suburbs lining the north coast, from Punggol in the east to Jurong in the west.[51] The new housing districts were thus, to varying degrees, exurban banlieue. The southern and central areas were to provide an economic "development zone" comprising a port, commercial/industrial and entertainment regions, and a nascent central business district built from the colonial city center. Although progressively modified by the URA, this plan continues to underlie the large-scale partition of the country's land uses.

While the sweeping renovation of Singapore created opportunities for "spec" development throughout the island, the greatest intensity was to be concentrated in the middle. These districts are home to the ultra-luxe malls and condo complexes that mushroomed during the postindependence years, particularly during the rise of the so-called tiger economies of Southeast Asia. The same period also saw the nation's retail boom, cementing one of the highest per capita shopping markets in the world—due in part to a high savings rate and disposable income enabled by subsidized housing.

This created spectacular fortunes for a number of private developers, who rapidly overtook Euro-American wealth at the top of international rankings in *Forbes* and elsewhere. Many of these remain active, fueling the phenomenon of local megawealth. Singapore, Inc. emerged as an engine for the coproduction of public and private value and made the government into a well-heeled organization—not least, as principal owners of the limited land reserves available for new malls and luxury towers. And while the PAP has never allowed direct parcel sales to subsidize its budget, the profits have formed an endowment that (as noted earlier) generates billions of dollars per year for operating expenses.[52] The state is also, in effect, a commercial landlord, one of the largest in a valuable rentier market. Receipts from an array of property investments have filled the coffers of the Government of Singapore Investment Company and Temasek Holdings, which has a portfolio worth more than S$300 billion.[53] This makes Singapore a world leader among sovereign wealth funds.

As abstract and diversified as this portfolio now appears, it must be remembered that it was the material stuff of the city-state—land and buildings—that first propelled it to affluence. Most of this was consolidated as eminent domain, under a 1966 Land Acquisition Act that was, like much of Singapore's law, built on the back of colonial emergency regulations.[54] It has given the PAP the right to claim private holdings on a compulsory basis, to set the purchase price, and to limit the means of legal appeal by the prior owners—justified, in part, by the need to eradicate crowded kampungs and clear sites for HDB blocks. From 1959 to 1984, the government acquired 17,690 hectares, which "constituted about one-third of the total land area of Singapore then."[55] Notably, by the 1970s, much land acquisition was being justified as a cooling measure to sap some inflationary momentum from the city's already booming property market. By the end of this period, the total ownership of land by the state equaled 76.2 percent, much of it purchased at bargain rates. A good proportion of this was also occupied by Chinese graveyards. The making-homeless of the dead, to make homes and money for the nation, is a significant part of this story—of that, later.

The state did not act merely to acquire and resell land, however. It was also an instrumental partner in allocating sites for new commercial ventures and frequently provided subsidized land and incentives. Although all developments were ostensibly "private" (or mostly so), the vast wealth realized by the pioneer generation of Singapore's speculative builders relied heavily on the cheap and lucrative opportunities offered by the PAP. Eunice Seng has chronicled the intensity of public–private partnerships in creating Singapore's first major urban megastructures, with measures like incremental payments for land and added salable floor area and property tax exemption periods that lengthened with every story of newly constructed buildings. For their part, the private firms were employed to extend the developmental capacities of the state. Seng argues that "this was the first programme in the world of its kind in which private participation on such a scale was promoted by a government."[56] The mantra of the time was that urban renewal could not be a state undertaking; it would need to be a transactional matter.

To this end, the government was intensively engaged in building the districts where private development was to take place. An early example was Shenton Way, the CBD strip housing the Singapore

Exchange and offices of global and local financial services firms.[57] This trend has continued, more recently with other economic sectors. The Jurong Town Corporation—another major landholding and development arm of Singapore—has acted as master developer for new industrial districts, building upon vast tracts in areas of the center and west districts.[58] Zaha Hadid provided an ambitious plan in the early 2000s for Biopolis, a pharmaceutical and medical research hub that today contains numerous firms and laboratories. Discoveries made here share intellectual property rights with the state. In 2014–15, Mediapolis opened on an adjacent campus, with facilities for film, digital media, video games, and special effects for television and Hollywood and Bollywood films. These are all "research incubators" that support the manufacture of products. It is notable that some of the major players in the development field—among them Capitaland—are now partially or mostly owned by Temasek itself. The development of the state was a boon for the state-as-corporation, and profits in this sector were typically reinvested in high-quality public amenities, housing, and infrastructure.

It is perhaps an unsurprising outcome that the state's megastructures, speculative products that house speculative activities, are increasingly marketed as sites of pilgrimage. Visitors from aspiring nations, from the region and from South Asia and China in particular, increasingly travel to see evidence of the Lion City's successes in the form of iconic and symbolic architectures. It is of no small consequence that the Singapore Tourist Board has made a go of marketing hotels and office parks, alongside attractions like Gardens by the Bay, to those who would wish to witness the miracle of state-sanctioned entrepreneurialism firsthand. In fact, some of the most fruitful ventures, like the interior forest of the Jewel Mall at Changi Airport, are built as self-serving destinations; increasingly, the function of the airport is to serve passengers arriving to visit the airport. Spectacular architectures commissioned from Moshe Safdie and Thomas Heatherwick play an outsize role in this touristic machine, reflexively monumentalizing their own successes.

PARAMILITARY GARDENING

Many of Singapore's landmarks use the spectacular medium of tropicality, of the largely invented equatorial landscape, to market the increasingly valuable concept of the "eco-city": a sci-fi utopia where high finance and technology sit, apparently without contradiction, in a verdant urban forest—a machine in a garden, where once was jungle.[59] The insistent leitmotif of tamed tropicality among these urban marvels is not chance, nor does it simply mirror the current vogue for "green" cities. As noted, Lee Kuan Yew—the consummate biopolitician—was acutely aware of what landscape could offer to the national project. In his own words, "the presence of ample greenery in an environment clean of litter would signify that Singapore was a well-organised city and hence a good destination for tourists and foreign investments."[60] Not only is nature a spectacle worth paying for, it is living proof of a place fit for speculation. Gardening was imagined as an index of environmental control and thus of securitization to sources of global capital. This was understood as an essential service without which the nation's planned economic future could not be realized. Lee often remarked that landscaping was an investment that brought the highest return and that Singapore's green was "bearing gold and silver underneath, invisible to all sight as cars went whizzing by."[61]

The Garden City has been, in its every aspect, an object of design attentions—and is one of the "concepts" most directly associated with Lee's command and the nation's image in its first fifty years. Party leaders discovered early that the tropical flora could provide a coherence to the spatial contradictions described earlier—the anxious contrast between proto-socialist public estates and glitzy downtown—while continually providing visual evidence of state capacity for potential investors. Equally useful was the very functional capacity of the garden to serve as both laboratory of governance and securitizing technology. Here, too, total design is equated with control over behaviors and outcomes—in the ongoing experiment with the national "garden," per Carl Trocki, "progressive evolution leaves little to chance and random factors."[62]

This process began in earnest in 1967 with the naming and articulation of a new vision for a disciplined landscape.[63] Trocki notes that "as Singapore became a global city-state, even its vegetation was brought under control, as specific varieties of trees, grass, shrubs, and flowers were selected for the carefully manicured parks and other public plantings."[64] As the HDB pursued its new mandate, the improvement of public greenery was increasingly entrusted to the National Parks Board ("NParks," formerly the Parks and Recreation Department).

From 1975 to 2014, the number of public gardens exploded from 13 to 330—a formalization of urban nature that came alongside an eradication of the small-scale agriculture and community gardens typical of the kampung.[65] Roadside plantings were given a uniform language, and interstitial lawns were cut to putting green length. Here, too, private developers were conscripted, leading to a ninefold increase in new trees from 158,600 in 1974 to more than 1.4 million by 2014—and a total stock that was nearly 25 percent greater than in the late colonial period.[66]

The reinvention of "natural" Singapore was no simple undertaking and had to be done largely without precedent. When Stamford Raffles landed in 1819, the bulk of the island was covered in dipterocarp forest and surrounded by coastal mangrove. During the colonial period, this was progressively cleared and recreated as agricultural landscape. Pineapple, coconut, tapioca, pepper, and rubber were grown in the interior, and the coastal mangrove was eradicated to create pools for prawn farming.[67] Variable demand wrought continual upheaval on the island ecology, but the effect on the dipterocarp was decisive. By 1850, the last remaining scraps of the indigenous forest stood around the Bukit Timah highlands, where steep topography made cultivation impossible. Concurrently, the broad exchange of plant species among the British colonies and those of other European powers, a practice termed "acclimatization," had flooded Singapore with flora from Southeast and South Asia, Africa, Australia, and Brazil. By the time the PAP set about replacing scruffy thickets with a tidy and consistent local style, virtually nothing on the island was native.[68] As ecologist Richard Corlett notes, very few of the species extant at the close of the twentieth century were there when Raffles arrived.[69]

This transformation was likewise fueled by the Singapore Botanical Gardens, an experimental engine of colonial agribusiness, plant creation, and dissemination. This complex institution—still a center of R&D for NParks—served to profitably combine the control and financialization of nature. An array of indigenes and foreign species were tested for their industrial and commercial applications, speed of growth, size, and hardiness. Other potentially lucrative products of its nurseries were, throughout the nineteenth and twentieth centuries, deployed locally to replace natives considered weak or without market value. More recently, the "Botanics" has become known for its new breeds of orchid, which are often named for visiting dignitaries and celebrities. *Papilionanthe* Miss Joachim, a novel hybrid propagated in the Singapore Botanical Gardens, is Singapore's national flower. Here, as in other aspects of statecraft, the PAP enthusiastically adopted Britain's experimental and commercial orientation. Lee noted the influence of this tradition, observing that the colonial administration had "done the basics" for the fledgling state in building the gardens.[70]

In the production of a local landscape style, the eradication of native forest provided a condition of great freedom for the new state, which was then in the process of splicing together available cultural and historical fragments—hailing from the Chinese, Tamil, Malay, Peranakan, Eurasian, and other ethnic communities—to create traditions and symbols that were recognizably "Singaporean" without being overly specific.[71] Likewise, a broad range of exotic species—canopy trees, ground covers, creepers like the ubiquitous *Ficus pumilla,* shrubs, and flowering hedges—were combined into an entirely novel series of combinations. All were common in their ability to survive locally, but few had previously coexisted. The new planting palettes were tidily composed and codified into standards and manuals of gardening for public space. The resulting landscape, marked by an appearance of deracinated tropicality, was a novelty. The Garden City is not formed of ecological unities. Its public parks and roadside verges are largely an invention, a kind of nonspecific equatorialism.[72]

Species are selected for ornamental features, hardiness, lack of fruit or leaf litter, or growth rate. Distinct ecologies—equatorial dipterocarp, coastal and riverine, subtropical—are forced together along abrupt lines of transition.[73] As a result of its unnaturalness, this is a heavily interventionist landscape. It requires a great deal of maintenance to keep from falling into imbalance, to preserve designed boundaries, to prevent fast-growing species from driving out weaker neighbors or merging into multispecial brush—as happened during the "anthropause" of the Covid-19 pandemic, when regular maintenance was impossible. Like the horticultural collections of the British, these are merely gardens of will: assemblages of plants that do not hail from coadapted communities and that would fall into disarray if not tended. These require, in effect, life support: the constant gardening and administrative care of the larger state. Their very survival is a daily testament to a competence and vigilance in maintaining collective order, to control destabilizing elements and a dangerous fertility. As Lee himself stated, you can't just plant a tree and walk away. The tree will die. . . . You need tree doctors, you need to understand what sound and how much sunlight it requires. . . . It's a very complex thing that all people who run big organizations will understand.[74]

Environment thus serves as both corroboration and index of the managerial capacity of the state. The survival of the planting design, with its orderly demarcations, indicates if the state is functioning effectively. It provides constant feedback regarding the capacity of its administration and serves as an early indicator of failure or inattention. Organisms need intensive upkeep, and Lee's recognition of this closely echoes Sheldon Wolin's assertion that "the political emerges, in the literal sense, as a 'culture,' that is, a cultivating, a tending, a taking care of beings and things."[75]

However, it is hard to overstate the transformative sociospatial violence that this procedure—the wresting of a garden from a dense, long-standing tangle of living beings—has required. In Singapore, landscaping borders on a paramilitary operation. Habitable space is torn back from nature; it must be bulldozed from urban villages, cleared from tertiary jungle, or "reclaimed" from the sea. Its reclusive topography must be unfurled and its flood-prone rivers canalized. Its air, which Lee considered soporific, must be cooled and dried. The environment is the enemy in a campaign, imagined as an insurgency or destabilizing threat. The presumption of constant insurrection by nature itself, a contra-modern force, provides an intense external pressure. It is a condition of perpetual emergency through which policies and technical capacities are sharpened, exercised, and extended. The Garden City requires landscape architects and planners, but also dedicated bureaucrats, horticulturalists, environmental engineers, architects, planners, policemen, former professional soldiers, tropical disease specialists, and housing policy experts.[76]

In the minds of its planners and technocrats, as well as in the public imagination, the city remains a jungle *ad esse*. Vegetation has long been cast by Lee, and others, as a negating aboriginal presence—as the essential tropical poverty against which Singapore's success is read. Nature abhors a vacuum, and the negativity of the jungle is always ready to assert itself. Pioneering flora encroach at the edges, and airborne weeds take root in closely cropped lawns and planting beds. Hundreds of gardening crews are dedicated, daily and weekly, to their subjugation. Turf must be trimmed to prevent the incursion of weeds, which can recolonize in less than forty-eight hours. Verges of shrub and vine contract and must be pushed back—and with them, threats such as snakes, insect pests, and the dengue-bearing *Aedes* mosquitoes that infest neglected areas. Weekly pest control sweeps and searches for standing water are conducted, involving mechanical trimmers and blowers, chainsaws and atomizers for fogging oils and pesticides. To the uninitiated, these appear like paramilitary operations.

The intensive nature of landscaping allows the state to control, in effect, which areas of the national landscape are inhabitable and which are not. This is dramatized by the many localized patches of "jungle"—encountered at sites within the urban fabric. Such pockets of free growth exist on sites earmarked for future development, alongside securitized zones.[77] Reservoirs, sand and gravel dumps, army camps, and military exercise areas are bounded by a cordon of untended forest, termed "green buffer." These punctuate the city center as well as outlying areas. In contrast to the lawns and bonsais and prim hedges, these are left to form a dense tangle. Only their edges are pruned, to avoid expansion into tidy neighboring areas. Their centers hold a tight compact of canopy trees, understory shrubs, and ghostly curtains of choking lianas. Passage into the interior is not advisable for the uninitiated, owing to swarms of mosquitoes, stinging insects, and reptiles. This forest figures in local discourse as a sinister intelligence. Ghost stories of former soldiers and national servicemen describe their encounter with nature in terms of a vegetal patience: an assumption that plants and their resident spirits await a recrudescence of the city's modern surfaces. Stands of jungle, whether by intention or not, have an intimidating or admonitory aspect. The convulsive forest, held in anxious stasis, also reminds the public of what will happen if the state fails or decides no longer to perform its duties as tender and gardener. Each tangle is a miniaturized apocalypse: a surrender of the equatorial city to external threat. This is a potential of the Garden City concept itself, a feature of its designed fragility.

The duality of clearing and jungle, inhabitability and its opposite, forms a powerful ordering technology. Zones of occupation are carefully planned, and there exist few gray areas—no greenwood pockets that would allow for informal or unscripted modes of occupation. It is a literal shaping of the island's "natural" body, directing flows of human traffic into prepared channels. The nation is not, as famously claimed by Rem Koolhaas, a tabula rasa. Rather, it is something akin to a hedge maze: a complex of living barricades. It gently supports the preemptive work of civil defense in a state that, despite strict regulations for public order, operates with a famously limited police presence.[78]

HOMELESS GHOST, UNHOMELY CITY

Of course, landscape alone does not suffice to ensure a quiescent, disciplined world city. Rather, the garden aestheticizes and reinforces homologous ordering relations that are constructed through architecture and planning and (as in any state) require legal structures to support the administration of action, speech, and biological life. A disciplined contraction of the body public created a Singapore well contained and conditioned, and dependent upon the benefits and entanglements of a formal wage economy. Literal and symbolic upward mobility required that seized land be dedicated chiefly to the pursuit of wealth, and to the large-scale imagineering of a city constructed within a garden. This model is not simply about security attracting foreign investment. Rather, it embodies a new economic order that balances volatility with security in all aspects, and in which security itself becomes a second-order structure for value. Securitization and speculation are, in fact, two halves of a common process and inseparable. From the early years, Lee astutely intuited that this paradox underlay an emergent world market in which lucrative sectors would be independent from industry—and in which mobile money would need safe harbor.

But again, not all goes according to design. The operations that cleared the low-rise, lateral world of kampungs and remnant forests were also explicitly understood as spectro-generative. In a historical irony, ghosts proliferated as ancestors were impoverished by the national project of enrichment. The asynchronism of risk capital required the past to be sacrificed so that the future might produce value in the present.

With this proliferation of ghosts comes an alternate conception of Singapore. This imagines spaces, forces, and values to be connected in a manner dramatically opposed to the metonymic structures of officialdom. Everywhere, we find spectral practices that would locate themselves *not* within the partitions and linkages of state planning but as arising from a cosmology that emphasizes holistic connections: flows, exchanges, and causal relations that bind national space as a totality, with those who live within it. These draw upon a recent history of contestation in which forces of secular modernization did not dispel the ghost so much as magnify belief in its powers. The imagined actions of *gui* rejoin places into a new spatial economy, crosscut the cellular honeycomb of Singaporean space, and posit, instead, a striated topology of connections and contiguities.

In the shadow history of the nation's spatial redevelopment, the social and spatial realm of the dead has been increasingly usurped. This is a process that, ironically, releases the ghost from a bounded "place" and into a public realm, as a vagabond drawn to sites of environmental disruption—which means, in effect, everywhere. The power of the ghost to ignore state-imposed boundaries and territorial taxonomy arises from conceptions of *qi* and spiritual disturbance that link the human body and psyche to an environment subjected to natural and social violence.[79] At the same time, this agency extends to the production of an alternative spatial order, one of localized expansions and convulsions, unexpected movements and diversions.

Ancestral practices within Chinese religion do not, by themselves, explain Singapore's spectral anxieties. The rise to wealth has come, also, at great psychosocial cost: the destruction of lived worlds. Release of land for speculative development and formalized housing was achieved, in particular, via the state's arrogation of burial spaces, bodily disposal, and funerary rites. This takeover sidelined a broad array of patriarchal, professional, and clerical bodies. In fact, this subject remains a controversial aspect of the transformation of Singapore.[80] Geographers Lily Kong and Brenda Yeoh, among others, have described the battle over funereal landscapes as one of the sticking points in Singapore's re-creation after independence. This remains a source of resentment that lies close to the surface.[81] We have seen how concerns about available land propelled a transition from the kampung to the modern high rise—a victory of the vertical over the horizontal, through which the government established a speculative property machine. In this same moment, the expansive Chinese graveyards that were scattered across large swaths of the city were dismantled, their human remains transferred to multilevel structures at centralized locations.

It is difficult to overstate the extent of such excavations. In addition to larger cemeteries like Bukit Brown and Tiong Bahru, Orchard Road, Novena, and Dhoby Ghaut, many smaller clusters of Chinese graves existed on higher, sloping grounds according to geomantic tradition.

These were ubiquitous, and one still can catch glimpses of remnant tombs in traffic islands and at roadsides, left isolated by infrastructure. Embankments along the Pan-Island Expressway, for example, still contain the resting places of some famous Singaporeans and are mentioned in tourist guides to the island. There are also sizable remnant sites that have been taken over by the state but have not yet been disinterred. The government policy on such land mirrors its approach to "protected" zones described in chapter 5; though remains have not been removed, these areas have been left for the jungle to reclaim. This makes them difficult to visit, and places a large burden of labor on those who would keep family plots clean and free of overgrowth.

A major loss of cemetery occurred with the extension of road and rail infrastructure—as in the case of Bukit Brown. The expressway and the MRT rail systems have both been directed through former burial grounds. A respondent familiar with geomantic practices told me that the creation of the MRT was regarded very negatively by feng shui practitioners, who saw it as "cutting the island into pieces." Ironically, the technology that planners imagined as unifying the island was viewed as a destabilizing influence upon its geobody—precisely the kind of disturbance that, we will see, is understood to attract unhappy spirits. There is thus a popular conceptual intimacy between infrastructure and lost graveyards, the one being a central cause of the other. Such exhumations are often seen as illegitimate and do not void the "ownership" of these lands by the dead. This is one of several reasons why railways and highways are thought to be haunted with particular vehemence.

The sudden mass eviction of the dead is a fact that still causes considerable unease.[82] The assumed "ownership" of former cemetery land, by those who were interred there, has a broader effect—as noted by many of my interlocutors, cemeteries are often *presumed* to have existed wherever a haunting is said to have occurred. The contemporary absence of the cemetery means that, imaginatively at least, it might have existed anywhere.[83] In a peculiar sense, the grave has become a sort of *topos* of origins for Singapore, a birthing medium—as claimed by Claudio Lomnitz for Mexico, the nation is understood as having been erected quite literally upon the foundation of death.[84] In a sense, the whole island is thought to have been preowned. Hui Ping, a young retail assistant, admitted to finding this amusing:

They'll say, "This school used to be a cemetery," or some war zone or something during the Japanese occupation. There are so many stories around. Whenever they have sightings of ghosts, they will say, "Oh, previously it was a cemetery, a mortuary, or something." Even if nobody actually knows this. It's funny how often you hear it.

Many Chinese ghost stories also involve Muslim burial sites. Mr. Kok, a property investor, recalled an incident that occurred while he was returning from a holiday with his family. They were driving home quite late, as the son was required to return to army service the following day. Their route passed through Margaret Drive—near the central Ayer Rajah Expressway—which, Mr. Kok noted, was "used as a Muslim cemetery last time." As he was turning onto this small road, he noticed his son staring intently out the window.

"I asked him what was the matter," Kok recalls. "He said to me, 'What are all these Malay people doing walking on the road at this time of night? Where are they going?'"[85]

In such narratives, there is often an implicit assumption that sites cannot be easily repurposed. Specific graveyards remain foci of debate over the value of redevelopment.[86] In this context, it is common practice for HDB, as well as other government authorities, to convert cemeteries to parks or fallow land for a period prior to allowing it to be redeveloped. This was the case with housing estates in Bishan and Tiong Bahru. In fact, Bishan was the subject of some concern after its eventual redevelopment, as "there were fears that it would face low occupancy due to its past."[87] This was also the case with the commercial center named Ngee Ann City on Orchard Road. As it was home to the former Teo Chew burial grounds, an elaborate prayer tent is erected on the forecourt every year at Qing Ming, although the graves have long been exhumed. The former Bidadari Cemetery was converted to a public park before its eventual re-creation as an HDB estate for forty thousand homes within the next decade.[88]

This was not merely about historical and existing graves; it was also about future ones. The new state mandated the rather un-Chinese alternative of cremation, and columbaria, as the only viable solution for the "land-scarce" island's future. Not only has land burial become difficult to obtain, it is also possible to occupy a plot for a maximum of fifteen years before being disinterred and cremated or reburied in a smaller soil volume (in the case of Muslims). Presently, only one cemetery remains. Bodies are deposited not in true soil but in a pre-fabricated "crypt": a cartridge-like unit that can be extracted when tenure is over.

The seizure of traditional burial grounds and practices was widely resisted by the clan organizations—in particular, the Ying Foh Fui Kun (or Hakka Association). As Teo and colleagues have noted, this was a moment in which "the state came in a direct confrontation with a complexly organized Chinese community, with its own communal perspectives and priorities not necessarily supportive of" the PAP's exhumation scheme.[89] The Ying Foh Fui Kun requested a number of concessions in exchange for their land—but the government denied most, relocating remains to peripheral columbaria in Mount Vernon, Yishun, Choa Chu Kang, and Mandai. Although clan organizations (or *gong hui*) still provide funerary insurance and distribute grave-yard plots to those who can afford the high costs, limitations of land put this out of reach for most Singaporeans.[90] In a 2008 article titled "Gravedigging: A Dying Trade," the *Straits Times* reported only nine active gravediggers employed in Singapore.[91] As Teo and colleagues note, this is a moment in which "the decline of ritual practice is itself inextricably linked to the diminished role that regional, dialect and clan associations play in Chinese social life after independence."[92]

Tong Chee Kiong has attributed this transition to centralized crematoria to a metamorphosis in Singaporean funerary practices, as well as in understandings of death. This is particularly evident in the contemporary experience of Qing Ming, the day when graves of ances-tors are traditionally cleaned and offerings are made by their descen-dants. The hyperdensity of columbaria like Mandai—an analogue, in death, of what is experienced by most HDB dwellers in life—makes Qing Ming into a rather hectic affair. This has affected notions con-cerning the visibility and "location" of the dead. As one informant told Tong, "one cannot see the ancestor while conducting the rituals."[93]

Of course, these concern only the *fixed* dead, that is, those who have been situated via proper rituals and appeased by regular offer-ings. "Hungry" ghosts are more problematically dislocated. They are described as "homeless" or "on the road," in contrast to wealthy spirits or those with family. They have been orphaned by premature or vio-lent death, the termination of lineages, or the drift of migrant populations, such as domestic workers.[94] Their graves are unmarked, and (at least during the seventh month) these may be understood to be anywhere, particularly in public and in "open" areas. As we shall see shortly, they make liberal use of routes of movement and exchange.

Though many informants specified violent death as a cause of hungry ghosts, common aspects of social change in Singapore were cited just as frequently. This would have been the case with Mei Zhen Jie's mother, for example, had she not bent the rules and decided to continue observance for her own parents instead of for her in-laws (as is traditionally the practice). Indeed, ancestors can easily be "orphaned" in families with only daughters. Veneration is commonly undertaken by the eldest son, and the ancestral altar would be placed in his home; this was described to me as a cause of the traditional Chinese preference for male heirs. Small families in particular run the risk of having no one to make observances. Childless couples are most vulnerable.

This type of problem is on the rise, as practices of ancestral observance evolved when Chinese families lived in large, intergenerational, rural households. These fit less well into the new Singapore of nuclear families and sixty-square-meter public flats. In contrast to the kampung era, when the Singapore population was rising through births and in-migration, growth has recently diminished. Rates are now the slowest in the nation's history and remain so despite government attempts to increase the population to 6.6 million by the end of the 2020s. Respondents expressed a fear that ghosts will increasingly become "orphaned" as fewer descendants remain to perform the rites. Moreover, as Terrence observed, the way in which the HDB system is organized—in terms of the maximum sizes, and the award of first flats by lottery—tends to divide families.[95] Young married couples purchasing units at subsidized rates have, until recently, had little control over the location. This contrasts starkly with the old kampung compounds, in which less privacy and personal space was expected and frequent, and small-scale additions to buildings allowed growing domestic units to remain under one roof. The result is a shift away from conditions that would allow for regular observances.[96]

Modernization policies thus "created" ghosts not only through disinterment but also in their effects upon living Singaporeans. Though multiple vectors of transformation are at work (involving religious demographics not least), the result is a widespread assumption of *gui* as variously "dispossessed" and adrift across the island. The irony of this, amid the wealth and secular modernity of the state, is not lost on the public. The resulting condition was perfectly expressed by "gardener auntie" Mrs. Tan—an avid believer who nonetheless expressed amazement at the ongoing presence of ghosts in the contemporary.[97] They are "*everywhere* now," she said. "My sister, her daughter can see. The mother is a medium. Her son goes to school, the school toilet got ghosts. In the carpark, in the lift, she says it is full of ghosts. Funny, hah. Singapore's so modern, still have all these things."[98]

SPECTRAL ECOLOGY, OR ANMETONYMY

The fact of ghosts being "everywhere," however, does not mean that their spatial habits are not precisely theorized. Nor does it imply that the razing and remaking of spaces is understood as spectro-generative only in terms of a generic presumptive logic, a kind of smoke–fire relationship. To close this chapter—and our account of the *unheimlich* doubling that links physical modernization to spectrality—it is important to clarify how spirits and material-spatial disturbances come to be theorized, in Chinese religion, by means of a "spectral ecology."

The dominant spatial logic of the PAP is often exerted through a variety of projects simultaneously. The trimming of untidy nature and conversion of the sprawling kampungs into delimited Cartesian flats, for example, came alongside efforts to discourage long hair in men—alongside wide collars and bell bottoms and other manifestations of an unrestrained bodily boundary. Such campaigns enforced a tightening of the spatial envelopes around the citizen at a number of scales, simultaneously. However, there have long existed other, more popular and expansive conceptions that purport to link the individual to their environment. I have written elsewhere about mass "body hysteria" during the 1960s and 1970s, in relation to anxieties about Singapore's nature (and, in particular, its coastline) during periods of tension with Malaysia and Indonesia.[99] Such collective panic, which assumes a direct link between the geopolitical and the biophysical, the island and the anatomical individual, can take place only when other ontologies of spatial order are in place. These ontologies arise from Chinese notions of *qi* and of environmental holism, and they inform also an ecological understanding of ghosts.

As parts of a holistic system, environmental and human well-being are seen, in geomantic and cosmological terms, to be inextricably linked. A general disturbance in the broader social or natural context is thought to immediately affect both collective and individual health, as flows of energy are constantly moving between natural context, our constructions, and ourselves. *Qi* passes through all of these, interchangeably, as instances of a common medium; it is understood to be energetic, but (as in quantum physics) its behavior forms the basic building blocks of matter as well. This is why feng shui—the orientation and materiality of architecture in context—is considered to have a direct effect on inhabitants' health and prosperity. We will see, in chapter 6, how this affects the haunting of sites and their remediation or augmentation via mediumship. In particular, the balance of male and female *jing* (animal life force, produced in the kidneys) is directly affected by unbalanced *qi*, with male *yang jing* falling to dangerously low levels. The total dominance of *yin* energy is associated with the condition of ghostliness.

Given this, assaults on the broader socionatural equilibrium may also upset the energetic equilibrium of the populace. Destruction of the natural environment or the historical synergies of buildings with their sites, disturbance of grounds or ecologies, interruption of flows or connectivity in the landscape—all these may operate negatively. Given this, it is not hard to see why Singapore has been perceived to be energetically "sick" in the postindependence decades and would continue to be so amid its ongoing urban churn. Upheaval in the destruction of traditional lifeworlds and the razing of homes and villages, combined with the disinterment of carefully placed spirits and their own powerful energies, have contributed to a massively imbalanced field of forces. In the Chinese medico-cosmological worldview, this is a landscape and a people in an extreme state of disturbance. This disturbance, moreover, has been (with a few exceptions) uniformly distributed across national space.

Via the complex relationships of energy and matter, Chinese medicine and cosmology hold to a vision of radical connectivity. Disruption at a greater level, in our world or in *di yu*, has the power to affect individual living bodies. This is because all are linked by common energetic flows and circuits. By the same token, disruption or destruction of *qi* in the natural environment can cause both social and biophysical unrest. As *qi* is a resonant phenomenon, bodily energy and that of a given place have interacting effects. As Scott Mendelson puts it, "chaos in society is a disturbance in the yang quality of order in the universe, which in turn resonates as disturbance of yang in the body."[100] This is one of the reasons that orderly and stable governance is so important in Chinese traditional thought. It is seen to keep the linked energetic interactions of the world in balance and to prevent chaotic and hazardous situations. As such, there is an immediate relationship between governance and health: the presence of unrest causes a disruption in the flow of yang (male, anodyne, orderly) energies and a disproportionate surge in yin (female, chaotic, spectral) ones.

Ghosts themselves have a very direct relationship to such tumult. *Gui* are themselves able to disrupt the flow of energies—especially as they are thought to be beings of predominantly yin (cold, damp, and antimasculine) energy. Through the contagious character of yin, they are assumed to bring infertility, ill health, and bad luck. Ghosts, especially hungry ones, are also thought to be attracted to sites of energetic imbalance and disturbance. The latter exert an almost magnetic effect.

This was a recurrent theme in the stories and explanations of my respondents. I asked Mr. Kok why he believed that national servicemen are thought to see ghosts and to be preyed upon by them (see chapter 5). He noted that this was only natural, as they are subject to hardships and upsetting experiences, that their "spirits are frequently low" and their energies depleted. He noted that "we have this idea, also, in Chinese religion, and also with *qi*, that when your strength is low you attract ghosts to yourself, and you can see them."[101]

Mei Zhen Jie noted, in passing, a variant of the same belief having to do with perception. She explained, "If your spirits are high, you won't see them. If they are low, you surely will." Eric offered another version of this idea, whereby "if you are lowly born [in Chinese astrological theory] you are more susceptible to evil influences, and bad luck, and all this sort of thing. If your star is shining very high, these negative influences would tend to steer away from you."[102]

For Jean, a doctor in her sixties, ghosts are opportunists. They reserve their visitations for moments when her life becomes hard to bear, when endurance is strained. She said, "They come to me when I am having problems anyway. And they come to test me; in that moment I will get through or I will sure fail."[103] Jean has a son who is seriously affected by anxiety and obsessive-compulsive disorder, who regularly sees ghosts around her. Though Jean herself cannot see them, her son is "constantly telling me, 'There is one behind you, he looks lost.' Or 'one sitting next to you who died violently, you can still see the damage.'" It is a common belief, also, that those who suffer from depression—alongside neurodivergent conditions such as autism—are attractive to ghosts and have the gift of sight. Famous spirit mediums often have such "burdens" (in much the same way that epilepsy and other conditions have traditionally been seen as problematical gifts from heaven). Children, also, are seen as energetically low and "open" to communication with the spirit world.

If *gui* are associated with any condition in which energies are imbalanced, low, or disrupted, we can understand how the influence of the PAP—and modernity at large—could be seen as ghost producing in perpetuity. Certainly this occurs via the disinterment of graves and in the destruction of the kampung, a process by which ancestors are displaced and the sociospatial conditions for their care are undermined. Less explicitly causal, but no less pervasive, is the prioritizing of speculative "creative destruction" and its climate of generalized upheaval. Owing to the restive forces of national development and the constant re-creation of the island's surface for profit, specters are continually "stirred up" by a widespread imbalance and the dismantling of established configurations of *qi* in both its material and energetic guises. It should be noted that, though ghosts are drawn to zones of disturbance, they are also seen to militate—at least, until convinced otherwise—*against* the transformation of prior formations of space and landscape. This has a direct effect, as we will see, on their perceived motivations in disrupting state projects. The dead are understood to jealously protect what remains and at the same time to protest against chaos that is inflicted on existing natural and urban conditions.

A vanguardist project of anxious future making, by contrast, is one in which present conditions are by nature unsatisfactory—in comparison to continually (re)imagined futures. The violence of the Singapore story involved a world literally upended: an expansive horizontal carpet translated into vertical slabs. The process typically involved demolition, deforestation, and fires (in the kampung) that destabilized the social balance, as well as that of the five phases of *qi*, or *wuxing*—wood, water, metal/gold, earth, and fire—necessary for geomantic harmony and the parity of flows in male and female energy.[104] This is hardly in the past; even within current HDB estates, a restless cycle of upgrading works means that the physical environment is never left in peace.

The assumed affinity of ghosts with disturbance also gives a Chinese explanation of the prevalence of haunted spaces associated with tragedy. Interestingly, this follows a logic of attraction that parallels Freud's conception of trauma—as unsettled energy.[105] Commonly, this invokes atrocities, both actual and assumed, committed during the Japanese occupation from 1942 to 1945. This is particularly the case in Changi—a site that the Singapore Tourist Board and the Economic Development Board have worked to make synonymous with a convenient and spectacular airport complex. Likewise, Sentosa—a place of massacres during the Second World War—has been converted into a pleasure island of golf clubs and international casino gaming.

Changi is a signal example, still remembered by the public as a place of massacres under the Japanese. As Mrs. Tan recalled, "they say Changi, because of the war, is the most 'dirty' one. They killed so many people, so bad energy is still all in that place." Mrs. Tan feared Changi Hospital, in particular, as a site of wartime atrocities *as well as* a decommissioned medical facility. She noted the Japanese history, but no less that "hospitals have the most [ghosts] because a lot of people pass away down there." Hui Ping emphasized the same thing in a millennial idiom, that Changi Hospital remains "spiritually unclean, with bad vibes," as she had recently been told by a friend who had trespassed into one of the wings at night. "The amazing thing was, she could somehow still smell this anesthetic smell—like the cleaning chemicals and all— even though it has been abandoned for a long time."

Mrs. Lee, a Peranakan woman in her eighties, told me,

> The Japanese time was awful. There are a lot of awful stories.
> My brother was one of the men that was shot. Machine-gunned.
> They lined them up on Changi Beach. My father-in-law, also.
> They would just go to the house, and they would just take the
> men and they made them stand along one of the streets, and
> gun them down.

A few of the roads where executions occurred, such as Lermit and Old Holland Roads, are still avoided by older Singaporeans, under the logic that their problematic histories could predispose them to future accidents and unlucky events. Beatrice, sixty years old, recalled,

> Mrs. Boon, she used to live near us, on Lermit Road, near where
> the Japanese had a gallows. Her husband used to go out for a lot of
> dinners. And she used to say, "[My husband] goes out for his din-

ners but I like to read and I'm never alone." And I said, "What do you mean you're never alone?" And she said, "Oh, they come into my room." "They," OK? So I said, "Your kids?" And she said, "No, my children are away at school. *They* just come in and they just sit there." And I said, "Aren't you scared?" And she said, "No, they're just sad. They are drawn here, but they are not out to harm me."

Such stories stress how violent histories hold a certain magnetism for ghosts. Importantly, *gui* at these sites need not have any relation to those who died there but may simply be drawn by the aura of the place. These unhappy spirits may, in turn, cause further violence in an ongoing cycle. As Hui Ping noted to me, "some particular roads are said to be quite scary, because of the number of accidents that happen. For no reason a car will just skid off the road."

This is particularly poignant in the case of Singapore, where tragic associations are carefully expunged from sites on which speculative regeneration—for housing, retail, or tourism—is planned. Sites of tragedy are determined by history and not by planning; hence they have no place in the order of the nation as designed. The success of the city relies, to a great degree, on forgetting. Interestingly, however, it is not the historical specificity of a tragedy that is important in the island's ghost-culture. The events of the Japanese period are not asking to be recalled, necessarily, in a precise manner. For the most part, historical tragedies do not "haunt the feast" in a plea for factual recollection. Rather, these exist alongside banal death or deforestation or social unrest in a general logic of disturbance, making invisible alterations to the fundamental substance of the contemporary city, a recalibration of matter and energy that influences its contemporary.

There is thus an invisible web of ecological relations linking governance, the physical environment, biophysical health, and ghosts—one that, moreover, assumes direct forms of causal relationality amid the turmoil of the postcolony. As a result of this spatiopsychological upheaval, ghosts are simply everywhere. They do not distribute themselves according to a model of compartmentalized nationhood in which a homuncular state is replicated at discrete locations. Rather, they are assumed to participate in a holistic system of flows, a spiritual current or liquidity. Like electricity or air, ghosts move in the differentials of high- and low-pressure zones: varying concentrations of *qi*, life essence (*jing*), and, as we will see, materials and landscape. And, not least, value—which is understood as a variety of energetic flow that can interact with both ghosts and *qi/jing*. An "anmetonymic" system is at work here: a type of fluid dynamics in which space is characterized by spiritual energies drawn to scars in the landscape and felled trees, to highways and rail networks and corridors of settlement and disruption. Seams of low or imbalanced energy become, in effect, highways for the spirit—much like ley lines or other occult shortcuts long presumed to bypass the distances and coordinates of Cartesian space.

So much, then, for Singapore's great renovation. As we shall see in the coming chapters, such an ecology presumes a universe in which the city can be bent or folded, pierced and short-circuited through the canny use of ritual forms and a tactical (if apparently back to front) deployment of money and surplus—that is, through the use of spectro-economic techniques introduced in the first half of this book. Such operations in situ work upon the energies of urban plots. These become both loci and substance for deals with ghosts and for improved human lives, within and beyond the frame of real estate and development. The ghost-world follows conceptions of space that emphasize not hierarchy but connection, reciprocity, attraction, balance, and dynamic causality. This system is hardly without contradictions, varied interpretations, or legalisms of its own. But crucially, in the confluence of energetic flows and coextensive natures and energies, no spatial point is isolated. Where PAP ideology imagines the state in plan and cross section, as distributions, the ghost-world posits a striated topology of laminar flows: pulsions of physical and cosmological connectivity. And although this conception rejects the assumptions of high-modern planning, it offers—as we shall soon see—a labile imaginary for the present.

5

Apparition and Insecure Space

> The problem is no longer that of . . . the colonial world and its barbed-wire entanglements, but of considering three times before urinating, spitting, or going out into the night.
>
> —Frantz Fanon, "On Violence"

It would be helpful, at this point, to briefly recount the story thus far. In its successful pursuit of national economic development, Singapore's government radically refashioned the island and securitized large swaths of its surface. This project ensured the conditions for the state to be viewed, as it is today, as a safe space for speculative late capital—global, regional, and domestic. Viewed through a Chinese cosmological lens, however, it produced a decidedly *in*-secure city: an epidemic of orphaned ancestors and hungry ghosts within the cityscape. This resulted not just from the excavation of land-intensive cemeteries but also from the collective trauma caused by the destruction of informal settlements and the destabilization of their ancestral practices. Matters were yet further exacerbated by widespread environmental disturbance and an explosion of infrastructures thought to be ghostly nonplaces: unregulated channels of yin energy and sites of violent death.

In popular accounts and urban lore, disgruntled spirits disregard the PAP's ordering systems and trespass its designed boundaries, compartments, and no-go areas. In fact, they appear *most* attracted to "black" sites and securitized areas, where red signs warn of arrest or other dire consequences. The ghost is likewise drawn to zones of damage and transformation, where balances of *qi* are thought to be in disequilibrium. These include roads and railways, reservoirs and canals and logistical corridors so closely affiliated with modernization projects. Likewise, particularly vengeful specters have a known affinity for the threatening jungle. The ghost within the forest enacts revenge against humans. And just like the living, the dead are drawn to the bright lights, loud music, and air conditioning of commerce and spectacle. Their existential poverty propels them everywhere, across the tended plantings and townscapes of a new order that does not apply to them and to which they owe neither gratitude nor fealty. Stories of their peripatetic behaviors suggest the reassertion of holistic, lateral connections across a numinous and fluid national space.

This chapter addresses narratives of this "insecure" city and how it is understood via spectral ecology and economy. This concerns, first, the apparition of *gui,* through spontaneous visitation and ritual summoning, within the traditionally "public" sphere: open spaces, streets, and nature. Second, and equally fraught, is the haunting of institutional and private architectures. Spaces marked by temporary or long-term insecurity are certainly feared and often avoided, but they are also considered places of opportunity. Read as vibrant and magnetic, their disturbances—present or historical, physical or social, natural or human—make them particularly available for reciprocal traffic and mutual gain.

GHOST MONTH AND THE INSECURE PUBLIC REALM

It is difficult to overstate the apparent ubiquity of ghosts in Singaporeans' perceptions. My interlocutors noted this fact, matter-of-factly, as one might point out the humidity. Winnie, an expatriate from Hong Kong, was surprised to find something like a "year-round Ghost Month."[1] In other Chinese societies, she had witnessed ancestral offerings and other practices only in the seventh month and Qing Ming or on significant dates like death anniversaries and birthdays. Similarly, oral surgeon Charles marveled at the local intensity of such concerns, noting (debatably) that they "do not worry about ghosts in China. That's a Singapore thing."[2] While certain older areas with tortured histories were mentioned repeatedly during interviews, very few areas of the city remain unmarked by spectral allegations. A series of ghost-tale compendia by author Russell Lee, the all-time highest-selling book series in the nation's history and its receptacle of local lore, recounts tales from nearly all neighborhoods and spaces.[3]

The pervasiveness of ghosts implies a need to be "respectful." This was the most common opinion in the construction industry, where shows of disbelief were seen to invite reprisal from the spirit realm. Johnny, a project manager for a large contractor, noted, "[The workers], even if they don't really believe, they *try* to believe, so they will not offend *them*. They say, during this month you should not do this, because the ghosts are around, nearby, you will easily upset them. Try not to go against the tradition." The ghosts are close at hand and would catch any discourteous behavior, especially by Christians or other doubters.

Statements about the ubiquity of ghosts were even voiced, unexpectedly, by those who also admitted skepticism about their existence. In several cases, disbelief was put to the test by inexplicable personal experiences.[4] After flatly observing that he "does not believe in such things," Dr. Ong—a surgeon in his seventies, a self-described "atheist" and "rational person"—related frightening happenings during his medical residency at the National University Hospital (NUH). He recounted that it "was a place where there were a lot of strange things. Because this is where the Japanese used to execute Chinese. Educated Chinese, professionals." During his residency, Dr. Ong slept alongside a few others in an empty ward, on the top floor of an NUH wing that was rumored to be haunted. He was astonished to wake from a nap to find that his bed, and those of several others, had been shifted several hundred feet to the far end of the ward. "I don't believe," he said, "but it happened; I could not explain this in any other way."[5] Andrew, an executive with Singapore's largest government-linked developer, was forced to adopt a similarly equivocal position after a collapsing beam killed two construction workers at one of his projects. This was a technologically advanced high-rise designed by Kisho Kurokawa. A cell phone video was passed around, purportedly showing a ghost moving through a wall in the basement parking level. Andrew's team investigated the CCTV feeds and concluded that it was "likely a hoax."[6] Regardless, ceremonial offerings were placed throughout the new megastructure, as "the ghosts can be anywhere."

Evidence of pragmatic caution can be found throughout the city, where ash and smoldering offerings are frequently visible. These appear throughout the year on curbs and corners, in parking garage spirals and food courts.[7] Some are made on the sites of former burial grounds disinterred or partially excised, in Chinatown and Tiong Bahru, downtown, and in the city's historic neighborhoods.[8] They are also positioned near homes and places of business and work, along streets and the open spaces of HDB estates. They are a commonplace of life in Singapore.

Such rites are performed far more frequently during Ghost Month, however, and take on a different affective coloring. They are made primarily for unknown ghosts, as opposed to familiar ancestral spirits or gods. The opening of the "gates of hell" allows an anonymous rabble to return in search of places and people, to drift, or to emphasize claims for what is rightly theirs. But also simply to drift, as many ghosts are thought to have been neglected to the point that they have forgotten their own identities and wander in a half-blind state of confusion and anger or dismay. As a result, they frequently join victims of violent death along roads, near bodies of water, or in other "attractive" zones of yin or energetic disarray—or follow their dim senses toward the heat, smoke, and light of the festival burnings.

Ghost Month is unarguably a time of fear, or at least of prudent caution. Few weddings are performed. Doctors and surgeons rarely see voluntary patients or perform elective procedures. Many business ventures are postponed until it is over. However, this period also incorporates an element of carnival, with outré performances and moments of public release. *Getai* (song stage) performances are held on makeshift grandstands, with scantily clad female singers pouring their hearts into sentimental Mandarin tunes.[9] These events are described as being for the benefit of the returning ghosts, and the first rows of seating are always kept empty for them. Regardless, these are important practices in the ritual vocabulary of the living, who integrate offerings and blessings amid the pageantry.[10]

Offerings made during the seventh month must be understood differently to those Qing Ming rites mentioned by Mei Zhen Jie and Mrs. Tan. The latter are understood as filial obligation, as remembrance. They are also considered a form of self-protection, as ancestral spirits that are uncared for become hungry and ghostly. While propitiating one's own predecessors may result in their favor, failing to do so will likely result in economic disaster of some sort. Sacrifices to hungry ghosts, by contrast, are attempts to provide them with what is missing in their painful, wasted existence. This, too, is an act of social insurance, as they are figures of some anxiety. But this is also understood to be a speculative, as well as protective, gesture—and the activities of the seventh month are characterized by "respectful" practices that are also understood to be at least partly gainful (see chapter 1). Importantly, such offerings have a different locational character—occurring in those edges, infrastructural corridors, and ambiguous zones that are the spatial analogue of this figure's existential condition. Whereas ancestors are situated and venerated at home shrines or in the temple, ghosts are typically associated with public spaces, the nonplaces of infrastructural limen and terrain vague.

While *gui* are frequently sighted in "protected" places (see later), and are known to trespass, they assert their own, alternate modes of territorialization. They produce their own spectral boundaries, carefully observed by believers. As a result, their peculiar agency is not asserted only in the rejection of securitized perimeters, and official internal borders. Ghostly confines are shifting and ambiguously demarcated, and a litany of practices exists for negotiating or avoiding them. As in the jungle, harsh penalties are said to await those who overstep or tread on offering sites. This understanding of the city involves unseen and ephemeral zones of danger, conjured into being through ritual.[11] The resulting alterations of movement are significant in this social context, in which uncommon value is placed on the logistical and the timely.[12] The state, like the proverbial Christian God, would make its roads straight—at least in their rational and unambiguous operation.[13] The city's spectral logics very often work contrariwise, however: slowing down time and increasing serendipity and detour. This occurs along two principal axes. The first is spatial and involves the impeding or redirecting of paths and passages. The second is temporal, whereby elasticity and arrhythmia appear in the time required for movements, communications, transactions, and deliveries. The resulting disruptions are productive as well as prohibitive. The blocking of a route causes a new one to come into being, like the "desire lines" of parks and gardens. These may be abbreviated: a short-cut or a jaywalking path.[14] Often they are longer or indirect.

Offerings to *gui,* though commonplace, are a pervasive source of dysregulation. These behave like expansions or contractions in the fabric of urban space, invisible but keenly felt. Whereas sacrifices of food and liquor with joss sticks tend to be constrained within small altars, more substantial burnings of *kimzua* money and commodities create considerable volumes of smoke that can saturate their surrounding areas. These are set alight in large metal drums that stand at strategic points near housing blocks and workplaces. These "incense burners" are placed by the state's town councils but are frequently moved by residents to alternate locations. Large quantities of paper are immolated in sessions lasting up to an hour, and the open-top charnels will billow heat, ash, and pungent smoke. Fires on one side of the street will typically impel passersby to cross over, where discomfort will still have them cover their mouths or shield their faces.[15]

The issue is more than discomfort, however. There is a long-standing belief that anyone other than the burning party should avoid contact with any aspect of the offering, which, strictly speaking, includes the ash as well. The cylindrical form of the drum creates a significant updraft, resulting in charred matter being buffeted around a street corridor or open space. Although many admitted that the cinders are nearly impossible to avoid completely, it is nonetheless seen as essential that one's feet not step on or kick them—a sign of clear and provocative disrespect.

This can have serious consequences. Hua, a self-described "older *tai tai*" (posh wife), offered the case of an irascible neighbor who found her path inconveniently blocked by a burning offering. "It happened many years ago," she recalls. "This neighbor, she stays in the kampung. And every evening, she will walk to our house to have dinner, and then she will walk back. She is such a fussy woman, quite [obsessive-compulsive], and she like to wash her hands, wash her feet. You know, in the seventh month, Chinese all like to burn. She was walking towards her house, and she saw this road-burning, and as usual you have all this ash flying. She says, 'Uh! What is all this ash?' and she kicked a pile on the ground in front of her. And you know what happened? She landed in the hospital for one year. From seventh month to seventh month the following year, she was [in and out of the intensive care unit] in Tan Tock Seng Hospital and nobody can tell what's wrong with her."[16]

This, too, is a familiar trope. Author Jonathan Lim notes that "those unfortunate enough to step on the remains of seventh month offerings on the pavements are often punished with sickness."[17] As respondent Alan warned, "when you see the offerings, you walk by and see this, the best thing is to avoid it. Out of respect." Harry agreed, noting that "they also have a practice that after they burn, when they make the offering and walk off, they won't even look back. But then a lot of people who are not the ones who pray avoid these areas." The offerings become temporary barriers, he notes, as "you find that people don't want to anywhere walk near it."[18] In denser, older neighborhoods, it is not uncommon to pick up the recognizable scent ahead and opt for a different street.

This is not only a matter of expressing disrespect. The paper, while burning, has a specific function: creating a temporary physical bridge between the living and the dead. This is because ghosts are thought to follow the odor of the joss—and odors in general. As Chu has pointed out, there is an oily smoke produced by this money matter that is in many ways akin to the presumed materiality of *gui* themselves. This extends to *all* of the detritus. Author Russell Lee demonstrates this in a story told to him by a young temp clerk, whose brother "had stepped onto a trail of papers left at a funeral site for the spirits to find its way into the other world. When my brother had stepped on the trail, the spirit, which at that time had been on its way into the other world, found its journey interrupted." Ghosts' movements through worlds have their own logic, and their circuits often intersect our own. And those whose paths are impeded become vengeful and must be propitiated with new routes and thresholds—as with the doorways drawn in military bunks to let trapped spirits return to hell.[19] Whereas *gui* frequently redirect human movements, they do not often tolerate the reverse.

Lee's confidant noted that the solution "was for him to retrace his steps, find the exact spot where he had stepped onto that paper trail and stand there." Only after he had made a new offering—which would serve as a kind of beacon—would the inconvenienced spirit leave him alone. It is common to hear similar narratives in passing. At a ritual in Chinatown, I was admonished against stepping on *any* paper in the street during this period, because "you never know why it is there." And, it is true, there were very often scraps of joss paper lying about, especially at significant times of year. As we will see later, paper in particular is understood to be a medium of transformation and communication between worlds, a radically labile substance and thus potentially dangerous.

An offering is considered the property of the spirits for the time it takes to be consumed by the flames. This creates an "unclean zone," briefly saturated by the contamination and energetic disturbance of death. The burnt offering will attract both ancestral spirits and unknown ghosts, who may be dangerous. The purpose of many street shrines is precisely to propitiate those who are unhappy and uncared for, and hence their operation is fraught. As described in the next chapter, the burning not only transfers value to *di yu* but also opens a connection to it. The boundary between worlds becomes thinner and more porous. Space expands and becomes fuller—becoming heavy with yin energy and those nonphysical beings drawn to the altar like a light in a dark, poorly navigable realm. The city appears to locally "dilate," to borrow Lewis Mumford's evocative phrase, and to become denser with nonphysical presence.[20]

There appear to be considerable discrepancies among understandings of the extent of this zone. Some individuals claimed that they would avoid a street where they see smoke, others that they would merely cross to the other side and feel safe to pass. Nearly all agreed that the offering produced a penumbra into which rogue spirits would be drawn and that thus it is best for bystanders to avoid attracting their attention.

Fruit and rice left on altars are also hazardous for a misplaced step— especially as these can remain for some time, positioned on the floor near the tables and chairs of the island's open-air coffee shops. This is a surprisingly frequent problem, especially as offerings for earth god Tu Di Kong—which, like all burnt offerings, will draw opportunistic wandering ghosts—are left on the ground. There are thus established protocols in the event that an offering is trod upon. Informant Kok advised me that, if there is a suspicion that one has stepped on something "bad," it is essential not to wear the shoe into the house before washing it thoroughly. In his youth, Kok lived near the former cemetery on Kiam Hock Road, where offerings were nearly constant. When he would return late at night, he would wash his shoes and leave them at the door before walking in backward, "because if you just walked straight something might follow you and be invited in."

As Kok's precaution makes clear, there are areas in the urban fabric that are particularly vulnerable and must be dutifully protected. Thresholds, openings and portals, stairs, roads, axes and alignments— all significant in geomantic tradition—are cause for the most concern, as they are seen to be attractive channels for spectral movements. Although it is acceptable to burn offerings for a well-tended ancestral spirit in the home, the broader city is open to the traffic of unknown and potentially hungry and vindictive spirits. There is thus a known spatial logic to the placement of altars and other preventive technologies. These are highly ambivalent, as a shrine that "stops" a ghost at the doorway—and prevents it from entering—also necessarily brings the unwanted presence close. Likewise, pungent smells and loud noises thought to repel evil spirits may drive them to other unwanted locations.

Given assumptions that *gui* are highly mobile, one must be protected from them at numerous points in the normal day's path. This requires gifts to be made at various key junctures, and observant Singaporeans note that the burnings may begin at the door and move concentrically outward to the city at large. Mei Zhen Jie observed, for example, that she would burn in the road in front of her home such that she might "go in and out in peace."[21] This is a matter of public order during the seventh month. A complex matrix of burning points—bins, altars, and urns—extends between the door of an HDB block and the public spaces beyond. The metal security gate over the front door often contains small joss stick holders. The common corridor will have a wastebin-sized burner, and others sit at the intersections of passages with major public spaces, such as lift lobbies or void decks. The larger communal drums sit in open spaces just beyond the perimeter of the building, to protect its perimeter at that point. There are thus multiple, imbricated scales of risk and protection that extend from the domestic to the public.[22]

I have noted that offerings to hungry ghosts are "unmoored," that is, not tied to a conventional location where the ancestor has been placed and, to a degree, domesticated. These do not take place in the home, the temple, or the columbarium. Owing to the anonymous nature of the hungry ghost, and to the fact that its histories are unremembered, such locating is not possible; like the value burned for them, they circulate endlessly. For this reason, they are "called" to unspecific places—office entryways, roads, and public spaces—to be appeased. Gifts on construction sites, for example, are distinct from main altars and are temporary. Johnny specified that these are placed in open areas that their recipients may easily discover.[23] Centralized fires will be started here, alongside smaller bundles of joss sticks placed in the ground at the margins and center on the lot. At the end of the seventh month, the dedicated altar will be removed and destroyed, to avoid attracting habitual visitors.

The burnings are created, of course, by people and not by spirits. Thus the obstacles of the ghost-world are, in a Durkheimian sense, social ones. This is plainly understood by Singaporeans. But the locations of the fires are seen as neither random nor simply subject to human will. The circuits of the ghost in the living world have a presumed spatial logic, based on the assumptions of conditions in the afterlife. The ghost moves through the city in a state of confusion and imbalance and thus seeks and follows overt signals or flares. These are the same elements that give legibility to urban space and are known in feng shui theory to create energetic harmony of which the ghost is painfully deficient: organizing axes, aligned roads and structures, clear apertures, monuments. These are also how the human city is organized. Hence the work of burning diverts the ghost to the margins of these spaces: the property's edge, the green patch lining the pavement, or the undefined and underused public plaza. An ironic effect is that such an action, due to the amorphous spread of smoke as a material, temporarily centralizes the ghost and forces the living to circumvent.

At the same time, this is attended by an anxiety: the widespread fear of contamination produces a concern to delimit these areas, to contain the fires within designated receptacles or chalk outlines, and to strengthen the boundary between temporary ghost spaces and the ongoing world of human affairs.[24] In reality, tidy burning seems nearly impossible, and official bins do not prevent detritus from settling nearly everywhere. The spatial unboundedness of burning, ash, and smoke—and the attempts to constrain spectral presence—merely dramatizes the larger problematic quality of both air and ghosts.[25] Ghosts, like airwaves, are in fact uncontained by the abstract dimensions or demarcations used in law or property. The ubiquity of oily smoke and ash merely underscores the imaginary of the ghost *itself* as a medium of pollution. This cannot be quarantined. Proliferation is central to its ritual vocabulary.

Seventh month rituals thus have a curious and contradictory spatial character. They are performed openly, in the street and across the extended public realm where ghosts are presumed to wander. And while these follow a known, consistent geomantic logic, they nonetheless remain mobile and flexibly open to interpretation at specific urban sites. Singaporean Chinese practices do not hold to a temple culture that would establish exclusive locations or even require priestly oversight. This lends the person conducting the rite a genuine, momentary power. They can conjure a space of danger and protection, as well as one of opportunity for personal gain, at the time and location of their choosing. The use of spirit money allows individuals to produce temporary nodes of heightened danger, to force together diverse modes of value and being, and to manufacture favorable distributions of probability. In practice, any urban clearing might be appropriated as a point of religious–economic convergence, whereby the rationality of planned space, its monofunctional partitioning and logistical hierarchy, is suspended. There is a flagrant kind of liberty being exercised here. *Kimzua* is a popular invention thought to move instantly beyond our world. As such, it exists both above and below the legislative frame of state. It is invested by the labor of belief, by a faith in the social to bypass gatekeeping authority and engage freely with its underlying speculative glamour. Its power is not exercised through fiat or design but (as we have seen in chapter 2) emerges from the voluntary and nonproductive release of value from a given form. The near immateriality of paper—its two-dimensionality, which stands at the horizon of substance and nothingness—is of the essence here. Combined with the restless potential of currency, it is a force that is liberated from spatial bounds and able to push and pull at the very concrete assumptions of illiberal state infrastructure.

The power of the offering opens a gateway, a capital circuit between worlds that is, while benevolent and generous, also a vehicle of risk management and potentially exponential profit. But the rite—as itself and as transaction—also makes use of the anxious and haunted character of the public realm as a site of value-production. The moment of mutual enrichment (or, at the very least, of spectral care) gains power precisely by drawing on the past sins of the city's production. In a profound sense, the Promethean "dead labor" of the state, as mass producer of lost souls and maker of spectral infrastructures, estates, and terrains, is the precondition for personal enrichment. As with so many aspects of ghostly economics, this would appear to fundamentally reverse the relationship between the work of living subject and ghost.[26]

THE EVER-SPECTRAL JUNGLE

The careful avoidance of offerings occurs alongside a more general concern about categories of commonly haunted locales. Clearly this includes troubled sites, such as massacre locations, former graveyards (which could reasonably be anywhere), roads with a history of accidents, and yin-dominant physical conditions, such as ponds and canals.[27] I have also heard concerns about Singapore's many areas of reclaimed land, as these bring soil from overseas and thus might also bring foreign spirits as fellow travelers. This avoidance has a temporal aspect, as the cautious will eschew certain places at night or during festivals (as earlier) associated with the tending of the dead.

In this context, "jungles"—loosely understood as any predominantly wooded area—are particularly fraught and exert their own spatial logic of boundaries and circumlocutions. A common subgenre of ghost stories concerns wooded army camps and rural operations sites. These are of the kind left tactically overgrown to avoid maintenance or as an obstacle to human ingress. Such zones are predominantly forested, some with old growth, and hence assumed to be densely inhabited by old spirits with similarly ancient claims of valid ownership. Tales dramatize horrific encounters: national servicemen, in a rite of passage to nationalized adulthood, come face to face with an illegible aboriginal nature—one that reasserts its power with astounding violence.[28] It is a case in which the soldier is completely out of his element, forced to perform dangerous tasks in an ecosystem only dimly apperceived. It is, in a sense, a spectral minefield that must be traversed. Soldiers are murdered or maimed for minor infractions, for sleeping or urinating in the wrong places. Many stories express an explicit terror of being lost in or consumed by vegetation. The ghostly antagonist, here, often does not present itself; rather, it is described as nothing other than nature itself.

The basic military training (BMT) camp at Pulau Tekong, among others, is surrounded by secondary and tertiary wet forest. Ghosts are thought to live among the flora, in trees and shrubs, and even in soil. The camp is seen to be in a condition of siege, and the spirits' behavior is used to explain BMT rituals such as a ban against training on Thursday nights. Stanley recounted to me that "every guy in Singapore who has been to Tekong knows this: you don't go training on Thursday nights because it's the night when the ghosts come out into the jungle."[29] Malam Jumat is a time when duties are canceled and troops stay indoors.[30]

In forest-ghost accounts, Singaporeans are typically represented as essentially urban folk confronted with a violent presence whose language and history they little understand. Many accounts begin with individuals lost or overwhelmed by their environs. A telling detail is that several of these stories involve conclusions whereby "local Malays" needed to be consulted to explain mysterious events or to help put things right. These somewhat shadowy discursive figures help to find the missing men or tell the commanding officers (who are as hapless as their charges) the "local" histories of inexplicable events or methods for rectification. The Malay here represents the aboriginal Singaporean, the wise and spooky landsman who instructs the modern urbanite in the ways of the woods. The invocation of the Malay often serves to dramatize the occult character of events.

In these narratives, Chinese Singaporeans often realize their lack of literacy the hard way. Contractor Mr. Chen described that "the jungle" demands specific rules of conduct that should be learned long before conscription age:

> When we are young we are already taught from parents, friends: don't just pee in the woods. If you have to do it you say "excuse me" and "sorry." That one I know from the army time. Some idiot guy go and pee or shit somewhere and got something. Suddenly he's crazy, raving mad, and we have to tie him up. So have to get the Malay guy in the kampung, the *bomoh* [Malay spirit medium].

Mr. Chen here explains a recurrent problem in military training areas, where an uneducated recruit may relieve himself in the woods without first propitiating the resident spirits. In punishment, he will be driven temporarily insane, or worse.

Dangerous natural areas are often associated with features that are illegible to most soldiers—in particular, large, old trees and tree "guilds" (clusters of corelated species), as well as notable topographical forms, such as mounds and ridges.[31] Within the undifferentiated conceptual complex of "the jungle," there is nonetheless a lexicon of problem places: clearings, tangles, and eroded paths. Installations that would serve to securitize regions of forest are also highly problematic—the worst being guard towers where servicemen must perform sentry duty at night. Ghosts seem to especially dislike such devices of panoptical military power, not least because they are typically constructed where vegetation has been cleared. Eric recalled to me that "the tallest tower in Changi still has a very old jackfruit tree next to it, inside the fence. You must never ever go and pick the fruit that is hanging around there. If you do that the spirits will come and really shake the tower."[32]

Jungle spirits are particularly violent, and narratives about them focus in detail on the abuses of the soldiers' bodies by a supernatural force. Men are casually flung into the jungle and eviscerated. It is important to note here that the individual recruits are explicitly understood to be property of the state. For example, a senior official at the Ministry of Defense told me that soldiers who are discovered to have contracted HIV while in the army are given heavy prison sentences—as the soldier is considered state property, venereal disease is tantamount to property damage.[33] Their bodies are "possessed" by a force other than the Ministry of Defense. In another frequent trope, they are immobilized by invisible forces. Stanley noted that "one of my company mates woke in the night and had the feeling that he was being sat on by an elephant. It was one of these ghosts, which were very well-known in the bunks to cause a kind of sleep paralysis. Every time he tried to push up, he was pushed down again. That's quite a common phenomenon. Sometimes they couldn't even rise for duty in the morning or for night exercises and got D.B."[34]

However, it is not only on military bases that a spectral nature behaves in this way. Army stories are merely a heightened variant of ghost accounts centered around the uncanny and dangerous presence of nature across the island more generally. Similar concerns fix upon those remnant urban forest fragments left idle by the URA. Mrs. Tan told me that her crews won't dare to enter these thickets. It's not because of the snakes but for fear that "all the city ghosts, killed in the road or wherever, will come to stay inside there." The affinity of ghosts with natural places—especially unruly ones—invests these stands, also, with a climate of dread.

Many Singaporeans confessed to avoiding heavily wooded areas—particularly at night, and without question during Ghost Month. This reinforces, perhaps, their official intention as devices to keep people out, as threatening admonitory objects. But concerns about jungle extend, also, to far less dense or overtly wild regions of the national landscape. Related fears were expressed about "nature" writ large: flora and earth throughout the city are seen with respect and fear. This extended, in narrative accounts, to "wayside" plantings like roadside trees and the flora beautifying condominium complexes and HDB estates. It applied also to public parks at night. Bishan and West Coast Parks, as well as the Singapore Botanical Gardens, are places to avoid after dark because, in the words of one staff member, "got a lot of ghosts there, also."[35] Even a single large tree, "nature" or "the jungle" in its most abstracted case, can be treated with wariness. Singaporeans claimed many individual specimens, especially older and larger and more spectacular ones, to be haunted, in much the same way that they enumerated specific houses or institutional buildings (see later).

Not least, trees have been known to resist their own felling, against the best intentions of modernization and urban renewal. Foreman Mr. Chen and medium Master Goh offered a case that is "famous" among contractors in Singapore, one that caused HDB—usually single-minded in the pursuit of a plan—to change course.

"This happens with government buildings sometimes," said Master Goh. "People say the government can do anything. But if they have a ghost-place they cannot do whatever they want. Toa Payoh, many years ago, was one of our first so-called New Towns. There is one tree down there, until now cannot touch. The first one approach the tree to cut, got heart attack. OK? People think it's a coincidence. Second go, this person also died already ah. Third one want to go, bulldozer never start. People think government one no problem, government also cannot."[36] The blocks were hastily replanned, Chen says, with the tree at the center. There is now an informal shrine to the goddess Guan Yin at the base.

Other famous "problem" trees have similar reputations. Mr. Kok, a businessman in his late sixties, felt that this was a common and predictable response of the spirit world to disturbance and upheaval. This is because "contractors, because of their work, they disturb a lot of things. They disturb the ground and entities get upset, and they fight back to protect themselves. This happens a lot, a lot. They want to go and chop down some tree, they can't do it—everyone who gets close gets sick."[37]

For architect Arthur, stories of haunted trees embodied "a kind of shared guilt." This was common in his native Malaysia also, where haunting has much to do with the erasure of natural places. He noted,

When [Malaysians] cut the tree, there will be erosion, the land falls away—they say that nature is fighting back. So, they will say that there is a spirit in the tree. For example, a strangling fig is supposed to contain a lot of spirits, and it's bloody hard to cut one down. Accidents happen. Trucks never get started. There are always things that look mysterious. Even the image of the dying tree, it looks skeletal, right? It looks ghostly.

Mr. Ong, a devout Buddhist, confirmed that many stories pit contractors against trees. In his experience, this was also "because the builder disturbs the ground. That ground is important because still owned by someone from last time. If you regrade it, you shift the topography, you had better watch out." Chinese tradition holds that the ground and the trees have designated spirits to take care of them. "So often, if you will see a shrine, it's under a tree."

For this same reason, it is a common tactic for a medium, priest, or monk to "relocate" a troublesome ghost into a tree by first luring the ghost to a shrine, which is then hastily moved to the base of a trunk. When a construction project is complete, for example, it is the job of the contractor's men to make a final offering to the resident spirits and to "just inform [them] that the job is finished, we have to move your home out from this site." The shrine or altar will then be customarily left under a tree near a temple, with some offerings and joss sticks. The shrines are never reused. Johnny recalled, with a laugh, that "if we go to a new job site, we will get a new shrine. We don't reuse the old one. Everything got to buy new, because it's considered a new project, must give the ghosts a new house. Old one is in charge of the old project."

It should be noted, also, that a number of the region's famous ghosts, ones that have entered into the Singaporean Chinese awareness—though not via the *gui-shen* axis of spirits—are likewise associated with flora. Most fearsome is perhaps the Pontianak, a vampiric female spirit thought to evolve from a childless woman or one who died in labor. She is thought to populate fruitless trees, such as ornamental banana variants—a clear symbolic analogism. The Pontianak often cannot be seen, but her presence is signaled by a cloyingly sweet smell of frangipani flowers. There is a double association here, as these are also used at wakes to produce a heavy fragrance, particularly around the body. This is similar to Bengali funerary traditions and a variant of Indonesian and Malaysian practices of planting the plumeria tree in graveyards. Though this species is often selected for its beauty in urban landscaping, it is often avoided because it is thought to attract ghosts.

Given the clearly frightening potentials ascribed to nature in Singapore, Lee Kuan Yew's valedictory claim that landscape was his "secret weapon" assumes complex ambiguities. Certainly the practice of cutting the tropical flora into bonsai, to show investors that his nation is well groomed and properly disciplined, appears far more strident and provocative. Nature-as-topiary is understood rather differently by the public, via an oral tradition that casts the island's flora as possessed of an old and deadly force and as vengeful when subjected to gestures of control.

This does not mean that natural spaces are avoided, however. Here, too, the prevalence of spirits—especially of the dangerous kind—translates to potentially powerful trading partners for the more overtly profit seeking. Jean spoke with great disapproval of visiting older, overgrown cemeteries to divine lucky digits for the national 4D lottery.[38] This wildly popular game is administered by the Singapore Pools company, a subsidiary of the government's Tote Board, which channels betting revenue into social welfare projects. Mrs. Tan spoke frankly of her own participation in this practice. It is believed that if offerings are made at burial sites, even of unrelated individuals, it is possible to ask for winning combinations. Aspiring diviners will sometimes purchase halal food to take to Muslim cemeteries that are less well guarded and where they can get uninterrupted access to the gravestones.[39] Mrs. Tan recounts that "some go to graveyard at midnight. They also bring [other] people to the graveyard, to ask for luck. Like we go there, every time got one whole lorry full of people. Go and burn and ask for numbers."[40]

As "lorry full" suggests, this is hardly a fringe activity. Such commerce continues a long-standing tradition, observed by gamblers also during colonial times.[41] This practice reflects long-standing beliefs that *gui-shen* communicate with the living through numerical sequences ascertained through yarrow stalk divination.[42] In Singapore, it is at least in part an outgrowth of the Qing Ming ritual: descendants would ask for lottery numbers while cleaning family plots. It was natural for ancestors to want their living relations to prosper, especially in a money-minded "meritocracy." Tramping among tombs in the expectation of personal gain is considered to be vulgar by some, like Harry and Jean—and among observant Christians, who seem to find this practice unsavory on principle. By contrast, Chinese religionists understood this as a time-honored exchange by which the lots of both parties are bettered.

The practice became a question of public controversy in 2006, however, when residents living next to Kubor Kassim Muslim Cemetery along Siglap Road complained to authorities of noise and disturbances at night. Visitors were entering via Siglap Close, to avoid the guard post at the cemetery's main entrance. Numbers written on paper slips were left atop the stones, and punters would chant for a sign that one had been selected by the spirit. A resident complained that

> some of these people would be here in the middle of the night in their big cars, Mercedes and BMWs. . . . I've seen groups of men sitting around a grave, as if they were having a board meeting early in the morning.[43]

It is an apt metaphor: speculators had pooled their spirit money and were meeting with their ghostly colleagues to, in effect, pursue a deal. At the time of writing, it was brought to public attention that "night tours"—of the type mentioned by Mrs. Tan—were being conducted, taking paying customers to remote Choa Chu Kang Cemetery in the wee hours. This phenomenon even came to be mentioned in a popular 2007 Singapore guidebook.[44]

Because ghosts are seen as most available for solicitation, there is a preference for divination at older graveyards where the dead have likely been forgotten. Likewise, places associated with violence and disturbance are popular for pilgrimages. Johnny noted, "There are people who believe in ghosts, especially gamblers will go to any place where someone was killed, they will go and pray and get the number." This means visiting accident sites, highway stretches with known histories of fatalities, and other macabre business. But it can also mean going to stands of urban forest and burning spirit money at the perimeter. This hearkens back to Mrs. Tan's assertion that ghosts killed in the road will sleep rough in patches of urban forest. Although such beings are highly dangerous—you must never reveal your name within their earshot—they are assumed to be the best partners in divination. As punter "Ah Tee" told a *New Paper* journalist, "the more violent the death, the more accurate the numbers will be."[45]

HAUNTED HOUSES AND INSTITUTIONS

Narratives of haunted places articulate another version of the alternative spatial order enforced by ghosts. This is evident, for example, in reports of strange events that took place from 2000 to 2005 at the Criminal Investigation Department (CID), an arm of the Singapore Police Force that prosecutes violent offenses, sexual assault, and "specialized" malfeasance like gambling and cybercrime.[46] The CID is headquartered on New Bridge Road in a complex of metal and mirrored glass that blends technology and Orwellian featurelessness. This building was plagued by paranormal incidents from the earliest days of its construction. Such events were perhaps not unexpected, as the department's previous base of operations—still standing on Eu Tong Sen Street—is considered one of Singapore's most haunted places, undoubtedly related to the dark nature of its mandate.[47] Most unsettlingly, when the foundations of the basement parking were being cast, an excavator unearthed a wooden Chinese coffin in the old style.[48] This was discovered thirty meters below the surface—far too deep for a normal burial. The object was sitting directly in the path of a main "pile," an anchoring column driven into the ground. The contractors immediately stopped work, unwilling to disturb it. This was in keeping with local construction practices, given the widespread belief that sickness and bad luck befall those who handle such artifacts. Their negative effects are considered highly contagious.

The story became yet stranger. The engineers were convinced, somewhat reluctantly, to reposition the pile. When the new location was checked on-site, however, it once again appeared to coincide with the coffin. It had somehow moved.[49] An architect on the project recalls,

> They thought they would modify the pile-cap, so as not to touch the box. The interesting thing is that whenever the surveyor came to do the check, and passed the information to the contractor, the piles [had] moved. And it continued to happen. They just could not cast those pile caps, because the piles moved. It is so incredible that they get another surveyor, a second. And it keeps happening.

The casket appeared to be exerting a transformative effect on the design, shifting the footings to avoid its location. To resolve this impasse, an exhumation consultancy was hired—a business specializing in relocating the dead without incurring their wrath.[50] This expertise was crucial, as "you don't know [who is buried inside]. It needs to be handled properly."

Construction was completed. But soon after, occupants allegedly began reporting unfortunate events: unexplained illness, freak accidents, infertility, and streaks of bad luck. The department responded with a standard Singaporean haunting protocol, hiring a team of religious "ghostbusters" to tour the interior and drive out malevolent spirits. This included a Buddhist monk, a Catholic priest, an imam, and a medium, who together blessed the space.[51] The medium later told me that he had located the source of the problem, a central depository where evidence from violence crimes was being stored.[52]

During the hauntings, however, the facility and its operations fell into a state of disarray. Employees took extended "sympathetic leave," worried about the risks to life and luck. The place was said to be *suay* ("unlucky" in Hokkien, the opposite of *huat*)—a property that, also, is understood as infectious when associated with spiritual or energetic disturbance. The branches of internal security that operated within this building were, in effect, barred from normal operation until the invasive spirits were convinced to leave.

This seizure of architecture is a commonly alleged pastime of the dead and a major focus of Singapore's paranormal discourses. For example, the MRT station at Dhoby Ghaut was built on a Jewish cemetery after 1983. Here, it is said, ghost passengers ride the trains in endless loops, restlessly moving yet going nowhere—their movements a very embodiment of the undirected and periodic character of a spectral existence overtaken by the tide of modernization. As noted, the construction of the mass rail system was also seen as a major violence perpetrated against the island and an invitation to haunting. More Jewish grave sites were disinterred to create the Novena area, now a modern health care hub and home to Tan Tock Seng Hospital, the nation's flagship public medical center. This hospital is avoided by many, and when a Covid-19 outbreak was followed by a dramatic suicide leap in May 2021, internet commentators speculated that this was due to the place's "dark past." Even buildings not associated with tragic events or disturbances can be taken over—even large parts of Yale-NUS College, the academic institution where this book was finished, are avoided by students at night due to allegations of hostile spirits.

The haunting of a building may cause its partial or complete abandonment or the collapse of its functions. As often, it causes irrational modes of occupation and an intrusive illogic in the actions of occupants. "Rightful" homeowners will find themselves abandoning their master bedrooms to sleep in the nursery or on the living room floor. Or the house may be avoided completely during certain times of day, when the ghosts dominate the space and its uses. Commercial tenants may be forced to avoid certain rooms or to work during truncated hours. The spectral presence militates against full ownership and use-value, causing occupants to divert and avoid.

This was the case at Stanley's house, where a "foreign" ghost claimed part of the domestic space for itself. He recalls,

> When I was nine I used to play at my grandmother's house where there were these terra-cotta dolls, like the warriors from Xian. I rode into one with my bike, and the head came off. I thought, "Oh shit, I don't want my grandmother to know." So, I rolled it up in newspaper and brought it home. I thought I would glue it back on and sneak it back, but of course I was lazy and never got around to it.[53]

A ghost was understood to have taken hold of the rooms around the garage, where the maids were housed. Spectral events were limited to this area, and none of the other household members were affected. Stanley's nanny would complain to him of a *ham sup* (perverted) ghost who would come in the middle of the night and pinch her all over her body. He laughs, saying, "We thought she was full of shit, but she rolled up her sleeves and there really were brutal blue-black marks all over her arms and legs. The maids had to all move out of their rooms, and sleep on the kitchen floor."

This forcing of residents to relocate in perverse ways is one of the hallmarks of domestic haunting. A similar account was given to me by a realtor who had lived briefly in the center of three compound houses, old bungalows in East Coast adjacent to Katong Shopping Centre, which was then being built. During construction, a site watchman had been killed, a Sikh guard known locally as a *jaga*.[54] His ghost was thought to have migrated from the scene of death to the home next door. After this, she told me, the center house was "so haunted that nobody can stay. Because when you are sleeping, the ghost takes you out of that room, and you wake up in the garden." This took place even when all of the doors and windows were locked. As this bungalow was uninhabitable at night, it was rented to a Montessori school and ultimately torn down during the housing boom of 2007.

In Stanley's case, his mother immediately called in a Taoist medium, who wandered around the house—mainly commenting on energy and feng shui issues, such as the proper placement of mirrors. But arriving at the garage, her attention was immediately drawn to the newspaper wrapping around the terra-cotta warrior.

"My mum said, 'Oh, that's just a doll which my son broke,'" Stanley remembers. "But the medium said, '*That* is the source of the ghost. He should never have brought this home. I'm going to take it out of the house.' So she took the newspaper with the doll inside. She said, 'Don't follow me,' and she walked down the road outside our house. And she walked outside my neighbor's place, where there was a big tree. She put the bundle with the decapitated doll under it, saying that the spirit was going to go up into the canopy. I thought she was fucking nuts, but after this the maids were fine—no more bruising."

Mrs. Tan[55] observed that an invasive ghost can be very *ma fan* (Mandarin for "troublesome") because they prevent the proper running of the household, not least because it is often the domestic helpers and maintenance staff who seem to be most directly affected by the spirit's malfeasance. Mrs. Tan ran a large household in Ewart Park, near Old Holland Road, with two "helpers," a cook, a driver, and an itinerant gardener with his crew. The house was built on high land above the road—in British colonial tradition, with the main house above and servants' quarters below. After a freak bicycle accident injured one of her sons, Mrs. Tan fetched the medium to see whether ghosts were involved. She recounts,

> I got a lady medium to come. And she told me that it is a haunted tree at the edge of the plot. She advised me to do some offering, on a Friday—because she said the ghost is Malay, and the Muslims usually worship on Friday. So every Friday I must go and make offering at the tree there, at the base. And I must not cook for the ghost with my own utensils, because the utensils have touched pork. Not halal. So I have to go all the way down to buy Islamic food. So one day we were driving to buy the ghost's dinner, and I told my husband, "Ayah, let's shift to another place, I can't take this hassle anymore."

But the husband did not want to leave. Life retained its former rhythm, until the gardener was found hanged in the garage. One of the two maids, a "very iconoclastic" Cantonese *amah* with one eye, went to scold the ghost. "She really went and berated them," Mrs. Tan recalls. "And she was very offensive. And you know the next day she came up covered with bruises all over!" In the wake of this, the running of the house collapsed—none of the staff wanted to work. Mrs. Tan convinced her husband to move to another large house nearby.

In these two stories, several similar spatial themes emerge. In both cases, spirits laid siege to the servants' quarters—in one case a liminal zone by a drain, in the other a space near the garage. In both cases, the maids, being either sensitive or bold enough to resist, were punished by pinching. And in both stories, it should be noted, the ghosts themselves were both foreign and mobile. They came from "elsewhere": in one case, the ghost was Malay and "out of place" in a wealthy Chinese housing tract; in another, it immigrated from China in a clay figure.

Ghosts may be benign and simply live alongside the living in a shared home. Typically, they are seen as the source of harmless mischief—lost keys, spooked pets, irregular TV reception or Wi-Fi connectivity—in much the same way that the British speak of "gremlins." In unserious cases, a medium will often advise the occupants not to attempt to drive away or disrupt the ghosts but to see them as inoffensive. The ghosts are particularly covetous of small household objects, often nonvaluable trinkets. Here, too, spectral behavior forces a kind of nonrational action on the part of those who should by rights have unfettered access and ease of use. Residents have admitted to leaving false sets of keys or other "decoys" of frequently abducted objects.

Many impassioned personal accounts revolve around reversals of fortune. Hua, for example, recalled that she became aware that her house was haunted when her husband, James, began to consistently lose bets on horses. At first this was not noticeable, but the evidence began to mount. She noted, "Whenever your house is haunted, your luck is very good, or very bad." For the year after moving in, her husband's was very poor. "Everything he touched, he was just losing money," she recalled. "Every weekend the bookie would come to the house to take money. How can my luck be so bad? How can I be losing money every weekend?" Hua pointed out that, with horse racing, luck will eventually turn around. "You may win some, you may lose some." But while they remained in the house, he consistently lost.

In some neighborhoods, reversals of fortune are associated with specific houses—especially when ill events were known to befall previous owners. Gossip identifies homes (and sometimes entire roads) where a series of owners lost money. In 2009, for example, rumors were fueled by media scrutiny of Ron Sim, a Singaporean technology millionaire who had lost much of his fortune in the end of 2008 on the acquisition of Brookstone's, the troubled American retail company. Sim's extravagant house was thought to be responsible and to have brought similar ruin to its previous inhabitant, a well-known entrepreneur.

At the same time, however, Singapore's tortured environments are seen—precisely due to their disturbed and haunted energetic characters—as fertile spaces for making money. Following Hua's preceding statement, the chemistry of spiritual presence vis-à-vis luck and value is complex and volatile. Although living with a ghost is undoubtedly uncanny, eerie, or even terrifying, it does not necessarily result in ill fortune or mishap—quite the opposite. As in Korea, Thailand, and other Asian contexts, a house spirit can be lucky.

This might seem counterintuitive, especially as famous examples have involved horrific events. This was the case in a seventh-floor unit of block 12, Lorong 7, Toa Payoh, which was the former home to serial killer Adrian Lim. Lim was a self-proclaimed medium who, with two accomplices, murdered a nine-year-old girl and ten-year-old boy and allegedly drank their blood in a sacrificial ritual involving torture and sexual assault. According to an article from the *Straits Times,* police discovered "crucifixes, blood-stained Hindu and Taoist idols, and a book on witchcraft" as well as "pills and hypodermic syringes, and a newspaper article on human sacrifice." Lim and his conspirators were hanged in 1988. A year before the execution, the highly pragmatic Tan family (Catholic) bought the flat for the bargain price of S$28,600. They were "aware of its dark history"—nearly all of Singapore was familiar with the salacious details of the case—but considered it lucky, as they struck 4D the month they moved in.[56]

Why would a home with such a traumatic history be seen as lucky? Does expectation not hold that such sites remain traumatized, melancholic, and disturbed by the unfulfilled desire of the dead for justice? Interestingly, the opposite rationality holds. The energetic disturbances taking place at troubled sites are assumed to attract ghosts. This is the nature of spiritual forces, and those drawn in are not necessarily malevolent. Meanwhile, the living who dwell in such places have great opportunity to appease *gui,* who are then predisposed to altering energetic forces toward benevolent ("lucky") outcomes. Even the willingness to pay for a flat that has been radically devalued by murder can be seen as a form of offering. In this sense, a lingering negativity can be recuperated. While a space may remain problematic, the energies surrounding its residents can become very *huat*. Ghostly magnetism is like the solicitation of custom at a shop; if one is prudent, and the visitors are correctly "served," then value will increase.

For example, even avowedly secular youths—who viewed Chinese religious practices as "superstitious"—admitted to performing rites when occupying new homes or offices. This occurred either at the urging of parents or out of fear that making a big change without ritual acknowledgment would be unpropitious. For example, Meizi and Jianhui, investment bankers and self-described "agnostics," leaped over a lump of coal at the threshold of their new house while carrying a bag of rice. They touched all domestic surfaces and appliances with notes of large denomination and made a large burnt offering in the driveway. When asked about it, Meizi laughed, recalling that her parents felt that it would have felt strange to begin living at the house "unceremoniously" and that there was "no harm" in the ritual. When young entrepreneur Ann opened a fashion boutique of a high-end French brand in the Raffles Hotel, her father was first to enter the premises, walking backward and wiping the racks of clothes with a thousand-dollar bill.[57] Some of these recall traditional symbolic practices to avoid bad luck. For example, there is a common belief that one should not sweep the floors during Chinese New Year, as this might serve to brush away luck—instead of sweeping out, people will sweep in.[58]

ECOLOGIES OF LUCK

What an initial exploration of insecure spaces suggests is a far more nuanced understanding of the process with which we began this section: of securitization as a strategy by the PAP to make a nation safe for speculative risk. Just as the government's clearings and jungles create openings and closures in the national landscape, hauntings and offerings produce local spatial distortions that alter movement and time. Conjured ghosts flaunt the limits of established order and enforce their own; they do so in a way that obliges an oppositional regime of indirect paths and closures, portals to the spirit world, and connections (via traumatic histories) between noncontiguous places in the national sphere. Troubled places are avoided and others occupied in strange ways that appear to undermine the logic of their design.

And yet, spectral interventions also have penetrating consequences for presuppositions of value and luck—producing, in their spatial contortions, a logic of opportunity. We will return, in the next and final chapter, to ghosts' seizures of buildings to see how their true value, both of use and exchange, will be radically affected via negotiation. Haunted houses, at the largest scale, are understood explicitly to be a form of development.

We find in the preceding discussion a pair of significant and recurrent themes. First, invocation of the ghost-world produces irrationalities of space, time, and action. To be safe against (and benefit from) spiritual influences, we must begin inhabitation on specific dates, leap across the threshold, walk backward or obliquely, set our money alight, or carry objects that embody puns or dramatize their own purposelessness.[59] In such acts, that ur-Singaporean logistical rationality, alongside the planned logics and conveniences of modern spatial inhabitation, come to be suspended—if only briefly. A second insight, familiar from chapter 2, is that the bill—be it SGD, *yin zhi,* or hell money—is an instantiation of value and thus gives humans a degree of influence over ghostly powers and future outcomes. Fanning surfaces and objects with a big note ostensibly makes them into magnets for ghosts, who are then served with generous gifts. The imaginary of monetary profusion, of high numbers, reserves, profits, and excess payments, creates a vocabulary for acts of numinous empowerment.

This, like all spectro-economic phenomena, rests upon a conception of luck that *contrasts* models of probability. To be *huat* is to be routinely subject to greater positive outcomes than could be expected. In Chinese popular conceptions, what appears to humans as chance is in fact the result of a complex and occult causality. There are, as Master Goh will tell us, inherently lucky and unlucky places—and here ghost-discourse begins to resemble the environmental determinist theories of state. Harmony and balance of energies will, like the proverbially rising tide, lift or lower all boats. Disharmony will thwart plans and processes. The decisive factors for futures are energetic, and these can be adjusted for good or bad via geomantic precautions or spiritual observances. A specific balance of elements and energies is required. Thus we might begin to understand the ghost's influence over risk. As beings of yin able to skew the energetic balance of a location, *gui*—alongside deities—exert powers of determination over environmental and personal conditions. Only those like the mediums, with their powers of sight and energetic sense, can "enter into" such places and bargain with their resident influences.

The crucial point, here, is that matters of luck (and hence of risk and value) are beholden to the proto-ecological model of ghosts and broader "spirit fields"—the expansive, yet localized, interplay of living and dead natures, materials and confluences. The foundational violence of the city's self-making acts as a form of infinite debt that must be continually ameliorated. As a result, bettering the energies of places through prayer and geomantic outreach is a work commonly undertaken by religious groups in the service of national prosperity. To this end, offerings are conducted with regularity at significant points in the landscape, to assist the glacial process of healing an environment scarred by modernization. For example, reports of prayers held at the foot of the Tourist Board's Merlion sculpture (positioned, importantly, at the mouth of the Singapore River) triggered great consternation for evangelical respondents who saw this as attracting satanic spirits to the city.[60] From a geomantic logic, this is understood as restoring harmony and safeguarding luck and profit by shoring up the river. The latter is a major geomantic feature that was disturbed in the large-scale geoengineering of the state's drainage network.[61] In the aggregate, however, we can see here a powerful explanation for Singapore's famous wealth: disturbance itself. Like Adrian Lim's troubled flat, Singapore's larger history of violence can be seen to predispose the place to opportunities for tremendous fortune. Luck must be understood here not as a transcendental force but as a social product set amid historical ecologies. This is an understanding with near-utopian consequences, and it is to the pursuit of these that we now turn.

6

Unreal Estate

BUILDING SITES AND SPIRIT FIELDS

It should be clear, by this point, that the spectropolis is deeply beholden to the many and diverse enchantments of the financial. One variety of Singaporean trade, however, exceeds all others in social importance. This is property development—an industry where wealth generation converges with nation building and modernization at the largest scale. It is perhaps not surprising, then, that this should be another major locus of ghostly practices and concerns.

It would be difficult to overstate the presence of speculative construction in Singapore. The quantity of new building, here, resembles the celebrated cases of Shanghai and Beijing in the early 2000s; one is unlikely to travel along a street without encountering at least one site where works are underway. The "hoardings"—tall perimeter walls of sheet metal that screen dangerous work from the sidewalk and road—present sophisticated, aspirational imagery of good living. Photorealistic renderings of upcoming projects occupy panels fifteen feet tall, alongside stock photos of spas, verdant landscapes, high-end shops, and lavish foods. In a city with relatively little billboard advertising, this cinematic presence exerts an indelible effect upon the experience of public space.

Given that climbing the property ladder remains a dominant aspiration of this society—and that the development sector generates billions in revenue—speculative architecture provides a potent medium for imagining rich national futures. Just as early HDBs were showcased as evidence of rapidly arriving modernity, luxe condos connote "global city" status. At the same time, and as noted in the introduction to this volume, such projects are integral to the ongoing production of Singapore's public and private fortunes.

However, there is an odd paradox to Singapore's new housing complexes. On one hand, these are incontrovertibly massive and material undertakings: towers of muscular concrete framing, which require vast inputs of sand, cement, water, rebar, glazing, stone, and timber. Their grounds are covered with paving and landscaping, fountains and pools. These are striated with piping and ducts and sit above levels of submerged parking. To benefit from economies of scale, such works typically occupy large, consolidated parcels and appear more like microcities than individual blocks.[1] A single one can house hundreds of families. At the same time, these retain an oddly provisional status—an impermanence that more commonly characterizes other forms of asset. They have rather short shelf lives, often standing fewer than forty years before being remade at higher intensities for refreshed profits. Their owners, moreover, treat them with straightforward pragmatism and calculation. Units flood the market in the event of rising prices, and residents are quick to form collective sale committees to transfer all back to the development sector for demolition and redesign. The monumental physicality of such buildings exists against the impression that they might, at any moment, "melt into air."[2]

This is because flats are understood to be sites of domesticity *and* speculative devices. On one hand, they are steeped in affective and intimate associations, in their role as household spaces. At the same time, however, they represent most Singaporean families' central savings vehicle. Property value necessarily remains at the fore, inseparable from class identity and wealth as proof of merit. Chua Beng Huat has pointed out that the emotive ideal of "home," here, cannot be disentangled from the function of capital accumulation.

This fact should not come as a shock. It is a tension that defines the commodity-form, of which the apartment is merely a variant. Likewise, it is integral to the capital process, which creates surplus profit precisely by circulating through material and immaterial phases. Analysis of, and moral panic about, such financialization is as old as Calvinism—condemnations of monetary derivatives of physical things, for example, predate their early appearance on the Chicago Board of Trade by hundreds of years.[3] It is nonetheless meaningful to consider how this ambivalence comes to roost in the often awkward design of the late modern home, and in the spectro-affective mediations that attempt to make sense of it. The desire to avail oneself of an investment *and* a lifeworld can be seen, for example, in the creep of commercial decor and treatments into residential spaces. The Singaporean condo is increasingly imagined as a shopping mall or hotel in miniature, projecting an uncontroversial (and globally fungible) luxury aesthetic that lends itself to reselling or renting.[4] Economic imperatives are found, also, in the shape of the interior, in the so-called bay windows that are a defining feature of many local units. This was an invention by architects, in response to the discipline of code and profitability: projecting ledges built on a plane above the floor resulted in additional, tax-free square footage and an appearance of spaciousness. The surfaces upon which family photos and greeting cards sit are ones that the owner pays for and the developer gets for "free."[5] The ticklish problem here is of life lived inside monetary forms; our domesticity accommodates itself, in every detail, with parameters of value-production.

The admixture of building with speculation is an anxious one. Procedures for realizing a new development are intricate and punitively expensive. This extends from land purchase—awarded by bidding exercises that require the presubmission of designs and financial models—to the management of thousands of independent factors, inputs, and potential risks during production. Singapore is one of the world's most intensively regulated building sectors. It is also, surprisingly, a highly decentralized one. Hence opportunities for vast, compounded losses are hidden within a labyrinth of construction, planning, and fire codes.[6] Profitability, moreover, often relies on getting grants of "waivers" that allow certain regulations to be ignored. This must all happen in the shortest possible time. Despite the pressing concern of opportunity costs for delayed sales, the government issues per diem charges and other fines for late completion.

To make matters yet more fraught, the outcome is not guaranteed success. Local developments are heavily exposed to what economists call "idiosyncratic risk." This means, simply, that individual projects may fare poorly in a booming market. It is surprising, considering the famous acumen of the city's property executives, that failures still occur and dramatic losses ensue. This happened at the 8 Napier condominium, for example, in 2010. Well-designed units on a prime site simply sat on the market. A common explanation, given by respondents and on social media, drew attention to the project's position beside Gleneagles Hospital; this was worrisome, as "many people probably died next door."[7] Suspicion was later considered to be confirmed when a unit sold at a loss of S$969,000—a depreciation associated with bad luck and death.[8] By contrast, several experienced players in the industry explained this to me in a secular way: the building simply had too many units at too high a price, in a moment when several other nearby complexes offered sales in the same range.[9] Extended lack of interest often results in cut-price purchases by funds, by real estate investment trusts, or by investors in "distressed assets" who feel that reputational issues can be managed (for example, by renting to "unsuperstitious" expatriates). Either way, the developer can expect to take a bath—especially if their product is positioned in the higher range.

Ghostly mischief is common in this charged context. Attempts to build mysteriously fail, workers are killed or injured, and spirits "reveal themselves" to unnerve workers or undermine morale. These incidents may be minor or disastrous, but allegations are nearly always taken seriously—because one paranormal event amplifies expectations of others and is linked to bad fortune in the sale or subsequent occupation of the project.[10] The most common hedge against this is to conduct highly conspicuous propitiations or to pay for visits by renowned mediums, monks, or interreligious organizations. This establishes confidence that the developer has courted the right kind of spiritual collaboration and that future setbacks are less likely.

Ghosts, through the trouble that they make, provide a discursive channel for varied concerns about risk in the development process. Most fundamentally, there is risk to life and limb. Construction remains a highly dangerous undertaking. People die or are seriously injured, and a kind of theodicy—the attempt to explain and justify the distribution of accidents—is linked to ghostly inhabitation and "ownership" of land parcels. Often, injury is ascribed to an individual or collective failure to follow religious protocols or to respect the invisible residents. This is seen not only as consideration for the ghosts but also as consideration for a broader collective belief.

"A lot of things, sometimes really you cannot imagine," Johnny told me.

> One of my building sites, ten, twenty-over years back. During one of these seventh month prayers. One of the workers, I said to him, "Hey, come over, let's pray, OK?" And he said, "No, lah! I don't believe all this mumbo-jumbo." So, he walked away. Just about thirty seconds from that, suddenly he fell into the channel drain. For nothing. I don't know if it's coincidence, or punishment, or what. We believe, you don't believe—never mind. But don't criticize. Keep quiet.[11]

Supernatural events do not appear to occur at random. Rather, they are overwhelmingly reported at certain acrobatic junctures within the construction sequence, when the project's capital assumes or sheds physical instantiations. In these fraught moments, the potentials and hazards of volatility are greatest.[12] One of these occurs shortly after the purchase of a site by the developer, either by private sale or through government tender. Problems are often reported during an initial reconnaissance, in cleanup and clearing of "jungle" or during the departure of old tenants. Others arise when demolishing existing structures, breaking ground for foundations, or completing the final "rectification" period, when the bulk of units become available for purchase and occupation.[13] This distribution of these is determined by the temporalities of design and construction and by the regulatory frameworks that determine when units can be sold and billed, at various percentages of the agreed price.[14] We will see, shortly, why this is the case. For now, it is enough to know that the larger venture, in its breathless moments of financial articulation, is seen to expose everyone involved—management, rank-and-file laborers, and future residents yet unknown—to a variety of unknown dangers and ill luck. Ghosts give comprehensible form to these and (as with spectro-economic practices) provide a protocol for intervention into what would otherwise remain incomprehensible and worrisome. A haunting or accident translates abstract risk into a legible event, which can be interpreted and addressed with well-known conventions. At the same time, anticipation of the paranormal at predictable moments provides an opportunity to secure the works by seeking the cooperation of resident spirits.

Similarly, ghosts provide a ready explanation for the mystery of what, besides death, is most feared—project failure. It is often hard to determine the exact cause of unsuccessful developments. Sometimes well-appointed units at good locations simply do not sell, even at a discount. Allegations of haunting during construction certainly anticipate such problems. Just as often, however, rumors of strange happenings are invoked retrospectively, as evidence of a hostile site. *Gui* may be the cause of this inhospitality, or they may be symptoms of a deeper energetic disturbance that would affect both developers and occupants. It is perhaps overdetermined that 8 Napier—which was constructed without incident—was diagnosed as haunted ex post facto.

Not least, ghosts offer a means to address those strange and potentially alienating qualities of Singaporean architecture with which we began: its extreme fetishism, ephemerality, and outsize impact upon personal fortunes. Spectral discourse rehabilitates these through two conjoined ideas. The first I will call *spirit fields*: energetic ecologies of sites, within which the valuation of the home is thought to affect the health, wealth, and luck of its residents. These sit, metonymically, as subsets of *da zi ran,* the ever-larger scales of a "greater nature," of which each site and dweller is a microcosm. Herein exchange-value is not simply a Marxian "fellow traveler," just as the dwelling is not simply a veil for the commercialization of the domestic. Rather, quality of life and property prices—in effect, use and exchange—are reconciled within a second, broader concept of *prosperity.* The value of real estate is understood as an index of existence faring well or poorly as a qualitative totality, reflecting an underlying harmony. Through the spectro-economic, via the collaboration of the nonliving, both harmony and prosperity can be dramatically enhanced.

All of this, too, is of political consequence. Hauntings present dangers that arise despite the would-be securitization of the "nanny state" and lie beyond its powers to dispel or arbitrate. Disruptions arise within matrices of popular belief, which also contains the occult knowledge needed for both the diagnosis and the resolution of dangers. Even more, ghost-practices suggest means for improving life that are social and nongovernmental in origin. This stands in direct contrast to the narratives of officialdom, which stress national enrichment via infrastructural advancements and architectural "upgrading."[15] By contrast, explanations of haunted places stress the management of environmental change—the need to acknowledge nonvisible forces and the long-span temporalities of the nation's grounds. The enterprise of building is plagued by concerns of these as profoundly unstable and vulnerable to energetic pollution. As a result, certain preventive measures—sacrifices and prostrations—are required to realize wealth from transactions based on real estate. *Gui* do not work to preserve urban memory, in any specific sense. Nor do their actions occasion an end to the destructive impacts of speculative construction. But they do create temporary disruptions, diversions, and apparent irrationalities that suggest the persistent power of preexisting modes of ownership and rules of conduct. Troubled sites—and the stand-offs that ensue upon them—emphasize popular agency over space and environment. This complicates the PAP's amnesiac, future-oriented approach to the island as an apparatus for the continual recycling of material and monetary inputs.

The status of this qua "resistance" is unclear. Certainly, spectral events appear to articulate concerns—which we have already encountered—about continual upheaval and transformation. However, Chinese religion should not be mistaken for a reactionary neo-traditionalism. It appears, more, like a strain of business-minded populism undergirded by Taoist conceptions of the world as a balance of forces that humans must maintain.[16] In certain respects, this comes to resemble a spiritual analogue of Singaporean capitalism: there is value to be produced, and prosperity to be created, in the amelioration of a landscape cyclically destroyed for gain.[17] Ghosts are both symptoms and agents of this disturbance, and they likewise provide the principal means for its restitution. They do not militate against the state's project of self-betterment—so long as they (like the common person) can be cut into the deal. To get rich is certainly glorious, if wealth is properly managed within an established cosmology and energetic ecology. This wealth wants to be free, to flow naturally, to improve all lives.

In this chapter, we look closely at this phenomenon of ghostly behavior on construction sites and the consequences of spirit fields for architecture. The building, like development more broadly, becomes a medium to transmit currents and essences and to triangulate capital, labor, and inhabitation in the production of good and ill luck. To this end, I introduce the accounts of those directly involved in these practices: the clients, the contractors, the architects, and the workers. Not least, we will examine the role of the medium, who assumes a central responsibility in mediating between living and dead, and among regimes of law and ownership. Through geomantic theory, this figure works to situate particular lands and properties within existing ecologies and among overlapping cadastral orders. The haunted site, in turn, elucidates other regenerative techniques of capital, in which the forms of life, value, and the city are simultaneously transfigured.

SECURING DEVELOPMENT

"Site ceremonies"—in which resident ghosts are appeased through sacrifice and negotiation—are not associated with a particular type of project, developer, or contractor. This fact differs considerably with their perception. Numerous informants told me with confidence that such practices are associated with "Chinese-speaking," uneducated, or "lower-end" builders and are uncommon in properly modern developments. In reality, these are almost universally seen as necessary precautions and appear to have no class character or cultural affiliation. I have attended such rites in projects ranging from large to small, from luxe to comparatively humble. These were undertaken by corporate contractors and small jobbers, of varying ethnic origin, and were commissioned by developers of all of Singapore's major religions (and secular individuals also). At the same time, these ceremonies are not associated exclusively with major environmental changes. Rather, we see similar rites—likewise understood as precautionary or appeasing—performed whenever an environment is in some manner subject to change or whenever a suspicious event has occurred in the course of work. Hence these are also deemed favorable when moving into a new home or place of work, just before or after redecoration, or when introducing a new resident or family member to a given home. Each change, no matter how minor, is assumed to cause changes to the spiritual environs—and thus to ask for a form of ceremonial address.

I describe here, in detail, one ceremony that was held on a site close to the west end of Orchard Road.[18] It was held at 8:30 in the morning, on a date selected by consulting the Chinese astrological almanac. This is used by feng shui professionals to determine auspicious dates and times for different types of endeavors.[19] A successful, Singaporean family–owned corporation was in the early stages of converting outmoded, high-density flats into large, triplex units under the name "8 Nassim Hill."[20] The new units were being created to compete in the ultra-high-end sector, with three-floor apartments retailing for approximately S$12–15 million each.[21] The design was provided by celebrated modernist architect Chan Sau Yan, with components sourced from a range of European and Asian manufacturers. Tokyu, one of Japan's largest construction and hotel conglomerates, had been commissioned to build the new structure, along with a submerged parking structure carved into the hill beneath.

Three weeks prior, an older condominium on the site was still partially occupied. By the time the rite began, it had been virtually erased. The building had been demolished, and even its subterranean structures—the concrete ground beams that lie beneath the soil—had been disinterred to make room for new excavation and piling. Early on the morning of the ceremony, the contractors erected a striped tent near to (but not directly on) the center of the site. This was to provide a base of activity for the performance of ritual components. The event itself was to be conducted throughout the site area, most notably at its geomantic middle and perimeter, as well as at past and future access points from the surrounding roads. The guests comprised members of the design team, structural and mechanical engineers, quantity surveyors, the client, and contractors. All gathered early to witness the proceedings. Chen, a senior project manager from Tokyu's Singapore branch, and organizer of the event, was pleased by the high level of attendance. He observed that a large turnout was important and that representatives from all trades and consultancies should be present. In Chen's understanding, the offerings and chants are principally about purifying the site and identifying possible problems. But they also, crucially, establish a sort of goodwill contract between any resident spirits and the living participants of the development process. Chen explained this as a strict requirement of the medium, Master Goh, who was to arrive later. The master later checked attendance and stressed that it was "most important" that client, contractor, consultants, and subconsultants all be present; if they are not, it is impossible to guarantee that they will be protected during the construction process or, on the other hand, that they will benefit personally or professionally from ghostly approval of the venture. Such success is a team effort.

The ceremony was likewise understood to be necessary by the many other parties involved, although differing reasons were offered as to why this should be the case. Beatrice, the daughter of a developer with the controlling share in the project—and the principal decision maker for the client's team—felt that it was important for the climate of sentiment on-site. At the least, she feared that the failure to make offerings would be poisonous for morale. As a devout Methodist, Beatrice stood to the rear of the tent and demurred when the organizers asked for her participation in lighting incense or joining chants. She believed, however, that not performing the obligatory propitiations would cast a pall over the enterprise and would lead the workers to feel that their safety had not been given proper consideration. Mr. Shinbo, the Japanese managing director of Tokyu's local office, felt that the blessings were to be respected as "local custom." Shinbo noted, moreover, that most Japanese construction sites host similar rituals at various points in the undertaking: at the outset, when final structural framing is complete, and at the conclusion. Some guests admitted to being skeptical of the literal "truth" of the rites, though most agreed that it would be bad *not* to hold them. Even among the relative skeptics, there was a sort of Pascal's wager in operation: although the whole thing might be mere superstition, there was nothing to lose in blessing the works.

Chen, by contrast, understood the ceremony in a much more explicit, and nuanced, manner. A believer and one experienced in spiritual matters on-site, he was not only convinced of its necessity but also able to read particular signs arising in the course of the ceremony. He was comforted, for example, that it was conducted during a brief torrential downpour (a clear sign of prosperity), and he broke into a broad smile when a bag of rice on the altar caught fire during one of the prayer cycles—this being a sign that the spirits had accepted the offerings.

As the collected group milled under the tent, a troupe of twelve others arrived carrying crates and plastic shopping bags and began to unpack the many components of the rite. All were dressed in matching white polo shirts and khaki trousers. This caused a distinct reaction (amusement or perhaps slight discomfort) among some of the assembled guests, as these informal cerements were almost identical to the famous uniform worn by the People's Action Party during reelection campaigns. With a wry smile, Chen pointed to the heavens and said, "Don't worry, they work for *their* party." Some of the polo shirts bore the logo of a regional cigarette brand. This later appeared oddly appropriate, given that smoking—as well as the burning of paper in multiple forms—was a habit of the master, and a repeated theme across the ceremony's ritual stages.

The men and women in white, who composed the altar and participated in the prayers, represent a loose association of Buddhist charitable volunteers. Most hold secular jobs or are supported by their families. They are disciples of Master Goh who understand themselves as working for the greater spiritual good. They are a community that undertakes these sorts of blessings in the public interest, ameliorating energetic environmental conditions. Some, such as a young woman named Lily, chose to follow the master after he was able to heal her long-standing physical ailments arising from an autoimmune condition. There are similar "fellowships" in Singapore that, in the organizational guise of Buddhist social foundations, care for the elderly and the terminally ill or teach meditation, tai qi, and feng shui to novices. Interestingly, Goh identifies himself as neither Buddhist nor Taoist but as open and unaffiliated—as do many others in Chinese popular faith, which is more of a syncretic spectrum than an organized sect.

The master describes his approach as a sort of spiritual pragmatism, used for the betterment of everyone. His services are in high demand, as buildings with bad energetic distributions tend to be both dangerous and heavily devalued. This emerged in public debate in 2007 when one old condominium complex, Farrar Court, was said to have very bad feng shui. As a result, a spate of incidents was reported: ill health, poor marks on school exams, suicides and accidents, and an inability by younger married residents to conceive children. The complex was up for collective sale to a developer, who spread the rumors to local news outlets to encourage some unit owners—holdouts opposing the negotiated price—to liquidate quickly.[22] This was a fraudulent practice, but it shows quite clearly what contractor Mr. Ong and other industry informants describe as a climate of extreme religious sensitivity surrounding houses and offices. By contrast, Master Goh observes that skillful work with the energies of the site, through chants and offerings, will not only avoid these problems but create the opposite effect. He explains that it is

> because of the energy. I work on it, it becomes comfortable. People will come in later, pay even 20 percent above the market price, because, you know, just feel comfortable, relaxed there.

Master Goh is quick to qualify that this should not be done merely to "add value" but must be taken on in good faith by all parties in the development process to ensure that positive energies are invested in the venture. Here again, we encounter the concept of economic success not as self-interested but as a positive-sum enterprise that is to everyone's benefit. For the site ceremony, Chen tells me, there is no fixed fee; the client pays the organization voluntarily, by means of a large *ang pao* ("red gift packet," containing cash).[23] A portion of these payments subsidizes the modest room and board of the medium himself.

Goh has nearly three decades of experience in these matters. He assumed his role at the age of thirty—considered rather old in Taoist tradition, where mediums tend to first experience ecstatic possessions and trance states in their teens and even earlier. Prior to this, he was, by his own description, a "lazy" young man, uninterested in and unaware of the numinous conditions surrounding him. After a seizure, however, he began performing site ceremonies and healings weekly, as well as teaching his disciples the methods of chants and the use of *qi*. Master Goh has been working with Tokyu Construction for over twenty years.

Chen recalls that their first collaboration "was at a project in Tampines. A very big project with a very deep basement for parking, so we had all the heavy machinery and we were beginning the sheet pilings, using a concrete vibrator. Big work. So, on the site they had the Japanese RE.[24] He was there to oversee all the works from the contractor's side. And he was standing there, and you know, the vibro collapsed. It fell right over and just missed him." Chen noted that "this doesn't just happen, OK? The vibro is clamped on with a metal clasp; it is tied, and there is a backup tie. So we knew, OK, we had to do something."[25]

Work was halted until a ceremony could be performed. The "vibro" incident was not the only problem; the Tampines site was plagued with an unusually high number of dangerous occurrences. Mr. Chen realized that "we cannot just get a monk to chant and solve the problem. Have to get something stronger." At the appointed time, when Goh began his work, one of Tokyu's visiting directors from Japan began behaving oddly. "It was very strange," Goh says, "like something took over him."[26] The young man had wandered away from the altar and the tent and had started weaving across the ground and performing spasmodic dancing motions. Master Goh recalled, "I had to sort him out. I asked later, and he said it was like arms were grabbing him, pulling him this way and that."

The types of ceremony Goh performs vary. Some, as at 8 Nassim—where no haunting or incident had been reported—are held prior to the inception of digging for foundation works. He insists that this is the most important moment if an accident is to be avoided; at ground breaking is when the disturbance of a site is most likely to manifest in negative consequences. This is the period when the "original owner" of the property may make their prior claim felt. It is a time when the "laws of the site" must be carefully observed. As he told me, "when you want to buy a site; you want to develop, they got laws. Must go to authorities, make application, get license, all of this. Site also got laws; different laws. These laws are not the same. You can follow Singapore laws, also have to follow site laws." He observed, with a smile, that he had done this many times for buildings housing the state's various bureaucratic ministries. "The government is very strong," he said, "but still, they have problems, they have to call me."

A haunted place is often addressed by bringing a Buddhist monk or a Taoist medium to the site to chant.[27] Master Goh and Mr. Chen feel that this is typically ritually formulaic and does not address the actual problems of a given space. Goh explained,

> A monk is like a policeman. A policeman comes, can chase you away. But after the policeman gone, what happens? You come back. Monk comes in and chant, and they can chase spirits away, but later they will come back. You must know the logic of the energy, cannot just chant. So when I chant, it's like I talk with them. I say, what do you need? Money? How much, is this enough? This? You need a passport, you need to go away somewhere? I help you. This way the site can be made all right.

Through his cycle of chants, but also his amalgamation of mediumship and geomancy, Master Goh works to "buy back" the site from its prior owners and enable their safe passage to a new home. In the same procedure, he identifies and works to rebalance local energies and elements.

This is done using an array of gifts, tools, and paraphernalia. At 8 Nassim, these centrally included food offerings—a bag of Thai rice, a one-liter plastic bottle of water, and small plastic cups (approximately the size of thimbles) containing cold tea and shots of brandy. Two large gold platters and a silver saucer held fruit, principally sweet pineapples and oranges. Two blue-and-white china vases contained marigolds. In addition, there were white jasmine flower petals in a clear plastic sack, later to be scattered on the ground, and an array of *yin zhi* notes. In addition to these rather standard ritual elements, there were a number of specialized geomantic implements, including a "sacred" hammer (wrapped in red ribbon) and wooden stakes. These allow key points to be marked on the earth, in a process not unlike civil preconstruction surveying.

Master Goh stood at the perimeter of the proceedings for some time while the items were arranged on the altar—a folding table skirted in red cloth, with a central bolt of white linen laid beneath the offerings.

FIGURE 13. Offerings at the Nassim Road ceremony included sacks of rice, fruit, and brandy. Also visible are some of the tools Master Goh used to work on the ground of the site. These are ornamented to indicate their special status.

He smoked constantly and occasionally approached the altar to make small adjustments to the offerings, incense, and tools. This chiefly included occasionally picking up and examining one of his wooden stakes and inscribing Chinese characters (one of the four cardinal directions and a number) on their sides with a red Sharpie. In contrast to the elegant image of the Buddhist monk, Goh presented himself with notable ordinariness. Prior to the ceremony, he wore a white singlet, and there was an untidy air about him. He was overweight, with multiple tattoos and scars, and chain-smoked between trance cycles.[28] Goh's exceptional, charismatic body is the means by which the spirits can make their presence and desires known. It is also, by all accounts, a sensitive receptor of energetic flows. But as is common in Singaporean mediumship, it is also abused and exposed with a casual disregard. The cigarettes were smoked quickly and with deep, aggressive drags; when not in the master's mouth, they lay on the bare earth next to the piles of burning paper.

At 8 Nassim, the setup took place for nearly an hour and a half, while the client grew visibly impatient. Master Goh briefly left the site and reappeared with a locked metal attaché, of the type seen in espionage films. He opened the lid and removed a series of instruments held within foam packing. First was a modified *luo pan* compass, used to locate the site within cardinal directions. Goh uses these to intuit the spirit field—yin and yang energies, in particular, which must be balanced by locating the eight directions, as well as the "center."[29] These inform the placement of the wooden stakes, which are driven into the earth by various project team members, at specific locations relative to the site and to each other.

The ceremony began not with a dramatic opening gesture but rather with a gradual coherence of chanting voices. The recitations were begun, in fact, while the table display was still being finalized, a practice that lent the start an informal flavor. While a cycle of chants took place, joss sticks were lit and placed on the fruit platters, into the sack of rice, and into bowls of sand and ash. The prayer cycles proceeded for approximately fifteen minutes. While the troupe continued to chant, Master Goh led the members of the construction team to the earth in front of the tent, to the pyres of spirit money. In contrast to typical ghost-offerings, these bills are burned in specific configurations. They are separated sheet from sheet, as burning in stacks or clumps is thought to devalue the offering. At one point, Goh and Chen became angry with the contractor's younger employees, who were dropping large wads onto the flames. Some *yin zhi* are folded into tight geometrical knots symbolizing Chinese ingots. Others are doubled over, corner to corner, and placed in a polar array that appears like a rosette—one of the many moments in the ceremony in which money is arranged in cyclical forms. Goh explained that this represents a kind of inclusion, the drawing together of all living and dead collaborators into the construction venture. At the same time, it signals reciprocity: the "wheel" is a cycle of gifted value that, as we have seen, goes into the spirit world and returns.

Master Goh then assumed a Buddhist posture to enter trance. He held an upright prayer hand to his solar plexus and continued to chant over the money, his voice an increasingly slurred rumble. The assistants echoed this in a slow crescendo, over a period of twenty-five minutes, creating a rather hypnotic effect. After the offerings had been burned completely, a silence fell, and Goh stood. High-ranking members of the project team were led from the tent into the middle of the bare site. The master's body language showed a heightened concern for the ground—he walked with a downward gaze fixed on the surface of clay and construction waste. Moving one bare foot forward, he made a series of hesitant, exploratory gestures before taking a quick step. Chen, Shinbo, two engineers, and the client's project manager

FIGURE 14. Master Goh leads several members of the construction management team in prayers.

followed in a slow, single-file procession. At each stop, a representative of the development team used Goh's hammer to drive a stake into the ground, under his guidance. These were distributed in the form of an elongated octagon. A final gift of money and fruit were placed in the middle and set alight. Subsequently, Master Goh explained that the center of the site had been "rediscovered," and its axis—a crucial geomantic entity requiring particular treatment—was reopened through the offering. It is the tendency of successive layers of building to block these important apertures, and the work of the ceremony is in part to restore these to prominence through demarcation. Not unlike acupuncture needles, each stake is understood to ease the passage of energies trapped within the ground at a particular point.[30]

Having established the center, the work of the group then turned to the perimeter. Again, accompanied by the project team, the apprentices walked the property line while continuing to chant, their hands in prayer position. This is performed barefoot, as both the medium and his assistants must maintain continual contact with the ground. The latter appeared distinctly dangerous, with its shards of waste and rusting metal fragments, but Master Goh claimed that this activity presents no risk. When performing a rite for Tokyu at a former Coca-Cola plant in 2005, he recounts, his team walked many rounds atop broken bottles without a single cut. At Nassim, each participant made

FIGURE 15. Master Goh enters a trance state, reading the energies of the site and making contact with its resident spirits.

a complete circuit. This is a ritual norm of geomantic ceremonies, which typically attempt to reinforce the perimeter using human prayer energy. Sites that are rendered incontinent—through axial alignments of doors and gates, for example, or the incorrect placement of water elements, which can allow unregulated flows in and out—are considered dangerous to their inhabitants. In particular, it is dangerous for their money, which is understood to find such openings and flee, like water from a leaky vessel.[31]

Particular attention was paid to the northeast and southwest corners of the parcel. In contemporary schools of feng shui theory, these are known to be gates in and out of the physical realm. Ghosts are drawn to these apertures, because this is where they may gain easiest access. There is a tradition of keeping children below the age of eight or sick and disabled adults away from these corners—as previously discussed, such individuals are seen as energetically low or compromised and attractive prey for spirits. "Floating" objects, like curtains and fish in tanks, are also said to call in ghosts and should be kept out of these areas. Of more immediate concern to Goh, these also should not be magnified by standing water, ponds, or other fluid elements.

FIGURE 16. The entire project team encircles the site three times by walking its perimeter. Only when this is complete can the excavator be started.

The process of defining central and peripheral points, and of marking these through prayer and offerings, was understood to create a "stable" ground for the new development to proceed. During the proceedings, one excavator was positioned near the center of the empty site, having been towed into place earlier that day. It was encircled by fires throughout, and its steering wheel and gear levers were "protected" with knots of red ribbon. After some two hours of chants, trances, and pacing, Master Goh entered the excavator and pressed a button to start its engine. The ceremony was over, and 8 Nassim was officially under way.

OTHER SITES, OTHER CEREMONIES

The preceding description is of a single ritual. There are many approaches to the ceremonial form, however, which has no prescribed content or sequence. The chanting cycles, the objects and foods offered—even the presence of the medium—all are variable. In fact, it is not clear whether two site blessings represent, strictly speaking, the same ritual; the differences can be very great. For example, some appear to involve a precise geomantic assessment, with a repertoire of acts addressed to the ground and to *qi* "phases" of earth, water, metal, and wood.[32] Spirits are not, here, at the center of the proceedings.[33] Rather, the center is the site itself, as an environment that is balanced to benefit living and dead. In other instances, the focus is more heavily on offering and prayer, with the greater objective being ghostly appeasement at a given moment. In the former cases, the distribution of joss sticks and sacrificial accoutrements assumes a more architectonic role. They are used to locate and reinforce the cardinal points, axes and accessways, low and high ground, and natural features. When offering to *gui,* these specific particularities of a plot are often treated as less important. Any nearby open space or grassy patch may serve for mass burning, as in seventh month events at building works. This is because the ghosts are assumed to be largely foreign and migratory; they are released from hell and find their way to unstable and imbalanced places where risk is afoot. What is addressed is thus not a specific location but a dispersed traffic.

Most rituals seem to mix these two tendencies. I saw this at another site, where the protocol embodied an approach different to Master Goh's. There, offerings were intended to protect the workers and proprietor of a new house on Belmont Road, in well-heeled District 10. This is a sprawling building that is, today, the developer's own home.[34] Though this was not a speculative product, its standing with the spirits was understood to affect the owner's other projects—not to mention his own well-being and that of his family. Uncanny incidents at a given property are seen to directly affect not only the construction crew but also the fortunes of its proprietor more broadly.

The main contractor, Mr. Choo, is Singaporean, with a good reputation in his field. The scale of the works was far smaller than at Nassim, the participants fewer. Choo did not believe that the efficacy of the ceremony would be undermined by some economy, and the event was liturgically simpler than that undertaken by Tokyu. It was held during Ghost Month, after initial demolition work had concluded (and, as such, was doing a kind of double duty).[35] Hell money and *yin zhi* were burned rapidly in large piles, rather than sheet by sheet, as Master Goh and other mediums insist on doing. Moreover, the mode of interaction with the spirits was notably different. No priest or medium was hired to lead the proceedings. Prayers were conducted in a flexible and improvised way, and a few of those participating knew the words to conventional chants. The majority of the laborers were migrants from South and Southeast Asia who followed the lead of their older, Mandarin-speaking colleagues.

Another difference, at Belmont Road, was the understanding of

FIGURE 17. At the site of a new house in the Bukit Timah neighborhood, a Chinese foreman explains ritual protocol to a group of workers. Many of the laborers hail from Bangladesh and Pakistan. When the rite concludes and the ghosts have "eaten," the food on the offering table is shared.

what was being blessed. Goh's geomantic approach places an emphasis on the site and the earth. Here the half-completed architecture was the focus and the stage upon which offerings were set. Rather than being placed directly on the soil, joss sticks and small pyres of ghost-money were used to demarcate the elements of the building's avant-garde form—at edges, apertures, stairwells, and transitional spaces. The architect had designed the house across multiple floor levels, platforms with stairs between, to negotiate the sloping plot. To address this peculiar condition, joss urns were placed on the edges of the unfinished slabs. The largest pyre, and ceremonial center, was positioned at the end of the building's central axis. Here a folding table was erected to hold plates of banquet foods—roast duck and suckling pig, Styrofoam packets of fried rice and *ngoh hiang*—alongside Choo's stacks of hell notes and *yin zhi*.[36] In addition, the building's angular geometry seemed to call for address. Clusters of incense were placed at the apices of its sharp projections, as these are thought to radiate bad energy (known as poison arrow *qi* due to its intensity).[37] Tang, the foreman, explained that "the angles look [stylish], but not so healthy."[38]

Choo is Christian, and his feelings about site ceremonies resemble Pascal's wager. He told me, "I don't directly believe in all of these things, but I do feel that it is quite bad not to do it." Choo did not feel

FIGURE 18. Small joss sticks are placed along the edges of main slabs, on paths, and around the perimeter of the site. Larger clusters are placed at the main opening to the road (what will later be the driveway).

that unpropitiated spirits were likely to cause site injuries but felt that "skittish" workers may well do so. Choo claimed that the offering was an expected practice and that something would be considered amiss if it were not to be held. This is the context in which "accidents happen." Choo claims that this is even the case with the large number of foreign workers who compose his team—hailing from Bangladesh, South India and Sri Lanka, Myanmar and Cambodia. Clearly the local Hokkien-speaking tradesmen would be expecting the offerings to be made. However, Choo told me that the foreign workers who have worked on Singaporean sites also come to feel that avoiding the ceremony is inauspicious.

Representatives from another contractor, Low Keng Huat, described yet another procedure for their own works. Two project managers, Chu and Yap, agreed that ceremonies are essential at project inception as well as during Ghost Month. However, it is not their habit to perform geomantic rituals involving a medium. Their standard practice involves purchasing a Taoist altar and statues from a temple. As long as the construction work is under way, the statues remain in place. As earth god, Tu Di Kong is very important to construction projects; Chu and Yap approach the ground with the same reverence described by Master Goh, Mr. Chen, and Mr. Ong. As foreman Johnny noted, the presence of Tu Di Kong is "very common because we believe that this god is in charge of all the earth and the ground. So, if you own a shop, a factory, you need him to protect you—protect your ground."

Chu and Yap noted that project managers from Low Keng Huat will also erect a second shrine, specifically for Toa Pek Kong. On construction sites, this deity is expected not to protect the workers but to bring good fortune and favorable outcomes.[39] As Johnny described to me,

> Toa Pek Kong is the one in charge of wealth and bringing wealth, prosperity. The other one is the god of the ground, the god of earth. That one you have to worship, because Tu Di Kong . . . is in charge of all the earth and ground. So on almost every construction site they pray to this, worship this. So these are the two.
> So over here [referring to a hotel project], you have one Toa Pek Kong at the second story carpark. And we have set up one *tay ji* at B1.[40]

> *How do you choose where to place them?*
> Actually, as long as we are concerned, the place that is quiet, protected, that is the place.

> *So even at the carpark is OK?*
> Ah, carpark. Exactly at the corner which is protected. [In] hotels and factories, they are normally at the basement, where the staff walk in and out. Because the staff come in and pray, and then go to work. And sometimes before they go back from break, they pray also. More for the safety of the place and so on. But here, they asked us to move because the owner is Christian. So, quietly we move it to second story, so nobody will know.

Chu showed a phone camera image of a shrine at another project that had been concealed to look like an electrical distribution box. Its front doors would be closed when the developer, who was evangelical, drove his Mercedes past.

When a project is complete, it is the job of the contractor's representatives to make a final offering to deities and ghosts and to "inform [them] that the job is finished, and that we have to move your home out from this site." The shrine will then be relocated to a temple. If there is no desire to adopt the effigy, the contractors will customarily leave it under a tree near the temple, with some apologetic brandy and joss sticks. Before this relocation can take place, indeed, before the contractor can consider the job finished, a representative must *da xin bei*, or use divining rods, to receive word from the gods that it is acceptable to conclude (the same method is used to determine whether ghosts have "eaten" food offerings). If divining rods are not available, Chu says that the *xin bei* will be performed with a coin toss. Heads must come up three times in a row, times three, or in nine tosses total, for Low Keng Huat to vacate the site.[41] It should be noted that the conclusion of works—and the beginning of the "defects period"—is another key moment in the development process. During this time, the architect and tenants will recall the contractor to make small corrections and improvements. More significantly, though, it marks the moment when inhabitants move in and the ownership of the new building moves into the hands of a tenants' management committee.[42] At long last, the developers' possession of the project is converted to liquid capital, once again.

DANGER, SPIRIT, AND SPECULATIVE PROCESS

It remains to ask, what does all of this symbolic work, these particular rites with their own symbolic emphases, address? What specific social concerns make them necessary? As I have argued, site ceremonies have much to do with transformations of places and the manifold dangers that are expected to result. This was very clearly the case at the 8 Nassim project. An unease lingered over the morning of the ceremony. This was quietly voiced by Jessie, the lead structural engineer of a London-based firm. She gestured toward the blanket of finely pummeled building waste that covered the earth. It was powerful evidence of destruction, residue of what went before. Shards of tile, hammered from the walls of kitchens and bathrooms, covered the ground. An atmosphere of violence resonated here, a shattering of the intimate and the familiar. In Singapore, such waste has traditional associations with potential physical and spiritual pollution. Such materials are thought to be channels of contagious conditions: illness, death, bad luck. This is especially true in those zones where resident spirits remain unreconciled with the ongoing rush of progress. In discussions with informants involved in the industry, I have heard repeatedly of worksites as loci of great hope and aspiration—but also of sickness and haunting, as forms of opportunistic contamination that prey upon them or find ecological niches within them.

Interestingly, there are layers of more mundane truth to this. As rain fell at 8 Nassim, those shards of ceramic and concrete were poisoning the earth. The landscape architect bemoaned the fact that this would leech salts and chemicals into the soil. The upper layer would need to be completely replaced before anything would be likely to grow. The puddles and rivulets forming amid the waste provided some concern for Goh, as damp and wet ground is imbued with yin *qi* and prone to ghostly infestation. For Chen, these are also breeding grounds for mosquitoes—a topic of some concern, as partially built parcels in the tropics are known to become hot spots for dengue, chikungunya, and, more recently, Zika. These are slow, invisible forms of site accident and are in fact more common and deadlier than more spectacular forms of physical trauma.

For the developer, these shards were also a disquieting reminder. The demolition of the former building represented the erasure of immensely valuable fixed capital: in this case, a condominium complex worth S$500 million. It is a form of destruction that is largely procedural and necessarily takes place before new value can be realized. Regardless, the moment at which work on the new building begins is also one of great risk. Although large sums have been paid out, the project has not advanced far enough that sales can begin. This is the period of greatest risk from financial leverage. Large changes to the market—such as those that befell the 8 Nassim Hill development in 2008—will leave the owner holding fixed assets that are not easily fungible in a sluggish market. Money invested in land and building contracts and materials cannot be banked and cannot accrue interest. The ceremony thus took place at a moment in which the equations of profitability contained the maximum number of unresolved liabilities.

In the peculiar business of real estate development, these are the most unreal moments, the instants of transformation in the developer's capital. What began as a series of financial instruments—bank loans, shareholder and profit-sharing agreements among investors and landowners—has suddenly become an investment in physical assets, that is, a building that has been destroyed and now cannot be resold. Those like Master Goh and Chen can understand, and articulate in the religious idiom, this problem. For them, the ritual moment is one of vulnerability precisely because it is an instance in which something has been destroyed and something else has yet to be built. Goh's own narrative uses energetics to describe this acrobatic moment: the uncertainty of the site, the immanence of its eradicated histories, and the as-yet-unrealized presence of a new object to anchor and shape the flows and forces of the place are precisely what make it potentially toxic. He translates, into ideas of elemental liquidity, in the freedom to move of spirits that are potentially problematic, an analogue of the financial situation that concerns the stakeholders. It is a moment in which ghosts, ancestors adrift, can interrupt the intended flow of monies as they prepare to move from one medium to another.

The ceremony, as well as those by Mr. Choo, Chu and Yap, Johnny, and others, addressed the anxieties of this moment on a number of levels simultaneously. Where Buddhist and Taoist practices draw on a rich conceptual vocabulary in dealing with concerns of the cyclical, of creation and destruction—and of moments and media of transformation—they are very much in sync with a mode of capital that prepares to reincarnate among past and future commodities, old buildings and "hot" properties, and oscillations of proportion between abstract finance and fixed investments. For this reason, the material practice of Goh's troupe replicates in its interactions with the spirit world the cycle of speculative capital. Master Goh "invests" objects with his blessings—paper money, rice, and food. These are used, or alienated, in the pursuit of a balance between the human world and the afterlife; this, in turn, is thought to bring profits, excesses, and surplus.[43]

Certainly these rites also address questions of "the becoming-past of places."[44] Ceremonies are not employed merely to secure monetary flows. Master Goh's language also addresses the problem of a certain vacuum created through near-instantaneous razing of sites. This vacuum is, as the phrase goes, "abhorrent" to spirits and energies as much as it is to nature and to a febrile human imagination. Certainly there seems a continued demand, even on the part of those who make their fortunes via the process of transformation itself, for a moment of restitution and reflection. The tools of the trade (the spirit compass, for example) work to address a larger field of spatialized history and to make certain acknowledgments prior to the endless re-creation of novelty for profit.

So much for the process, then. What about the product?

From a ghostly perspective, architecture appears to retain a problematic status. It is just as common—in fact, more so—for Master Goh to be called in to completed buildings when strange events take place. I have given an account of his visit to the Central Intelligence Department, a case in which troubles during construction led to others later. Finished structures live on as environments, which attract incidents by virtue of their own particular imbalances, orientations, locations, and adjacencies. Architectures of state, as bureaucratic centers of transformative violence, are major attractors of haunting. Speculative structures likewise deal with turmoil that extends to different owners and users after the initial profit models have been safely actualized. Certain typologies, like hotels, appear to be in a continual state of spiritual upheaval—due, perhaps, to their association with alienation and ill event, and their deeply contradicted conflation of public, commercial, and private spaces. Older informants, such as Hilda and Hua, exemplified a common belief that "hotels are haunted because you have no idea what happened there."[45] Harry, who works for a corporation that develops and manages hotel property, likewise noted that "ghosts in hotels, there are a lot. . . . If you believe in ghosts, in hotels there will be ghosts."

As noted, the assumed nature of the ghost appears to address two key concerns in the spectropolis. The first involves the status of the building as a spiritual-geomantic fact, with deep implications for luck and prosperity. Here architecture and site, as material things, cannot be ontologically extricated from their histories as environmental disturbances. There are no "accidents": fate and ecology are conjoined. The second question is that with which we began this chapter: the problem of the building as a commodity, as an economic operation sitting uncannily at the core of the lifeworld. The resolution of these, for Chinese popular religion, lies in the fact that they are one—that the environmental and the pecuniary can be shown to be deeply embedded within each other and mutually constitutive.

As an intervention in a spirit field—which quickly becomes part and parcel of that same res extensa—the work of architecture carries implications extending far beyond both domestic harmony and value or, rather, which give these a rather greater role and significance. Here Singaporean Chinese folk practices sit within a heavily Taoist and geomantic worldview, in which a given building stands within the expansive notion of *da zi ran* (greater nature). The principles ordering the universe imbue the new structure, just as the latter creates localized effects in the world that preceded it and which surround it. The environmentalism of this tradition remains, in a powerful way, immanent in its conception. The whole of the universe is in the site; in it, all things are connected. We, as humans, influence nature in ways that in turn influence us.

And while many contemporary Asian feng shui practitioners reject "black hat" or other traditions that emphasize money magic, it is nonetheless an essential aspect of this tradition that luck and prosperity are energetic matters responsive to the precise location, orientation, and design of a house—and not least with the dangerous fluidity of yin energy, which can wash out wealth as easily as it can carry it in. For this reason, Master Goh was heavily preoccupied with areas of ponding, with drains, and most of all with the location stipulated by the Singapore Land Transport Authority for the main gate and drop-off at Nassim Hill Road. Streets, from a geomantic perspective, are rivers: aqueous channels of energy. They are thus major sources of volatility—both dangers and potentials. Here, also, we see another world of associations with the ghost. Like streets, spectral beings are yin. Their appearance on a site does not merely threaten misbehavior or aggression. Rather, their very energetic basis is associated with a possibly negative liquidity—with literal fluids—and suggests the outpouring of the developers' investments into the surrounding network of drains and byways.

Crucially, this affects everyone. There are fears, all the way down the line, about the building as an economic operator, as a successful product and venture but also as a space that will be lucky for those who inhabit it. This is what underlies Goh's claims in transforming the "energies" of a building and the resulting jump in prices. There is encoded, here, a sense of the home not merely as a capital investment but as a determining factor in one's economic fortunes. This again goes back to the conception of both landscapes and constructions as, essentially, spirit ecologies. The safety of the workers, smooth construction, and the profitability of the venture all indicate that the project has been carried out correctly with respect to numinous influences of energy and spirit. This benefits all—capital, workers, contractors, suppliers, and designers. By the same token, the failure of a project is also seen to have a contagious effect, and so the venture affects everyone for the worse. This explains why it was so important to Goh and Chen that all parties join the ceremony. It is a broader social contract, and the project's ultimate production of value plays a double role: as evidence that relations with the netherworld were handled properly and as an investment that will benefit the spiritual-geomantic condition of the place going forward. It will bolster the residents' prosperity and that of everyone who worked on the job. This makes sense of a curious fact about Singaporean construction, which is the heightened care of the workers for the success of a project that offers them no additional benefit. This explains, also, another unexpected phenomenon: although gossip within the construction industry is a perennial fact, most contractors will jealously guard knowledge of paranormal incidents within the team, as if the developer's vast profits were their own.

In this sense, we might understand the purpose of the spectral incident and the site ceremony as performing ritual work familiar from classic anthropological texts. As ritual, it gathers a provisional social collective into a common defense against risks, real or perceived. No wonder that this should occur at times when such dangers appear to be at their most acute; nor, in Singapore, that the rite should have a capitalist spin, providing not only numinous insurance but the potential for an amplification of value. We may recognize in the alleged haunting one of Max Gluckman's "trouble cases": threatening events that provide an opportunity for reaffirmation and renewed affiliation.[46] In this same moment, the problematic relationship of the ghost to the construction industry's many migrants is adressed. While beyond the scope of this book, it is a long-standing assumption in Singapore that foreign workers are understood as particularly susceptible to possession and spectral encounters.[47] While I have not found this to be a particular discursive focus of incidents on job sites, it is nonetheless true that contractors and foremen are very careful to make sure that foreigners are included in the rituals.[48]

This ghost-culture of architecture has one final notable effect. This study is concerned principally with the influence of ghosts on speculative building. The notion of a *da zi ran* embodied in each architectural instance, however, introduces forms of perceived risk that extend beyond profits and loss. Many individual futures are influenced by the production of new towers and houses, of which the sale price is seen more as an indicative measure of broader fortunes and exchanges. In this cultural understanding, *all* Singaporean buildings are speculative—in that they are thought to have direct and uncertain effects on the futures of those linked by association with them.[49]

This might, at first, contradict their oddly "thin" appearance. These seem to be homes only incompletely: there is a sense that such structures exist in an alien zone of exchange and "at two" with presence or function. Here design leaves telltale traces. The profit motive disincentivizes the use of actual stone, brick, or wood. Developers typically opt for plastered and painted concrete instead, rationing the budget for decorative features at areas of high visibility and traffic. The anemic character of Singapore's industrial-productive economy means that "real" volumetric substances, like solid wood, are difficult to acquire and too costly for budgets premised on profitability. Instead, structural frames are pasted up with laminated cladding made optimally thin: from paint to ceramic tile to veneers that create a clever imitation of materiality.[50] Through innovative factory processes, these may be made to asymptotically approach depthlessness—a process by which the real house for the Singaporean and the paper one for the ghost gain a striking resemblance. Both are understood to have an existence in thrall to delayed forms of surplus-value. Both, likewise, represent temporary vehicles that must be destroyed to release value and capture it anew; like *gui*, Singaporeans (indeed, all of us) live in houses made of money, actualized through creative destruction.[51]

However, we should not identify this merely as the wasting effects of alienation or the failure of a "real" or authentic being. Rather, we might now imagine a wholly different view of such architecture: as a temporary instantiation of value, as a transmitter of forces that link home life with Greater Nature's fluid dynamics. Ghosts, after all, are energetic forms that interact with others and have qualitative effects. Happiness, health, social harmony, fertility, good grades—the whole aspirational-affective world of middle-class life—do not and cannot separate themselves from value. That which would stand in absolute contrast to the monetary, to the speculative, is here frankly and fundamentally conjoined to it via the concept of prosperity. Understandings of matter, energy, and spirit dramatize and recoup this odd contradiction at the center of the architectural commodity. Those of the Chinese faith do not simply ignore its central "theological" contradiction. Nor do they merely put up with its *unheimlich* aspect. Rather, the discourse of value as energy, and its role amid balances of forces that intimately affect human lives, works to reconcile the equivocal nature of the house-as-property with the house-as-home. Exchange-value exists in a building but functions as a down payment on futures and outcomes. This is produced through an influx of investment, which works to improve *sheng qi* (growth/prosperity energy) and also, in money, is used to strike a bargain with its unseen residents. The *price* of a property is not a source of alienation but a lever of numinous agency, both acting on lives and interpreting their ups and downs. As in Hua's example, concepts of devaluation, personal power, comfort, and luck become entwined via the unknown specters of an old house.

Moreover—and of no small consequence for the ephemerality of local buildings—value must be put in motion. Undoubtedly, deep discomforts arise from the disturbance of environments. But there is also an understanding, embedded in the logic of Taoist assumptions, that the value instantiated in architecture needs occasional release, either through reconstruction or by the partial bloodletting of "upgrading." Old buildings, especially ones without perceivable heritage-value, are often viewed with a kind of suspicion. They are "run down" in the sense that their inherent value is trapped and stagnant. Peggy, a realtor in her forties, joked to me that many bungalows from the early 2000s are a pain to sell because "people think they're so old, haunted already." These are assumed to attract ghosts for two reasons: first, stagnant energy leads to imbalance, which acts magnetically, and second, they are the site of prior human event and emotion, themselves having energetic consequences. This is why older hotels are treated with fear and distrust and why so many "listed" buildings in Singapore are alleged to be haunted. The process of construction is both anodyne and dangerous in this respect. It can clean the slate but also must reckon with the fact that older events and energies, and the ghosts that they draw in, do not go away easily. Regardless, a collective sale on a condo complex is described by its proponents as a fresh start, and the decrepit character of older architectures is always central to discourse of justified demolition. Here we can see an evident contradiction. On one hand, transformation of places is a source of disturbance; on the other, the built and natural environments must be disrupted for the "natural" flow of value to occur. Here, again, Chinese cosmology à la Singapore is brought into alignment with a capitalist ethos—the shibboleth of creative destruction.

Conclusion

GHOST-MODERNISM?

> You know, it starts off and particularly with those who like
> to put money on horse and numbers. They go to a tree and
> the word spreads around that if you go and pray by that
> tree and offer penance, you will be a rich man. And after
> a while, candlesticks appear. Then a tablet appears; then a
> table appears; then a roof is put over it. And ultimately, we
> get permanent building, right in the middle of a circus or at
> an important junction. I am not against anybody wanting to
> seek solace from spiritual sources. If anyone can get spiritual
> comfort or psychological release by either striking the four-
> digit numbers or praying to the Infinite, I say, good luck
> to him!
>
> —speech by Prime Minister Lee Kuan Yew, October 31, 1965

We might ask, finally, what is at stake in considering Singapore's ghosts, as we have in the foregoing. What insights do they offer to an emerging picture of the contemporary?[1]

By now, I hope to have established the spectral imaginary as a means to conceptualize contemporary economy and address epochal anxieties about value at the mercy of unknown outcomes. It enables a vision of utopian striving within a humanistic, socially embedded capital—offering resources that are at once epistemological and participatory.[2] Herein, *gui* transcend their roles as melancholic revenants, to appear as curious amalgams of Nietzsche's "free spirits" and the modern market's free agents.[3] As such, they provide a magical means to introduce equivalence in Singapore's experience of late capital—granting entrée to worlds of speculation and being a hedge for reaping reward without risk. This extends beyond questions of money and profit to animate complex and malleable logics of prosperity and personal–cosmological–socioecological balances. As beings beyond the order of society, state, and time, ghosts also perform as speculative modes of subjectivity. They are invoked for the fear that they inspire and the mischief that they make.[4] Amid the discursive effervescence of haunting narratives, spirits are known to determine the course of events and to halt (if only temporarily) the authoritarian machine in its path. Most significantly, perhaps, they have come to embody a single nexus of risk *and* security: as those who cause ruin or wealth, who weaken and empower, who prey upon *and* protect the worker, and so forth.

Encrypted in this figure, moreover, are lessons about late capital itself. Even if we eschew literal claims that contemporary economy "is" spectral, there is a great deal about it to fuel ghostly interpretations. There is, as we have seen, the ascension of probability and uncertainty. There is likewise, as illustrated by Singapore's speculative properties, the problem of abstraction and the stubborn resistance of the material. There is the haunting presence of catastrophe and collapse, dramatizing the brutal fact that our expansionist markets *require* damaged, ghostly ecologies.[5] Equally undeniable, as Mbembe has pointed out, is the dilatory presence of death within all future scenarios of value-production. A kind of dark anti-utopianism is on the march, once again, and it is not hard to detect a literal necropolitics growing within both the ideology and the realpolitik of much neo-neoliberal ideology.[6]

The figure of the ghost is of importance, likewise, in considering pressing questions of history, the increasingly precarious status of the future, and the possibilities left for praxis in the present. It is in these questions that the Singapore case speaks perhaps most directly to spectral theory. On one hand, we cannot ignore Derrida's formulation, mentioned earlier, in which the reappearance of the ghost signals an extended, disjointed present. Such disjointedness does not appear to offer any clear resolution. Derrida makes quick work of neoconservative claims about the "end of history." However, from the standpoint of the early 1990s and the apparent triumph of capital, the endgame of *The Communist Manifesto* is likewise replaced by a condition of revolution in perpetuity, whereby the true "spirit" of Marxism is a constant hauntological engagement with the spectral regime of value. We welcome the ghostly—invite it, even—by committing to the attitude of dialectical engagement, "the critical idea or questioning stance."[7] This occurs, necessarily, without any eschatological timeline and in full awareness of the failure of "actually existing" socialism(s). A similarly compelling, if more depressive, vision was offered by Mark Fisher, for whom this present was haunted by "the slow cancellation of the future."[8] Fisher argues that a widespread cultural malaise arises, not least, from the recognition that our many progressive and utopian visions have themselves become ghosts, sacrificed to a single, neoliberal inevitability. "Cancellation" does not mean that there will be no future but rather means that there can be only one.

Both conditions—the spectral present and the extinction of alternatives—are all too clear in the Singapore model. The quality of daily life seems dominated by the paradoxes of fetishism (see chapter 3) and by instrumental, productive logic. Fisher's endgame might resemble, quite literally, the photorealistic urban renderings delivered, year after year, by the government: disciplined, "green," and beholden to the cause of accumulation above all else. There is, here, an exclusive orientation toward the future, inherent within the developmentalist ethos—not least in the forward gaze of speculation. This is a culture of anticipation in which true modernity is always in (to use the PAP term of art) the "next lap." Fisher would recognize, all too well, a cruel avant-gardism that makes of the present a treadmill, an accelerating pace of labor in pursuit of unending downpayment. The corollary of this futurism is a kind of dementia. Singapore's official discourse appears invested in a vague and fragmentary recollection of the national past and in a mythos of origin: a "third world" outpost, a "tiny island" or "fishing village." By the same logic, *kampung* life is depicted via caricature, as a mix of communitarian bonhomie and squalor.

However, the "problem" of Singapore's present, as an acute case of a global condition, appears magically reversed—enchanted and radically benign—in the light of local spectral discourses. Chinese religion has little concern for world-historical drama, modernist stadial history, "end times," or divine apotheoses. By contrast, its cosmological vision emphasizes the cyclical and the eternal persistence of a dynamic unity between continuity and change that is manifested in the contemporary.[9] These are, as we have seen, open to limitless improvement: the underlying expectation of spectro-economic activity is that the conditions of both living and dead can be bettered, *within the now.*

In this present, the repressive and disempowering mechanisms of capital are reversed—made benevolent, positive sum, and all enriching—via ghostly agency. The *huat* life, the prosperous and happy one, is achieved in a holistic sense by performing apparently irrational economic actions: by reversing the relationship between capital and profit; by seeking occult reconciliation between use- and exchange-value; by overpayment and seemingly unproductive expenditure; and last, by reemphasizing the market as a space of social interactions not among objects but among persons, living and dead. What is surprising about Singapore's ghosts is the degree to which their variety of presentism contradicts the disjointed, claustrophobic conditions described by Derrida and Fisher; by contrast, they animate a phantasmagoria of popular control, flattened hierarchies, and defiance against the grinding wheels of money and time. An ecological vision, theorizing the play of energies, monies, interactions, and representations, reorders and makes coherent the structural underpinnings of the real itself. What Singaporean respondents describe is what we might (semiseriously) call "ghost-modernism": a structure of belief that eschews world-historical futures or revolutionary-eschatological redemptions in favor of an enchanted present.[10]

Of course, this better and more accessible world is conjectured within—and not against—contemporary economy. In being so, it echoes another strand of Fisher's work: as a worldview that remains, in many aspects, constrained by a capitalist realism. Viewed in such a light, it might appear as a wild and populist analogue of the reformisms and "accelerationist" positions that seek to amplify or temper existing dynamics *within* the present mode of production. However, the moral order of the spectropolis must be seen as highly ambivalent with respect to the dominant, value-driven regime. On one hand, there is an ecstatic embrace of money, the commodity, and schemes of finance and securitization. Getting rich is, at all times, seen as glorious. On the other, ghost-practices cannot be divorced from nonmonetary notions of betterment: luck, health, and generalized prosperity. Most importantly, the spectro-economic expectation is of radical accessibility; as with other forms of prosperity gospel, anyone can become wealthy.[11] This goal is pursued through an almost satirical reversal of rational economic logic. The paradise of Chinese religion is imagined *within* capitalism, but only by *transforming* the very nature of its basic processes and instrumental requirements.

The figure of the ghost itself embodies this immanent counter-economy and inhabits it via a kind of total ecological condition (see later). It is exterior to time, a condition that comes with power over earthly matters. It is also exterior to the order of governance by state or market. Its role thus inverts many of capital's dynamics and offers a promise of popular accessibility, while also asserting an alternative authority over formal economic projects. At the same time, the ghost's "untimeliness" allows it to be seen as an aggressive advocate for the value of the old and the obsolete. While ostensibly tickled by novelties, the commodity for the ghost remains, in a sense, ever young. It performs that quiet praxis theorized by Walter Benjamin and Max Pensky: denaturalizing the regime of novelty and obsolescence, the endless and needless destruction of qualitative wealth.

The ghost, then, may or may not signal the worrying shift identified by Fisher, in which neoliberalism has foreclosed any notion of collective progress beyond the bounds of capital. All plans, it would seem, must now be made from within a state of capture. Spectro-economics does not embody the aggressive hostility of so-called revenge capitalism—as embodied by certain subcultures surrounding cryptocurrency. Though it involves the creation of alternative currencies, markets, commodities, and transactions, it does not preclude participation in more formal channels, such as the stock market or the formal development trade. In this reading, our ghosts might be seen to embody a kind of "spirited pragmatism": an admixture of enchantment and acceptance. At the same time, we must view their insistence upon inversions and analogism and imagination, and upon the social, as drawing attention to the necromancy of capital itself—its own dark fictions, phantom equivalences, and perverse irrationalities—so as to struggle with them.

The particular nature of this imaginative take on capital leads, necessarily, to a third matter of consequence: the embrace of urban space as a wildly complex, extrahuman field of engagement and relation. Where Chinese religion offers no eschatology, it has ecology of a most remarkable kind. This is not a typical, "naturalist" approach—though it remains largely compatible with discourses of environmental science and often reinforces, via its own physical and metaphysical theories, biochemical accounts of the health of flora and fauna or their interactions. It is an extraordinary systematization, both in the breadth of its holism and in the detail of its analytical capacity. For this reason,

I have only been able to touch on certain features in this book—in effect, those that relate ghosts to matters of space and economy. In summary, however, we should note a few of its relevant principles.

In essence, sites are seen as porous loci in which plant and animal life interacts with materiality (wood, fire, earth, water, metal) and with their corresponding energetic "phases." The presence and configuration of multiple living species, alongside varied inorganic matter, cause "balance" insofar as phase cycles of *qi* can continue to circulate. Opposed qualities—night and day, wet and dry, male and female, expansive and recessive—should be balanced as yin and yang. Equanimity, in a given locale, will largely determine health, wealth, and luck in human life and add a positive or negative magnifying factor to value-production there.

This discourse concerns not merely physical quantities but—as we have seen with Master Goh's site analysis—alignments and positions, openings, and axes. All of these influence the magnetism of a site for ghosts. For example, in geomantic theory, the "gates" to the spirit realm exist at the northeast and southwest of the home or plot, and for this reason, the placement of yin elements there (water, willow trees, and other "fluid" elements) encourages passage in and out. Placement of yin elements in alignment with front doors and principal elements can also signal "openness" and vulnerability. As in chapters 5 and 6, this may bring good or bad consequences, depending on how the owners and occupants manage a high degree of spectral traffic. At the same time, the placement of objects with human qualities—that is, mimetic representations of people—can attract ghosts, if the latter feel that the objects are being "venerated."[12] Such objects should be kept away from yin corners, centers and axes, and other areas of significant attraction or perceived "importance" within spatial hierarchies. What this demonstrates, in a rather extraordinary manner, is that *forms and representations* are not excluded from this ecological system either.

Likewise, human events may produce chains of disturbance in their reordering of material landscapes and the relative positions of their elements. For example, a concrete-and-glass condo or HDB, replacing a swatch of tertiary forest, adds dramatically to metal and mineral phases, often to the detriment of wood—with its necessary life-producing, expansive qualities. Elaborate gates, aligned with front entrances in Western style, invite problems: inflows of ghosts and outflows of value. Such anthropogenic factors occur alongside social unrest (in both "big" historical tragedies and private microtraumas) that likewise upsets the equanimity of energies. Disequilibrium draws spectral activity, because ghosts, as yin beings, can move easily in yin-heavy environs. At the same time, they will search for yang energies as a symptom of their "hunger." This means that sites of wartime tragedy are as apt to be haunted as those of modernization and development.

Last, and perhaps most remarkable, is the fact that this ecology is not seen to be distinct, either spatially or causally, from economy. As we have seen, value becomes a lever to interact with this complex eco-logical system—to repair or take advantage of imbalances, encourage troublesome spirits to leave, or seek their cooperation in making luck. In this sense, as I have noted, traumatic events or disturbance of a site's physical properties can be seen (in properly late capitalistic terms) as a source of both risk and opportunity. As much as ghosts act as "agents of recollection," they respond to environments in which past events are preserved and encoded. Viewed in this way, spectral "trouble" is merely a kind of sedimentation within the social-material landscape of the city, amid its labile configurations.

I would argue that such a model should be taken very seriously by those who urgently seek new, paraecological models that do the ur-gent work of relating human and nonhuman lives and experiences. In a profound sense, the holist orientation of geomantic theory in Chinese religion bridges differences between methodological orientations of object ontology and the "multispecies turn" in the social sciences.[13] Each element of the system—be it a stone or an abandoned wrist-watch, a person or an animal, a unit of money or an image—is integral to relations affecting the well-being of the cosmic totality. The living and the dead, social history and daily life, animate and inorganic mat-ter, substance and image, are brought into a field yet more expanded than many of those proposed in contemporary models, post Donna Haraway. Questions of "touch" here appear less like epistemological barriers—because questions of mutual understanding are deem-phasized in favor of those concerning mutual health and flourishing. While obviously anthropocentric, such an ontology is not "flat"— because the powers of certain actors are acknowledged to determine, above others, the presents and futures of sites. In a broad sense, this raises questions about whether the social sciences should in fact be adopting ways of seeing from their sites of inquiry, rather than simply "decoding" them.

Singapore's ghost-economy and ghost-theory thus involve an expansion from time to space, from history to ecology or geography. In a very clear sense, this mirrors the environmental determinism of the Singapore state's ideology and its intensive attentions to the city's natures and architectures—albeit *without* its futurism and temporal discipline. This in no way invalidates the well-established chronopolitics of ghostliness. Rather, it adds a novel dimension of *the present as an environment*: a site that serves as a locus of temporal predicaments.

Is the Singaporean believer "at home," then, in a world of alienation and abstraction, one increasingly available to spectral associations and interpretations? Perhaps. At least, there is a mature discourse here that is of use when trying to make meaning from a peculiar state of things. But local narratives of the dead are never homely, in any abiding sense; they are not a place to get comfortable. The numinous is, here, a state of permanent upheaval as well as possibility—it explains and allows action while remaining deeply dangerous, fearful, and unknown. Such popularizing tendencies do not work against the ultimate mythos of Singapore's state or of capital: of the value of value or of a prosperous futurity. Hauntings do not cancel projects; rather, they slow them, contort them, or make them locally ineffective or irrational. Given appropriate forms of ritual action, the bulldozers are able to be started again. In the process, however, acknowledgment must be made of dissenting visions of the future and its production.

Against the emergent order, however, it is the perverse optimism of the specter that gives hope—not least in its indefatigable sociability. Against an ever more gleefully anomic cultural imaginary, whether neoliberal or populist, the pestering spirit would speak of obligation, mutuality, and the common weal. These, like Herbert Marcuse's thoughts of freedom and happiness, continue to "haunt the mind."[14] Behind the apparently naive faith in expansive and proliferating value, in alignment with the cosmic will, is the shape of something both radical and anthropologically familiar: an affirmation of continuity, reciprocity, and life well lived. Death-as-negation and death as a world-making force are locked in a pitched struggle, and ever more so. In between stand the ghosts.

Notes

PREFACE

1. "Slavoj Žižek: Capitalism with Asian Values," *Al-Jazeera,* November 13, 2011, https://www.aljazeera.com/program/talk-to-al-jazeera/2011/11/13/slavoj-zizek-capitalism-with-asian-values.

2. "Asia lite" has appeared in a broad range of publications, including *The Washington Post* and *Times Higher Education.* "Disneyland with the Death Penalty" was the title of an article by William Gibson in *Wired,* April 1993.

3. https://annual.cfainstitute.org/2013/05/16/10-facts-about-the-singapore-financial-market/.

4. David Martin, *Singapore on the Thames: Model for a Post-Brexit UK?,* https://www.rsis.edu.sg/rsis-publication/rsis/singapore-on-the-thames-model-for-a-post-brexit-uk/#.XrtgLsYRU6g.

5. "Where Public Housing Apartments Can Go for More Than $1 Million," *New York Times,* May 24, 2024, https://www.nytimes.com/2024/05/24/world/asia/singapore-public-housing-program.html.

6. According to the *Economist* Intelligence Unit's Worldwide Cost of Living Survey. Janice Lim, "Singapore No Longer World's Most Expensive City, as Prices Fall amid Pandemic: Survey," *Today,* November 18, 2020, https://www.todayonline.com/singapore/singapore-no-longer-worlds-most-expensive-city-prices-fall-amid-pandemic-survey.

7. Most famously, with some of the smaller Riau Islands. This was a cause of serious environmental concern; see Deni Ghifari and Fadli, "Return of Sea Sand Exports Sparks Controversy in Indonesia," *Jakarta Post,* May 30, 2023, https://asianews.network/return-of-sea-sand-exports-sparks-controversy-in-indonesia/. See also Joshua Comaroff, "Built on Sand: Singapore and the New State of Risk," *Harvard Design Magazine* 39 (2015).

8. Victor R. Savage, "Human Environment Relations: Singapore's Environmental Ideology," in *Imagining Singapore,* ed. Ban Kah Choon, Anne Pakir, and Tong Chee Kiong (Times Academic Press, 1992), 200–201.

9. Brigadier-General George Yeo, at the Harvard Club of Singapore annual dinner, January 27, 2007.

10. Ian Hacking, *The Taming of Chance* (Cambridge University Press, 1990). It is an interesting fact that Singapore is increasingly in the business of exporting its own models of governance and development, across Asia and beyond. See Chua Beng Huat, "Singapore as Model: Planning Innovations, Knowledge Experts," in *Worlding Cities*, ed. Aihwa Ong and Ananya Roy (Wiley-Blackwell, 2011).

11. This period is most commonly referred to, simply, as Ghost Month.

12. *Eurasian* is an official racial category in Singapore, referring to a long-standing community of mixed South Asian, Chinese, Malay, and mixed European ancestry. Portuguese surnames are common among these families, which hearken back to the expansion of colonial settlement into the straits from Goan outposts. More recently, the term has come to refer to anyone with mixed ancestry and most commonly to children of Chinese and Anglo-American parents.

13. "Drivers" plural, as more than one attempt was made to raze the old structure. This is a common trope of ghost interventions that we will encounter again. The comparison of bruising, fatigue, and nausea to radiation sickness is borrowed from playwright Jonathan Lim, *Between Gods and Ghosts: Our Supernatural Skyline* (Marshall Cavendish, 2005), 53.

14. For a detailed description of this historical relationship, see Joshua Comaroff, "Ghostly Topographies: Landscape and Biopower in Modern Singapore," *Cultural Geographies* 14, no. 1 (2004): 56–73.

15. Thorough engagement with this subject required a kind of "whole of society" approach, as participation in ghost-practices is not—as often believed—confined to lower-middle-class Taoists, educated in Singapore's Chinese-language schools (education in English, as opposed to Chinese, is stereotypically considered to be of higher status). The reality is much more complex. Among those I have interviewed on this subject, fewer than a quarter of believers were from the lower income brackets. The rest hailed from all points along the nation's economic scale.

16. This is described in Comaroff, "Ghostly Topographies."

INTRODUCTION

1. The term was coined by Susan Strange in *Casino Capitalism* (Blackwell, 1986).

2. This notion will return later. This analysis of Singapore as a system dependent on the ongoing creation, sale, and rental of lucrative land and architecture is proposed in Anne Haila, *Urban Land Rent: Singapore as a Property State* (Wiley-Blackwell, 2015). Further clarifications and extensions of Haila's argument are given in Ho Kong Chong, "Land and Housing in Singapore: Three Conversations with Anne Haila," *American Journal of*

Economics and Sociology 80, no. 2 (2021): 325–51. Importantly, the tender of sites has also served as a lever for the state to control the nature and quality of development through tight regulation. See Lee Kah-Wee, "Regulating Design in Singapore: A Survey of the Government Land Sales (GLS) Program," *Environment and Planning C* 28, no. 1 (2010): 145–64.

3. Prime Minister Lee Hsien Loong's statement, and its consequences for the spirit world, are discussed in chapter 4.

4. A number of these authors' works have informed what follows. Those looking for an introduction to forms of ancestral and deity worship should see Tong Chee Kiong, *Chinese Death Rituals in Singapore* (Routledge, 2004); Terrence Heng, "Hungry Ghosts and Urban Spaces: A Visual Study of Aesthetic Markers and Material Anchoring," *Visual Communication* 13 (2013): 147–62; Heng, "Interacting with the Dead: Understanding the Role and Agency of Spirits in Assembling Deathscapes," *Social and Cultural Geography* 10 (2020): 1–24; Heng, *Of Gods, Gifts, and Ghosts: Spiritual Places in Urban Spaces* (Routledge, 2020); Kit Ying Lye and Terence Heng, eds., *Death and the Afterlife: Multidisciplinary Perspectives from a Global City* (Routledge, 2024); and Jack Meng-Tat Chia, "Who Is Tua Pek Kong? The Cult of Grand Uncle in Malaysia and Singapore," *Archiv Orientální* 85, no. 3 (2017): 439–60.

5. This book concerns Chinese discourses about ghosts as the subject of a systematic financial imaginary (and again, not in any general ethnological sense). This is not the result of a Sino-centric perspective. My fieldwork made clear, time and again, that a Singaporean Chinese is as likely to exchange stories of smelling a Pontianak as of seeing a putatively "Chinese" ghost; however, they will not attempt to court a Pontianak with hell money. It should be noted that studies of spirits, cosmologies, and ancestral practices among Singapore's Malay and Indian cultural and religious traditions involve other questions and hold other consequences for the consideration of the present. These have been the subject of excellent research across fields. For example, see Kenneth Paul Tan's "Ghosts, and the Possessed: Female Monstrosity and National Anxiety in Singapore Cinema," *Asian Studies Review* 34, no. 2 (2010): 151–70, Ad Maulod's "The Haunting of Fatimah Rock: History, Embodiment, and Spectral Urbanism in Singapore" (BS thesis, National University of Singapore, 2009), or Nicholas J. Long's "Haunting Malayness: The Multicultural Uncanny in a New Indonesian Province," *Journal of the Royal Anthropological Institute* 16 (2010): 874–91.

6. *Hantu* denotes a world of ghosts and demons native to Indonesia and the Malaysian Peninsula. A few of these, including the Pontianak, commonly appear in Singaporean ghost stories and are discussed later.

7. I use this term as defined by Mark Fisher in *Capitalist Realism: Is There No Alternative?* (Zero Books, 2009).

8. As discussed in part I of Herbert Marcuse, *Eros and Civilization: A Philosophical Inquiry into Freud* (Routledge, 1956). Marcuse argues, from Erich Fromm, that dissatisfaction "haunts" the successfully internalized subject. We return to this principle in the conclusion.

9. See the conclusion.

10. For the notion of the hauntological as concerning the failure of progressive and utopian expectations (and the melancholia of radical movements), see Mark Fisher, *Ghosts of My Life: Writings on Depression, Hauntology, and Lost Futures* (Zero Books, 2014). For the dysregulating temporality of dead labor, see James Tyner, *Dead Labor: Toward a Political Economy of Death* (University of Minnesota Press, 2019).

11. L. Randall Wray, "The Origins of Money and the Development of the Modern Financial System," Working Paper 86, Jerome Levy Economics Institute at Bard College and University of Denver, March 1993; David Harvey, *The Enigma of Capital and the Crises of Capitalism* (Profile Books, 2010); Stuart Banner, *Speculation: A History of the Fine Line Between Gambling and Investing* (Oxford University Press, 2018); Gayle Rogers, *Speculation: A Cultural History from Aristotle to AI* (Columbia University Press, 2021).

12. Fredric Jameson, *Postmodernism; or, The Cultural Logic of Late Capitalism* (Duke University Press, 2007), xix.

13. Harvey, *Enigma of Capital.* See also Michael Hudson, "Finance Capitalism Versus Industrial Capitalism: The Rentier Resurgence and Takeover," *Review of Radical Political Economics* 53, no. 4 (2021): 557–73. While some representatives of industry (notably James Dyson, who later relocated to Singapore) argued for Leave, a groundswell of Remain sentiment was expressed by "business." This was repeatedly highlighted by the BBC and others. "EU Referendum: More Than 1,280 Business Leaders Sign Letter," BBC, June 22, 2016, https://www.bbc.com/news/business-36592782.

14. I refer here to Ron Sim, founder of personal technology company Osim (known for its massaging devices), and Sam Goi, so-called "Popiah King," who sells the skins used to make southern Chinese–style spring rolls (*popiah* in Hokkien dialect). Goi is famous for his huge home—often confused with the embassies located nearby—and collection of Ferraris.

15. For example, many Singaporeans suffered during the 2007–8 subprime implosion, as they did during the 1997 tiger markets crash. The problem, in the more recent cases, did not arise from "pure" finance. Rather, it was the repackaging of near-worthless loans on real-world inputs, through layers of "securities" that appeared to make them both safe and valuable. The complex relationships between productive economy and finance are well understood, if only in general terms, among Singapore's financially literate public.

16. Youyenn Teo, "The Singaporean Welfare State System: With Special Reference to Public Housing and the Central Provident Fund," in *The Routledge International Handbook to Welfare State Systems*, ed. Christian Aspalter (Routledge, 2017).

17. David Harvey, "The Geography of Capitalist Accumulation: A Reconstruction of the Marxian Theory," *Antipode* 7, no. 2 (1975): 9–21, and Harvey, *The Condition of Postmodernity: An Enquiry into the Origins of Cultural Change* (Blackwell, 1991); Edward Soja, *Postmodern Geographies: The Reassertion of Space in Critical Social Theory* (Verso, 2011).

18. We need not argue with Moishe Postone, or others, who hold that labor is still the root of value under capitalism. This is an important argument, made in Postone's *Time, Labor, and Social Domination: A Reinterpretation of Marx's Critical Theory* (Cambridge University Press, 1993). Of course, it is possible to object that money markets and abstruse "products" produce money, not value, or that labor serves as a variable standard for general *social* value, or that price and value are distinct and often confused.

19. Allison Schrager, *An Economist Walks into a Brothel: And Other Unexpected Places to Find Risk* (Portfolio, 2019). Of course, the perception of contemporary existence as saturated with risk was clearly articulated by Ulrich Beck in *Risk Society: Towards a New Modernity* (SAGE, 1992) and more recently in Zygmunt Baumann's study of precarity, *Liquid Life* (Polity, 2005).

20. See Roger Farmer, "Confidence Crashes and Animal Spirits," *Economic Journal* 122 (2012): 155–72; Timothy Geithner, *Stress Tests: Reflections on Financial Crises* (Crown, 2014); Benjamin Friedman, "A Predictable Pathology," keynote address at the BIS annual conference, Lucerne, Switzerland, June 27, 2014; Charles Calomiris and Stephen Haber, *Fragile by Design: The Political Origins of Banking Crises and Scarce Credit* (Princeton University Press, 2014); Martin Wolf, "The Challenge of Halting the Financial Doomsday Machine," *Financial Times*, April 20, 2010.

21. Anne Fabian, *Card Sharps, Dream Books, and Bucket Shops: Gambling in Nineteenth Century America* (Cornell University Press, 1990); Jonathan Levy, *Freaks of Fortune: The Emerging World of Capitalism and Risk in America* (Harvard University Press, 2012); also Banner, *Speculation*.

22. Because risk has become so fundamental to most forms of contemporary value, it must increasingly lie at the heart of any Marxian analysis, alongside labor. Increasingly, economy is marked by a "two-tier" class system, divided between those who contribute value through work in service and production and those whose income is tied to probability. This should be put in dialogue with David Graeber's "bullshit jobs" theory, which fails to explain *why* remuneration should be inversely related to "useful" work, in *Bullshit Jobs: A Theory* (Simon and Schuster, 2018). Probability is of no use;

it is gaming. Regardless, it sits at the center of modern capital. Those who increasingly participate in the perpetuation of its dealings are thus disproportionately rewarded, and their work retains a certain glamour. Production, by the same logic, becomes infinitely devalued, and service jobs are merely grist for the continuance of the system.

23. This is described by Benjamin Lee and Edward LiPuma in *Financial Derivatives and the Globalization of Risk* (Duke University Press, 2004). Of course, it may be objected that this has long been the case. And certainly modes of capitalism and proto-capitalism based on risk are as old as the hills. Weber provides a summary of adventurism going back to the *commenda* and before. See Max Weber, *The Protestant Ethic and the Spirit of Capitalism* (Routledge, 1930), xxvi. However, as a burgeoning literature (see note 20) makes clear, this is ever more a problem of generalized national and global concern. As risk-based trade occupies an increasing—and increasingly integrated—share among dominant economic practices, the dangers of risk become highly acute and pervasive. At the same time, the glamour of disproportionate rewards appears increasingly difficult to resist.

24. The difference between these techniques is poorly understood and almost always discussed incorrectly in popular analyses. Diversification might include a varied portfolio, in a common market of industry, of assets that might all be subject to devaluation from a common influence—as a range of different stocks might be to a market crash. Hedges typically split risks into nonrelated fields; this would be the case, for example, if one bought stocks and invested in real estate.

25. The name, perhaps, should have raised concerns—despite the claim that this system was derived from consistent wins in the casino of the same name. Zack O'Malley Greenburg, "Bye-Bye, Billionaire: Ryan Kavanaugh's Relativity Media Files for Bankruptcy," *Forbes,* July 30, 2015, https://www.forbes.com/sites/zackomalleygreenburg/2015/07/30/ryan-kavanaughs-relativity-media-files-for-bankruptcy/.

26. Strange, *Casino Capitalism.*

27. Securities are based on stocks and shares, not on the underlying companies (as stock and shares ostensibly are). The advent of complexities like "put" and "call" prices and horizon timings for sale or purchase makes these far more complex than traditional stock positions.

28. Lee and LiPuma, *Financial Derivatives*; Benjamin Lee and Edward LiPuma, "Cultures of Circulation: The Imaginations of Modernity," *Public Culture* 14, no. 1 (2002): 191–213.

29. Simon, interview, April 22, 2019.

30. This quote appeared in Berkshire-Hathaway's annual letter from 2002. However, Buffet is known to have openly used options in his

long-range financial strategies. Mark Sebastian, "Warren Buffett Loves Quietly Using These Financial Weapons of Mass Destruction," *The Street*, March 16, 2018, https://www.thestreet.com/investing/options/warren -buffett-loves-quietly-using-these-financial-weapons-of-mass-destruction -14525447. While participants in this sector in Singapore have told me that so-called day trading (comprising short-term positions by retail investors) is a gamble, others employ long-term derivative strategies that bet on the continuous growth of the market.

31. Mervyn King made this argument in *The End of Alchemy: Money, Banking, and the Global Economy* (Abacus, 2016) and later, with John Kay, in *Radical Uncertainty: Decision Making Beyond the Numbers* (W. W. Norton, 2020). King's point is that national banks were seen to be making global markets more secure, while they were in fact providing incentives for ever-risker bets.

32. Lydia Lim, ed., *Singapore's Economic Development: Retrospection and Reflections* (World Scientific, 2015), 8.

33. Clearly two of these would be the disavowal of so-called big government and the privatization of industry (or, at least, of keeping the state out of the life of business). As we will see, Singapore's approach has been built on public–private partnerships, and the government is heavily invested in a range of private firms. Although the latter would appear to be a contradiction, it is important to note that Singapore's avowed ideology of "pragmatism" has historically allowed for a mixing and matching among philosophies and policies. The PAP remains fully committed when it comes to other cornerstones of neoliberalism: ideas of personal responsibility (as against welfarism), value-production above all else, and the elevation of corporate management technique as a model for areas of statecraft. When it comes to "small government," several authors have pointed out inconsistencies within strains of neoliberal thought, some of which are far less averse to state interventions in economy or personal life. Jamie Peck, Nik Theodore, and Neil Brenner, "Neoliberalism Resurgent? Market Rule After the Great Recession," *South Atlantic Quarterly* 111, no. 2 (2012): 265–88. We might also point out a shift in many neoliberal nations toward illiberal governance; see note 42.

34. Gavin Peebles and Peter Wilson, *The Singapore Economy* (Edward Elgar, 1996); Linda Low, *The Political Economy of a City-State Revisited* (Marshall Cavendish Academic, 2006).

35. https://yaleglobal.yale.edu/content/singapore-local-switzerland -asias-wealthy.

36. Government-linked developers and their role in nation building are discussed in chapter 4.

37. Tiffany Fumiko Tay, "Gaming Remains Main Revenue Driver for IRs amid Expansion," *Straits Times,* April 5, 2019, https://www.straitstimes.com /singapore/gaming-remains-main-revenue-driver-for-irs-amid-expansion.

38. See Lee Kah-Wee, *Las Vegas in Singapore: Violence, Progress, and the Crisis of Nationalist Modernity* (NUS Press, 2020). For more on the expansion into casino capital, see also Derek Da Cunha, *Singapore Places Its Bets: Casinos, Foreign Talent, and Remaking a City-State* (Straits Times Reference, 2010); Joan Henderson, "Betting on Casino Tourism in Asia: Singapore's Integrated Resorts," *Tourism Review International* 10, no. 3 (2006): 169–79; Lionel Wee, "Neoliberalism and the Regulation of Consumers: Legalizing Casinos in Singapore," *Critical Discourse Studies* 9, no. 1 (2012): 15–27. Daniel P. S. Goh has argued that the integrated resort at Marina Bay Sands has come to play a central role in the image of the city itself in "Choreographing Singapore's Utopia by the Bay," in *Tourist Utopias: Offshore Islands, Enclave Spaces and Mobile Imaginaries,* ed. Tim Simpson (Amsterdam University Press, 2017); see also, on this subject, Erica X. Y. Yap, "The Transnational Assembling of Marina Bay, Singapore," *Singapore Journal of Tropical Geography* 34, no. 3 (2013): 390–406.

39. See Chua Beng Huat, *Public Subsidy, Private Accumulation: The Political Economy of Singapore's Public Housing* (NUS Press, 2024).

40. A BTO flat can be resold after a minimum occupancy period of five years—increased to ten in 2024 for Plus and Prime flats, which are in more attractive locations—and almost always generates profit. https://www.hdb .gov.sg/residential/selling-a-flat/eligibility. Life decisions are, increasingly, made around this timeline. Cara Wong, "BTO First, Propose Later: Young Couples Don't Regret Applying for Flat First," *Straits Times,* June 4, 2017, https://www.straitstimes.com/lifestyle/entertainment/biting-the-bto-bullet.

41. Interestingly, in HDB literature, the three- or four-year wait for one's BTO lottery number to come up is described via a rhetoric of planning, not of chance. The young couple is supposed to marry early—an incentive, supposedly, to increase the birthrate—and to "BTO" at the right stage in their life-building plans, alongside career advancement and savings through the CPF scheme.

42. This is the source of highly sensitive debate around the success of the savings scheme. See Chia Ngee-Choon, "Adding a Basic Pillar to the Central Provident Fund System: An Actuarial Analysis," in Lim, *Singapore's Economic Development,* and the introduction by Lydia Lim in the same volume. Certainly the overwhelming emphasis on homeownership by the PAP has led to many purchasing homes to the detriment of liquid retirement savings.

43. At least, there is a sense of a crisis in confidence in long-standing Western models. See Cherian George, "Neoliberal 'Good Governance'"

in Lieu of Rights: Lee Kuan Yew's Singapore Experiment," in *Speech and Society in Turbulent Times: Freedom of Expression in Comparative Perspective*, ed. Monroe Price and Nicole Stremlau (Cambridge University Press, 2017).

44. Daniel Bell, David Brown, and Kanishka Jayasuriya, eds., *Towards Illiberal Democracy in Pacific Asia* (St. Martin's Press, 1995); Fareed Zakaria, "The Rise of Illiberal Democracy," *Foreign Affairs* 76, no. 6 (1997): 22–43; Václav Štětka and Sabina Mihelj, *The Illiberal Public Sphere: Media in Polarized Societies* (Palgrave Macmillan, 2004); Boris Vormann and Michael D. Weinman, eds., *The Emergence of Illiberalism: Understanding a Global Phenomenon* (Routledge, 2021).

45. This can include such acts as drawing a sketch, dancing, or looking around. See Nick Hayes, *The Book of Trespass: Crossing the Lines That Divide Us* (Bloomsbury, 2020).

46. Jacques Derrida, *Specters of Marx* (Routledge, 1994), 7 and 11.

47. Derrida, 9.

48. Martin Jay, *Cultural Semantics: Keywords of Our Time* (Athlone Press, 1998).

49. See, e.g., Bessel van der Kolk's *The Body Keeps the Score: Brain, Mind, and Body in the Healing of Trauma* (Viking, 2014).

50. With these authors, we see, I believe, a contrary tendency—the application of the spectral to lives grounded in material conditions. For Mbembe, the ghost becomes (not metaphorically) a category of person in the contemporary dispensation, a being that has slipped beyond the stabilizing bounds of ethnic nationhood and human reciprocity. What is expressed through Tutuola's work is a lived human condition that simply cannot be described otherwise. Achille Mbembe and R. H. Mitsch, "Life, Sovereignty, and Terror in the Fiction of Amos Tutuola," *Research in African Literatures* 34, no. 4 (2003): 1–26.

51. Achille Mbembe, *Necropolitics* (Duke University Press, 2019).

52. Frantz Fanon, *The Wretched of the Earth* (Penguin Modern Classics, 1963).

53. Appadurai's analysis deals with the spectral in a manner similar to Derrida in the chapter of *Specters of Marx* that considers exchange-value. It is interesting, however, that fictive or projective valuations here are "fixed" to specific buildings and places—and the recitation of these becomes a mode of social performance. See Arjun Appadurai, "Spectral Housing and Urban Cleansing: Notes on Millennial Mumbai," *Public Culture* 12, no. 3 (2000): 627–51.

54. This stands in rather marked contrast to a dominant strain of spectral studies that operates primarily through representations of the ghost or the uncanny in arts, literature, and media.

55. Aihwa Ong, *Spirits of Resistance and Capitalist Discipline: Factory*

Women in Malaysia (State University of New York Press, 1987); Erik
Mueggler, *The Age of Wild Ghosts: Memory, Violence, and Place in Southwest
China* (University of California Press, 2001); Andrew Alan Johnston,
*Ghosts of the New City: Spirits, Urbanity, and the Ruins of Progress in Chiang
Mai* (University of Hawai'i Press, 2014); Joseph Bosco, "The Supernatural
in Hong Kong Young People's Ghost Stories," *Anthropological Forum* 13,
no. 2 (2003): 141–49; Julie Y. Chu, *Cosmologies of Credit: Transnational
Mobility and the Politics of Destination in China* (Duke University Press,
2010); Tine M. Gammeltoft, *Haunting Images: A Cultural Account of
Selective Reproduction in Vietnam* (University of California Press, 2014);
Kenneth Dean and Peter van der Veer, *The Secular in South, East, and
Southeast Asia* (Palgrave Macmillan, 2019); Kenneth Dean, *Taoist Ritual
and Popular Cults of Southeast China* (Princeton University Press, 1993).
Though perhaps less intensively ethnographic, this book has benefited from
the methodological examples of Steve Pile, *Real Cities* (SAGE, 2005), and
Karen Till, "Mapping Spectral Traces," in *Mapping Spectral Traces* (Virginia
Tech College of Architecture and Urban Affairs, 2010).

56. See Émile Durkheim's *The Elementary Forms of the Religious Life* (Free
Press, 1995), 47, and Victor Turner, *The Forest of Symbols: Aspects of Ndembu
Ritual* (Cornell University Press, 1967). It is perhaps obvious that this distinction denoted categories into which actual objects, spaces, and practices were
divided, as well as modes of parsing abstract natures. Like Pierre Bourdieu's
Kabyle house, the physical arrangement and demarcation of spaces are sometimes tightly interdigitated, to the point of being inextricable. In other cases,
structured oppositions are far more abstract in character and loosely/variably
joined to the physical world or built environment (as in day/night, dry/wet).
In Derrida's taxonomy, the "outside" of death—as beyond or external to the
realm of the living or the social world of human life—is rather different to the
space "outside" the city wall or the national border.

57. In effect, the conceptual connections of the ghost are at once symbolic and ecological—and, as such, operate in two very different registers to
the ordering of state. This is discussed further later. For a helpful definition
of the distinction between metonymy and other modes of connection, see
René Dirven and Ralf Pörings, *Metaphor and Metonymy in Comparison and
Contrast* (de Gruyter, 2004).

58. Derrida, *Specters of Marx,* 42.

59. In *A Sense of Things: The Object Matter of American Literature* (University of Chicago Press, 2002), 28, Bill Brown insists that the resistant
physicality of the table contributes a great deal to its awkward and contradicted nature. Hence Marx doubles down on the materiality in his
description, its "wooden brain," and so on. In *Reassembling the Social: An
Introduction to Actor-Network-Theory* (Oxford University Press, 2007, 85),

Bruno Latour argues that the example of fetishism here contains a surfeit of meaning that extends beyond Marx's example—suggesting, in a Derridean sense, a kind of textual surplus and indeterminacy that cannot be resolved.

60. As opposed to a traditionalist, "concrete" notion that would see the object as an isolated, idiographic instance. Postone, in *Time, Labor, and Social Domination,* has emphasized that the universal aspect of both labor and the commodity—the abstract character that builds on, and elides, the concrete—operates as a "total" form of social mediation.

61. Derrida, *Specters of Marx,* 45–46.

62. See chapter 2.

63. Spectropoetically, it is a "becoming-god." Its godhood is fetishism. Derrida, *Specters of Marx,* 42.

64. Derrida, 41. In this account, "Marx always described money, and more precisely the monetary sign, in the figure of appearance or simulacrum, more exactly of the ghost" (45). Money and the monetary sign are the same, and this only moves further into the realm of simulation.

65. These are, in fact, merely two ways of saying the same thing. As we will see, the buyer causes an object to be haunted by overpaying for it; by the same operation, the object comes to be valuable because this process "haunts" it (so to speak).

66. There is no account in which such houses are resold in the ghost-realm. To the contrary, these appear to be what blockchain programmers call "soulbound": the inalienable property of a particular being.

67. This is why, for example, paper money must be burned only after being distributed in circles and rosettes. The notes are understood to embody value (the cost of their purchase in Singapore dollars) and are thus a "real" substance, from the ritual standpoint. Fire—alongside paper, in its role as potential fire—is also assumed to possess unique physical properties essential to the exchange. At the same time, the fact that this is a cyclical and reciprocal gesture must be represented by the form, or arrangement, in which the notes are offered. This is not mere politesse; the arrangement of the bills is assumed to have a direct effect on their efficacy. See chapter 6 for discussion of this rite. This "technical" relationship between materials and signifying forms would not have surprised Durkheim at all; his comments on the instrumental character of magic in *Elementary Forms of the Religious Life* define this logic precisely.

68. An insightful summary can be found in del Pilar Blanco and Esther Peeren, *The Spectralities Reader: Ghosts and Haunting in Contemporary Cultural Theory* (Bloomsbury, 2013), 57. This is also a recurrent theme in Avery Gordon's *Ghostly Matters: Haunting and the Sociological Imagination* (University of Minnesota Press, 2008) and in discussion of depression and failed utopian subjects by Mark Fisher.

1. SPECTERS AND SPECTRAL ECONOMY

1. See Wang Gungwu, *China and the Overseas Chinese* (Times Academic Press, 1991); Kwa Chong Guan and Kwa Bak Lim, *A General History of the Chinese in Singapore* (World Scientific, 2019); also Donald Nonini, "Shifting Identities, Positioned Imaginaries: Transnational Traversals and Reversals by Malaysian Chinese," in *Ungrounded Empires: The Cultural Politics of Modern Chinese Transnationalism,* ed. Aihwa Ong and Donald Nonini (Routledge, 1997), and Chang Chak-Yan, "The Overseas Chinese," in *Fujian: A Coastal Province in Transition and Transformation,* ed. Y. M. Yeung and David K. Y. Chu (Chinese University Press, 2000).

2. *Tang-ki* is a word in the Hokkien dialect meaning "divining youth." The mandarin cognate is *jitong.*

3. Russell Kirkland, *Taoism: The Enduring Tradition* (Routledge, 2004).

4. Durkheim, *Elementary Forms of the Religious Life.*

5. Home and temple can be, in fact, very blurred in function. See Goh Ze Song Shawn, "Making Space for the Gods: Ethnographic Observations of Chinese House Temples in Singapore," *Religions* 11, no. 7 (2020): 349.

6. Margaret Chan, *Ritual Is Theatre, Theatre Is Ritual: Tang-Ki—Chinese Spirit Medium Worship* (Singapore Management University Press, 2006).

7. https://www.singstat.gov.sg/publications/cop2010/census10_ stat_release1.

8. In the same census, the number of identifying Buddhists was 1,032,879.

9. These occupy adjacent sites, and worshippers visiting one and then the other to light joss sticks is common.

10. https://soch.wordpress.com/2006/07/03/a-visit-to-waterloo -street-kuan-yin-temple/. I have even seen Yoruba statuary on altars in small eateries along Rangoon Road. When asked, the owner of one told me that Nigerian workers in the oil industry would eat lunch there, and this was a sign of respect.

11. Mrs. Tan owns a landscaping company with her husband and identifies herself as Taoist and also "a little bit Buddhist." This was common to many respondents, who would list aspects of these faith traditions that they believed in. The question of Taoism's polytheistic emphasis appeared to be an important determinant. Interview conducted April 2, 2009.

12. Interview conducted June 20, 2010. *Rojak* is a popular local dish, a "salad" of fruits and vegetables that is covered in a dark prawn paste and tamarind dressing. The term is used in Singlish to refer to a "hodgepodge."

13. An interesting aspect of Chinese religion is that individuals often self-identify as being closer, in orientation, to one contributing tradition than another.

14. The generic ghost tends to be characterized primarily through the notion of hunger (see later). This tends to apply to unknown ghosts, the "mob" considered to be "out there," and less in the case of familiar spirits.

15. We will see this in the coming chapters with conceptions of the death process; of the afterlife and conditions of ancestor and ghost; and of health, cosmology, geomancy, ritual protocol, and spirit money. While these carry clear influences of Chinese conventions, we see a great diversity in knowledge and understanding that a traditional Chinese might see as "confused" or underinformed. This stands in contrast to belief systems chronicled in Anna Siedel, "Review: Buying One's Way into Heaven: The Celestial Treasury in Chinese Religions," *History of Religions* 17, no. 3–4 (1978): 419–32; Evelyn Sakakida Rawski and James L. Watson, *Death Ritual in Late Imperial and Modern China* (University of California Press, 1988); Joseph Needham, *Biology and Biological Technology,* vol. 6 of *Science and Civilization in China* (Cambridge University Press, 2000); and Chu, *Cosmologies of Credit,* or, alternately, by Robert P. Weller's "Bandits, Beggars, and Ghosts: The Failure of State Control over Religious Interpretation in Taiwan," *American Ethnologist* 12, no. 1 (1995): 46–61, or in Malaysia in Ong's *Spirits of Resistance.*

16. Such accommodations are reminiscent of those in Korea between shamanic practices and Christianity. See Andrew Eungi Kim, "Christianity, Shamanism, and Modernization in South Korea," *CrossCurrents* 50, no. 1/2 (2000): 112–19.

17. Charles D. Orzech, "Mechanisms of Violent Retribution in Chinese Hell Narratives," *Contagion: Journal of Violence, Mimesis, and Culture* 1 (1994): 111–26.

18. This comment was made by Arthur, March 23, 2009. This reflects more the cosmologies shared by Chu's respondents in China, who understood spirit money as contributing to a reserve of credit in the afterlife. Arthur saw the remission of "money" not in literal terms but as a means to elevate the dead through displays of respect and remembrance. This allows them to rise on the *gui-shen* spectrum, which connects well-tended and -situated ancestors, poor ghosts, and gods.

19. See the next note. Such understandings of the spatial structure of the afterlife, oddly, have also been heavily influenced by dioramas of Haw Par Villa, a "theme park" in Singapore that depicts cautionary moral tales based on Chinese lore. These are, however, subject to wild imaginative license— but are seen multiple times by most Singaporeans during their childhoods. These leave an indelible imprint, and I have noticed that unconventional visions of Chinese hell often reflect what is on display here. https:// theculturetrip.com/asia/singapore/articles/a-guide-to-haw-par-villa -singapores-nightmare-theme-park/.

20. Again, here, it should be noted, with Russell Kirkland, that the repertoire of ideas that compose the afterlife is highly varied among Singaporeans, and there are differing ideas of the nature of this debt. In recent discourses, this is seen in highly financialized terms (a view not commonly shared, for example, among older Singaporeans). See Kirkland, *Taoism.*

21. Tong, *Chinese Death Rituals in Singapore.*

22. Hui Ping, interview, September 30, 2009.

23. The "spectral turn," as Martin Jay has correctly observed, coincided with a moment of particular interest in the more troubled aspects of history and memory. Jay, *Cultural Semantics.*

24. In this sense, they resemble the recently dead of the Ndembu, as described by Victor Turner in *The Forest of Symbols: Aspects of Ndembu Ritual* (Cornell University Press, 1967), 8–10. As still-social beings, they remain interested, and likely to meddle, in the ongoing matters they have left behind—such as the remarriages of their widowed spouses. The Singaporean case also very closely resembles Ndembu belief that "forgetting" of the dead results in a loss of social status.

25. Philip Lim, "Dead 'unable to rest in peace' in Singapore," *Sydney Morning Herald,* March 15, 2009, https://www.smh.com.au/world/dead -unable-to-rest-in-peace-in-singapore-20090315-8yuc.html.

26. This is a popular conception expressed in many informants' accounts and illustrated in public media such as Singapore's Haw Par Villa theme park. More can be found in Ken Brashier's explanation of the Taizong Hell Scrolls in Chris Lydgate, "To Hell and Back," *Reed Magazine,* December 1, 2009, https://www.reed.edu/reed-magazine/articles/2009/brashier -hell-scroll.html.

27. This term refers to seeing without being seen. Derrida, *Specters of Marx.*

28. Likewise, this echoes Freudian interpretations in Sigmund Freud, *Civilization and Its Discontents* (W. W. Norton, 2005), and in Freud, *The Uncanny* (Penguin, 2002), or in the charismatic Christian tradition of "spectral evidence," which is physically absent but appears to the witness in the form of dreams or visions. Pragmatist Charles Peirce theorized conjectural knowledge as abductive logic or the "educated guess" in *Collected Papers of Charles Sanders Peirce,* ed. C. Hartshorne and P. Weiss (Harvard University Press, 1934), 2:17ff.

29. This is described by Tom Gunning, citing Jean-Claude Schmitt, in del Pilar Blanco and Peeren, *Spectralities Reader,* 217. This was an occasional theme of Singaporean accounts also—at least, of the broader issue of the ghost's problematic visuality. Transparency or an impression of "emptiness" (much like *kimzua* and sacrificed objects) was mentioned by some, but by no means by all. It should be noted that, in much traditional media, Chi-

nese ghosts have a conventional "outfit," complete with a ribbon in front of the face. None of my respondents spoke of this in their own accounts.

30. Interview conducted September 30, 2009.

31. Interview conducted October 28, 2009. The friend was later found, confused and febrile, in a stand of trees.

32. Mr. Ang, interview, February 10, 2009; Father JP, interview, October 3, 2009.

33. David Toop describes this effect in "Chair Creaks, but No One Sits There," in *Sinister Resonance: The Mediumship of the Listener* (Continuum, 2010), 144ff.

34. A more precise distinction between seeing and sensing was expressed by respondent Charles (see later), who noted that the former is rare and (in adults) requires a gift, illness, or unusual circumstance. He stated, "Many people can sense ghosts, but far fewer can see them." Interview conducted January 14, 2007.

35. Tom Gunning, "Uncanny Reflections, Modern Illusions: Sighting the Modern Optical Uncanny," in *Uncanny Modernity,* ed. Jo Collins and John Jervis (Palgrave Macmillan, 2008), and Gunning, "To Scan a Ghost: The Ontology of Mediated Vision," *Grey Room* 26 (2007): 94–127.

36. Much nineteenth-century haunting in fiction articulated this ineffability. Edgar Allan Poe, "MS Found in a Bottle," in *The Complete Tales and Poems of Edgar Allan Poe* (Penguin Classics, 2011), 122. Poe reiterates this concept repeatedly, also describing an "indefinite awe" and "a sentiment ineffable" (124).

37. Brian Massumi, *The Politics of Affect* (Polity, 2015).

38. See Henry James, *Turn of the Screw: Norton Critical Edition* (W. W. Norton, 2020); Rudyard Kipling, *Rudyard Kipling's Tales of Horror and Fantasy* (Pegasus Books, 2008); and Edgar Allan Poe, *The Complete Works of Edgar Allan Poe* (Penguin Classics, 2020).

39. Mark Fisher, *The Weird and the Eerie* (Repeater Books, 2016), 61.

40. Gothic fiction in the Victorian and Edwardian modes described both visible and nonvisible ghosts, but the visible became dominant with the rise of photography. See Gunning, "To Scan a Ghost."

41. Interview conducted March 15, 2009.

42. Interviews conducted October 22, 2009, and April 15, 2013.

43. This is akin to the ambiguities described by Hylton White, "The Body of the Spirit: Post-Funerary Embodiment in Zululand," workshop on "Ghosts, Ancestors, and Archives," Archive and Public Culture Research Initiative, University of Cape Town, August 26, 2014.

44. One, the late geomancer and *qigong* teacher Master Timothy, said that "a ghost just wants attention; it will say anything to get it." Interview conducted December 8, 2016.

45. Some examples of this, as are discussed in chapter 6, could be explained in a secular interpretation as the violence of modern construction processes and the risks to laborers—such as being crushed by large objects, cut, or run over by heavy equipment.

46. For a discussion of weak messianism, see Walter Benjamin, "Theses on the Philosophy of History," in *Illuminations: Essays and Reflections* (Houghton Mifflin Harcourt, 1968).

47. This occurs in many ways, but we will see a signal case with property development in chapter 6—a space of giddy and often fetishistic depictions of commodified futures.

48. Lila Abu-Lughod, "The Romance of Resistance: Tracing Transformations of Power Through Bedouin Women," *American Ethnologist* 17, no. 1 (1990): 41–55. We will hear a bit more about what the ghost "wants" in chapter 6.

49. It should be noted here that ghosts are treated with extreme caution by the secular state—as are all matters of religion. The latter are seen as a powder keg, and interethnic violence in the nation's history has been understood, in large part, as dividing along lines of faith. In two decades of following this subject closely, I have never witnessed an allegation of haunting that has not been taken seriously by officialdom. Likewise, for reasons that will become clear in chapter 6, I have seen representatives of private firms dismiss spectral allegations only from within the framework of evangelical Christian belief (and only rarely).

50. I describe this in "Ghostly Topographies." In this sense, Singapore stands at the recent end of Foucault's timeline of power—and supports his depiction in *History of Sexuality, Volume 1* (Vintage, 1978), 135ff., that modernity represents a transitional mix of these two modalities.

51. Made famous, in part, by the controversial caning of Michael P. Fay for vandalism offenses in 1994.

52. Chan, *Ritual Is Theatre*. This "theater of pain," a gruesome spectacle, exists also in Hindu communities in Singapore. In the Taoist version, the medium is burned, bludgeoned, and pierced, as well as whipped. They rarely show any reaction. This is but one example of a common attitude of opposition often found in religious groups that see themselves to be at odds with the repressive hand of a secular state. This was a common sentiment in my research among evangelical Christian groups, who saw themselves as (in the words of one cell-group leader) "answering to a higher authority." It occurs in other areas of Taoist practice; see, e.g., Chia Jie Lin's "State Regulations and Divine Oppositions: An Ethnography of the Nine Emperor Gods Festival in Singapore," *Religions* 11, no. 7 (2020): 330.

53. It should be noted, however, that "female intuition" was a common presumption also and that (like "Lady Luck" at casinos) it was assumed that

women's "sensitive" natures predisposed them to correct speculative guessing. The centrality of womanhood among speculative notions is discussed in Rogers, *Speculation*, 165.

54. See Tabitha Stanmore, *Love Spells and Lost Treasure: Service Magic in England from the Later Middle Ages to the Early Modern Era* (Cambridge University Press, 2022).

55. This group was founded by Anat Rosenberg of Reichman University, Kristof Smeyers from the University of Antwerp, and Astrid Van den Bossche at King's College London. Their website is https://economic-enchantments.net/.

56. Although Derrida reads widely across Marx's writings, the book pays particular attention to Marx's *The Communist Manifesto* (Penguin Classics, 2011), *The Eighteenth Brumaire of Louis Bonaparte* (International, 1994), and *Capital, Volume 1* (Penguin Classics, 2004).

57. Tong, *Chinese Death Rituals in Singapore,* 139, focuses on these in particular, but there are many other types of objects also; see chapter 3 for discussion of auctions and their role among seventh month events.

58. As of 2024, an increasing proportion of these payments are made through PayNow and other digital peer-to-peer platforms.

59. These were the going rates for packages in the year of writing; 888 represents an auspicious number in Chinese, as *ba* (eight) is a homonym for *fa* (grow prosperous) in Mandarin.

60. At the time of writing, there are several established specialist sites for ancestral items, such as http://www.kimzuadiam.com.sg/, https://kimzua.com.sg/, and https://po-pi.com.sg/. More general distributors, like Lazada.sg, fulfill orders for local brick-and-mortar shops.

61. Interview conducted December 4, 2014.

62. Tong, *Chinese Death Rituals in Singapore,* 87.

63. http://taoist-sorcery.blogspot.com/2013/07/secret-to-strike-4d-lottery-on-hungry.html.

64. https://stomp.straitstimes.com/singapore-seen/singapore/machine-churns-out-lucky-lottery-numbers-at-maxwell-food-centre.

65. This was commonly performed by yarrow stalk divination. There appears to still be an active readership in this area, with books like Cook and Zhao's publishing translations for contemporary study. In this sense, divination practices resemble, to a lesser degree, the contemporary interest in feng shui. Constance Cook and Zhao Lu, *Stalk Divination: A Newly Discovered Alternative to the I Ching* (Oxford University Press, 2017).

66. Tong discusses this in his chapter "Unnatural Deaths," in *Chinese Death Rituals in Singapore.* The proportionate relation between the power of the ghost and the violence of its demise appears to be assumed by many respondents in Singapore. I did not find corroboration of this among

Malaysians or mainland Chinese—leading me to wonder if this is the result of some other influence or merely a unique development of Singapore's ghost-culture.

67. Hence the common tactic of spreading rumors of haunting to injure rival developers or by potential buyers in the hope of falling unit prices. See "Unfair Scare Tactics at Farrar Court," *New Paper on Sunday,* March 18, 2007.

68. Peter Geschiere, *The Modernity of Witchcraft: Politics and the Occult in Postcolonial Africa* (University of Virginia Press, 1997); Peter Geschiere and Francis Nyamnjoh, "Witchcraft as an Issue in the 'Politics of Belonging': Democratization and Urban Migrants' Involvement with the Home Village," *African Studies Review* 41 (1998): 71; Jean Comaroff and John L. Comaroff, "Occult Economies and the Violence of Abstraction: Notes from the South African Postcolony," *American Ethnologist* 26, no. 3 (1998): 279–303.

69. Weber, *Protestant Ethic,* xxxii.

70. This term was, in fact, the title and central topic of King and Kay's 2020 book *Radical Uncertainty.* See also Hacking, *Taming of Chance*; Gerd Gigerenzer, Zeno Swijtink, Theodore Porter, Lorraine Daston, and John Beatty, *The Empire of Chance: How Probability Changed Science and Everyday Life* (Cambridge University Press, 1990); Nassim Nicholas Taleb, *The Black Swan: The Impact of the Highly Improbable* (Random House, 2007).

71. Interview conducted March 20, 2012.

72. https://www.statista.com/statistics/966747/population-living -in-public-housing-singapore/.

2. HELL MONEY

1. This aspect, of faith, is a staple observation of most histories of money and currency. We see this argument reappear, for example, in King, *End of Alchemy*; Niall Ferguson, *The Ascent of Money: A Financial History of the World* (Penguin Books, 2008); Tom Nicholas, *VC: An American History* (Harvard University Press, 2019); and Larry Neal, *A Concise History of International Finance: From Babylon to Bernanke* (Cambridge University Press, 2015). It is the subtitle of Jacob Goldstein's *Money: The True Story of a Made-Up Thing* (Atlantic Books, 2020).

2. This is particularly well articulated by Jack Weatherford, *The History of Money: From Sandstone to Cyberspace* (Methuen, 1997).

3. In this sense, paper money is merely a more terrifying instance of money, a categorically frightening and devilish thing. This is a global phenomenon, hence (for example) its association with the demon El Tío

among Bolivian miners or with the devil's labor in Colombia. See Michael Taussig, *The Devil and Commodity Fetishism in South America* (University of North Carolina Press, 1980). Even when not perceived as overtly satanic, money may have magical associations; see Hans Binswanger, *Money and Magic* (University of Chicago Press, 1994), and Fernando Coronil, *The Magical State: Nature, Money, and Modernity in Venezuela* (University of Chicago Press, 1997).

4. Weatherford, *History of Money.*

5. As opposed to money on the gold standard, for example, where an amount is held in reserve for each bill.

6. Rogers, *Speculation,* 54.

7. This was the apt description of accountant Roger, interview, August 7, 2019.

8. Resemblance to American money, and the significance of this in China, has been investigated by Julie Chu with great insight. Chu, *Cosmologies of Credit.* Likewise has been the role of this type of spirit money versus others. From her research, there is a clear distinction made between type of currency and recipient—whether ghost, ancestor, or god. Likewise, according to Chu, many see hell money as having a "low-class" association as compared to traditional forms. Again, here, Singaporean understandings seem rather different, in two major respects. First, there is a general maximalism that comes from a loose adherence to mainland traditions. Although some were aware of a difference between what is sacrificed to whom on the *gui-shen* spectrum, others were not aware or did not see this as important. In fact, when asked which spirit money they chose to burn, the logic of the response was to make use of as many varieties as possible. This is true of forms as well as denominations. Here the U.S. greenback has status but is placed in a kind of cosmopolitanism of forms, images, and associations. Second, the Singaporean case was far more financialized; the dominance of hell notes was understood, in part, via a literalization of ghost-sacrifices qua investment, and the "debts" of *di yu* were seen to be explicitly financial. The notion of hell having a central bank, in the sense of a national treasury, was in no way understood as a metaphor. See Hill Gates, "Money for the Gods," *Modern China* 13, no. 2 (1987): 239–77; Anna Siedel, "Review: Buying One's Way into Heaven: the Celestial Treasury in Chinese Religions," *History of Religions* 17, no. 3–4 (1978): 419–32; Stevan C. Harrell, "When a Ghost Becomes a God," in *Religion and Ritual in Chinese Society,* ed. Arthur Wolf (Stanford University Press, 1974); John L. McCreery, "Why Don't We See Some Real Money Here? Offerings in Chinese Religion," *Journal of Chinese Religions* 18 (1990): 1–24; Gary Seaman, "Spirit Money: An Interpretation," *Journal of Chinese Religions* 10 (1982):

82–87; Gray Kochar-Lindgren, "Trans-Rational Cash: Ghost-Money, Hong Kong, and Nonmodern Networks," *Culture, Theory, and Critique* 58, no. 1 (2016): 94–106.

9. Walter Benjamin, *Reflections: Essays, Aphorisms, Autobiographical Writings* (Schocken Books, 1978), 87.

10. It is impossible to ascertain the actual market share of Chinese products, but it is certainly true that these are ubiquitous. Discussion with a local *kimzua* seller revealed that "around half" hails from the PRC. Lim, interview, August 6, 2022.

11. This statement was by Chee Wai, mid-twenties, who works in sales; interview conducted June 28, 2016.

12. The graphic language of spirit money is discussed extensively by Chu, *Cosmologies of Credit.*

13. Although he admitted with a laugh that "a very poor ghost, very poor thing one, might still take it." Interview conducted October 9, 2019.

14. In one sense, this is very illuminating—it is an interesting fact of discourses about ghost-exchanges that people speak of this value in qualitative as well as quantitative terms. That is, certain streams or inputs of value were of higher quality because they were offered with the best of intentions, by individuals of piety.

15. See Georges Bataille, *The Accursed Share,* vol. 1 (Zone Books, 1991).

16. This reflects Derrida's analysis in *Specters of Marx,* where he notes that "the metamorphoses of commodities . . . was already a process of transfiguring idealization that one may legitimately call spectropoetic" (45). While Derrida's analysis touches on this only glancingly, I feel that the Singaporean case presents a rich circumstance of this symbolic process, what Paul Ricoeur would call "predication." Ricoeur, *The Rule of Metaphor: The Creation of Meaning in Language* (Routledge, 2003), 154.

17. This is likewise not unlike monetary remission, a "service" in which one pays to move value over geographical space. The latter, however, is associated in Singapore with relative poverty and foreign labor and is a transaction that certainly does *not* result in surplus for the sender.

18. Alongside other kinds of offered objects. Bending space is, to a degree, thought to be inherent in the rite of offering (for example, with food and liquor as well as money). In this sense, the note works as a kind of subcategory of a given mode of ritual power.

19. Germaine, associate in a public relations firm, interview, February 23, 2018.

20. See essays by W. J. T. Mitchell and Elizabeth Helsinger in *Landscape and Power,* ed. W. J. T. Mitchell (University of Chicago Press, 2002). This same principle is dominant in Chinese notions of environmental and human health. Needham, *Biology and Biological Technology.* Stagnation

of flows is a principal source of pathology and may be addressed through acupuncture—or, in Singapore, via the enormously popular foot reflexology.

21. See Hillel Schwartz, *The Culture of the Copy: Striking Likenesses, Unreasonable Facsimiles* (Zone Books, 1998).

22. In fact, *prosperous* is often used as a euphemism for *fat*. When one "looks prosperous," it is a polite way of saying that one has put on some weight. Prosperity can mean a wedding in the family, having many children (an expanding household), or rude health in old age. Here the local usage of this term more closely resembles the traditional sense of "to prosper" than the more modern, financial sense.

23. Under the 1994 Maintenance of Parents Act, https://eresources.nlb .gov.sg/infopedia/articles/SIP_1614_2009-11-30.html.

24. Mrs. Tan's Singlish is rather heavy, and this statement requires some translation. I would translate this statement as follows: "That's why we go! We thought this kind of thing only existed in the movies. So, when I was there, there were the priest and priestess who were routinely at the temple, and I asked, 'Can you give me luck?' And they replied, 'Do you mean money? 4D? No, now we are curing you. But when you are cured, you will have luck.' Really! When I was cured and returned I won twenty-five thousand dollars at 4D. Really, but it's true. They have these things [in Thailand]. [We see these sorts of things] every time we go."

25. Interview conducted June 20, 2010.

26. Interestingly, I have frequently heard the reverse also.

27. During research at City Harvest Church and New Creation Church in Singapore during 2006–8, I regularly heard similar explanations followed by the time-honored "the Spirit moves in mysterious ways."

28. Many of Singapore's banks' "private" departments offer arrangements of large deposits for dramatically increased annuities, including Overseas Chinese Banking Corporation and Standard Chartered Bank. These are a common topic of discussion among wealthy Singaporeans.

29. For example, Weatherford notes in *History of Money*, as does Jacob Goldstein, *Money*, that there were once more than eight thousand currencies circulating in the United States, requiring an industry simply to provide valuations. Almost none of these traded were worth their printed denominations. The same occurred, even, for coins—the practice of "sweating" money, of rubbing coins in a pouch to shed the metal as powder, meant that these gradually lost value over the course of their exchange.

30. See Lim, *Singapore's Economic Development*.

31. In fact, four recessions between 1998 and 2009. See Tan and Bhaskaran, "The Role of the State in Singapore: Pragmatism in Search of Development," in Lim, *Singapore's Economic Development*, 72.

32. Tan and Bhaskaran, 74.

3. SPECTRO-COMMODITIES

1. Cherian George, *Singapore: The Air-Conditioned Nation—Essays on the Politics of Comfort and Control, 1990–2000* (Landmark Books, 2000), 15.

2. C. J. W.-L. Wee, "Staging the Asian Modern: Cultural Fragments, the Singaporean Eunuch, and the Asian Lear," *Critical Inquiry* 30 (2004): 777.

3. As Cherian George puts it, "the end is a high level of material security for Singaporeans." George, *Singapore,* 15.

4. See Chua Beng Huat, *Life Is Not Complete Without Shopping: Consumption Culture in Singapore* (Singapore University Press, 2003), 3. More recently, Singaporeans' online shopping has become something of a cause célèbre. See https://www.visa.com.sg/about-visa/newsroom/press-releases/singaporeans-are-southeast-asias-top-online-shoppers-visa-survey.html.

5. Chua argues, helpfully, that retail in Singapore acts merely as a programmatic basis of public life and that much happens in shopping centers that is not shopping. This argument stands as a healthy corrective to the dismissive accounts of other critics, who have suggested that commercial activity had replaced other, more authentic aspects of civic life on a European model. This is discussed further in chapter 4.

6. The vaccine, in a paper syringe, created a stir in Malaysia and was soon after spotted in joss paper shops in Tiong Bahru market. https://www.asiaone.com/malaysia/ghosting-covid-19-spirits-get-vaccinated-offerings-jb-store. One might well wonder what use a ghost has for this item. The maker specified that the purpose of paper commodities is simply to give the dead what they most desire—which often involves unsettled business or feelings of unjust death. His assumption (probably correct) is that many people died during the pandemic wanting a medication that would have saved their lives.

7. This complex relation has been worked through in great detail, and a full discussion is beyond the scope of this chapter. The duality of the commodity, and thus the labor that produces it, is a crucial factor. See Postone, *Time, Labor, and Social Domination.* A key observation is how the fetish appears to animate it into life. It is this autonomy that is relevant, in particular, to arguments about the commodity's spectrality. See Derrida, *Specters of Marx,* and Slavoj Žižek, *The Plague of Fantasies* (Verso, 1997). Also see Katja Diefenbach, "The Spectral Form of Value," *Transversal Texts* (blog), January 2006, https://transversal.at/transversal/1106/diefenbach/en.

8. Marx understood market-oriented exchange-value, the spectral fellow traveler, as something in need of exorcism. When the illusion of the fetish is dispelled via the revolutionary process, so, too, will the ghost be.

9. See also Postone, *Time, Labor, and Social Domination.*

10. Such objects have an interesting sociolegal history. The lost term *deodand* referred to beasts and inanimate objects that caused human mortality. Teresa Sutton has examined this concept in terms of the responsibility for death, which goes back at least to Plato's *Dialogues*. Sutton, "The Deodand and Responsibility for Death," *Journal of Legal History* 18, no. 3 (1997): 44–55. William Pietz also discusses this with respect to monetary valuation of life in "Death of the Deodand: Accursed Objects and the Money Value of Human Life," *Res: Anthropology and Aesthetics* 31 (1997): 97–108.

11. Theodor W. Adorno, "Theses Against Occultism," in *The Stars Down to Earth* (Routledge, 1994), 174.

12. Jonathan Sterne, *The Audible Past: Cultural Origins of Sound Reproduction* (University of Minnesota Press, 2003); Neal Kirk, "New Media Hauntings: Digital Aesthetics of Haunting, Context Collapse, and Networked Spectrality" (PhD thesis, Lancaster University, 2017); Gammeltoft, *Haunting Images*.

13. Gramophone and microphone inventor Emile Berliner claimed that the microphone would eventually pick up the dead, as they simply vibrate at a lower frequency than the living. See Sterne, *Audible Past,* and Friedrich A. Kittler, Geoffrey Winthrop-Young, and Michael Wutz, *Gramophone, Film, Typewriter* (Stanford University Press, 1999). See also Kirk, "New Media Hauntings."

14. Indeed, there is a rather busy emerging field of practice in digital engagements with spirits in Singapore. See Alvin Lim Eng Hui's fascinating *Digital Spirits in Religion and Media: Possession and Performance* (Routledge, 2019) and Lim, "Live Streaming and Digital Stages for the Hungry Ghosts and Deities," *Religions* 11, no. 7 (2020): 367.

15. Here they resemble conditions documented by Elizabeth K. Teather in "High-Rise Homes for the Ancestors: Cremation in Hong Kong," *Geographical Review* 89, no. 3 (1999): 409–30.

16. Playing one's IC number is a common way of gambling on 4D. The government IC is issued to all citizens and permanent residents of Singapore and is one method of tracking the populace.

17. It should be noted that the character of 4D lends itself to this kind of speculation. Unlike Lotto, where occasional winners face immense odds to win enormous payouts, 4D is structured such that many winners (who present partial number combinations) win far smaller amounts. Many people thus have stories of winning a few hundred or a few thousand; relatively few win more than this. 4D is thus a system that lends itself to pragmatic, small-scale speculation.

18. Marcel Mauss, *A General Theory of Magic* (Routledge, 2001).

19. Pierre Bourdieu, *Outline of a Theory of Practice* (Cambridge University Press, 1979).

20. This term, which is highly pejorative, is usually used by primarily English-speaking, middle-class Singaporeans to describe "Chinese" tastes among a variously imagined working-class population. It is used, for example, to describe the tastes of *ah beng* and *ah lian,* the male and female urban lumpen-proletarians—depicted as Chinese-educated (or undereducated), superstitious gangsters who speak a ludicrously dense Singlish patois. Cheena is also used as a signal of contempt and differentiation from mainland Chinese, who are subject to overt discrimination and a stereotyping that borders on racism.

21. *Helper* here refers to a migrant domestic worker; the term has come to replace *maid.* Interview conducted October 3, 2018.

22. These observations were made in 1947. They are reprinted in Fei Xiaotong, *From the Soil: The Foundations of Chinese Society—a Translation of Fei Xiaotong's "Xiangtu Zhongguo"* (University of California Press, 1992). The ideally "open" nature of reciprocal exchange is likewise described in Yan Yunxiang, *The Flow of Gifts: Reciprocity and Social Networks in a Chinese Village* (Stanford University Press, 1996).

23. Tong, *Chinese Death Rituals in Singapore.*

24. The popularity of items for students, discussed by Tong, was confirmed by Gan, who mans a *kimzua* shop in the Tiong Bahru neighborhood. Interview conducted June 3, 2020.

25. For example, in 2013, a businessman paid a record S$488,888 for a "lucky" urn. The record-setting bid was reported in the Singaporean daily *The New Paper* on August 22 of that year (2–3).

26. This has been repeatedly described to me as the signal moment of Ghost Month, a sort of climax.

27. Mr. Lim, volunteer auction leader, interview, December 8, 2017.

28. In the contrast of these understandings, we see a repeated bifurcation of approaches to the ghost-economy. One tends toward narratives of occult power and mystification, while the other is loosely rationalist.

29. And this, of course, speaks to the powerfully arbitrary nature of exchange-value itself.

30. For this reason, the provenance of the objects (by means of a particular temple or organizer) and the identities of the buyers are prominently displayed, and winners and prices are sometimes reported in the newspaper and online.

31. Because, as we know, the exchange-value originates in socially necessary labor time.

32. Max Pensky, "Method and Time," in *The Cambridge Companion to Walter Benjamin,* edited by David S. Ferris (Cambridge University Press, 2006), 187.

4. GHOSTS IN THE GARDEN

1. See Albert Lau, *Moment of Anguish: Singapore in Malaysia and the Politics of Disengagement* (Times Academic Press, 1998).

2. This telling phrase was used in "The Returned Student," a powerful speech to the Malayan Forum at Malaya Hall, London, January 28, 1950.

3. As do *hantu* (Malay) and *pey* (Tamil).

4. This phrase was used by "LHL" on April 5, 2018, at the Singapore University of Technology and Design (SUTD) Ministerial Forum. The transcript is publicly available and makes clear the degree of state intentionality: https://www.pmo.gov.sg/Newsroom/pm-lee-hsien-loong-sutd-ministerial-forum.

5. For an account of housing as a broader economic lever, see Lee E. Goh, "Planning That Works: Housing Policy and Economic Development in Singapore," *Journal of Planning Education and Research* 7, no. 3 (1988): 147–62; Augustine H. H. Tan and Phang Sock-Yong, *The Singapore Experience in Public Housing,* Occasional Paper 9, Centre for Advanced Studies, University of Singapore, 1991; and Stephen H. K. Yeh and Pang Eng Fong, "Housing, Employment and National Development: The Singapore Experience," *Asia* 31 (1973): 8–31.

6. George, *Air-Conditioned Nation,* 14.

7. Clarissa Oon, "Singapore's Green Trump Card," *Straits Times,* May 7, 2009.

8. Savage, "Human Environment Relations," 200.

9. I discuss this with respect to Cuba in "Terror and Territory: Guantánamo and the Space of Contradiction," *Public Culture* 19, no. 2 (2007): 381–425.

10. This strain of socialist reformism (popular with Lee and early PAP elites) followed many of its predecessors and contemporaries in emphasizing the power of environment. In this case, determinism was an aspect that survived its schism with the Fellowship of the New Life. See Kevin Manton, "The Fellowship of the New Life: English Ethical Socialism Reconsidered," *History of Political Thought* 24, no. 2 (2003): 282–304.

11. This can be seen with absolute clarity in Rodolphe De Koninck, Marc Girard, and Thanh Hai Pham, *Singapore's Permanent Territorial Revolution: 50 Years in 50 Maps* (NUS Press, 2017). "Permanent territorial revolution" is perhaps the best descriptor for this postcolonial condition. See also Peter Ho, Liu Thai Ker, and Tan Wee Kiat, *A Chance of a Lifetime: Lee Kuan Yew and the Physical Transformation of Singapore* (Singapore Centre for Livable Cities/Editions Didier Millet, 2016).

12. See Chua Beng Huat, *Politica! Legitimacy and Housing: Stakeholding in Singapore* (Routledge, 1997), and George, *Singapore,* 189.

13. Thongchai Winichakul, *Siam Mapped: A History of the Geo-Body of a Nation* (University of Hawai'i Press, 1994). Thongchai uses this term to refer to the image of the national perimeter, which was an emotive aspect of Thailand's anticolonial media. I have discussed this with respect to Singapore's coastal land reclamation and bodily dysmorphia among its menfolk. Joshua Comaroff, "Coastlines of the Self: Body and Geobody in Singapore," lecture presented at RMIT, Melbourne, Superterrestrial lecture series, September 1, 2020. Where Thai examples communicate a sense of threat to a natural and eternal boundary, the Singaporean case would appear to emphasize uncertainty and malleability. This reflects a more general epistemological instability with respect to the coastline, as discussed by Paul Carter, "Dark with Excess of Bright: Mapping the Coastlines of Knowledge," in *Mappings,* ed. Denis Cosgrove (Reaktion Books, 1999).

14. See Comaroff, "Ghostly Topographies," and Chris Hudson, "Romancing Singapore: Economies of Love in a Shrinking Population," paper presented at the fifteenth biennial conference of the Asian Studies Association of Australia, Canberra, June 29, 2004.

15. Lee, speech at SUTD.

16. Arjun Agrawal, *Environmentality: Technologies of Government and the Making of Subjects* (Duke University Press, 2005).

17. In this sense, Singapore's pragmatism resembles Deng Xiaoping's famous political dictum of "crossing the river by groping for stones" *(mo zhe shi tou guo he),* or constructing policy through discovery of a path in the midst of administrative circumstances. The PAP early leadership were skillful improvisers, and the concept of pragmatism as against fixed ideologies, either communism or Western liberalism, was invoked to justify changes of course. A good account of this approach is given by Boon Siong and Geraldine Chen in *Dynamic Governance: Embedding Culture, Capabilities and Change in Singapore* (World Scientific, 2007).

18. See Cedric Pugh, "Housing and Development in Singapore," *Contemporary Southeast Asia* 6, no. 4 (1985): 275, and Pugh, "Housing in Singapore: The Effective Ways of the Unorthodox," *Environment and Behavior* 19, no. 3 (1987): 311–30. Pugh raises the ticklish question of ethnic quotas in HDB neighborhoods in particular. An account of the sensitivity of the PAP to housing is given by Tai Ching-Ling, *Housing Policy and High-Rise Living: A Study of Singapore's Public Housing* (Chopmen, 1988), 107. Tai points out that the relief of the housing shortage left by SIT was a major platform in its first electoral campaign, in 1959. The party swept to victory on this platform, and "delivering the goods" (to use Goh Chok Tong's oft-repeated phrase) has been an essential element of claims to legitimacy ever since.

19. Goh Keng Swee's role in the housing story is an important one, as he occupied the post of assistant director of social welfare (social research) in 1953, when the first social survey of the Department of Social Welfare was conducted. The latter was the first PAP analysis of urban housing and living conditions and, according to Tai, "the first comprehensive analysis [of this subject] ever made in Singapore." Tai, *Housing Policy and High-Rise Living*, 45. For an account of administrative roles among the "pioneer" generation of state, see Lam Ping Er and Kevin Y. L. Tan, *Lee's Lieutenants: Singapore's Old Guard* (Allen and Unwin, 1999).

20. Chua, *Political Legitimacy and Housing*, 130.

21. A concern that is still regularly voiced, in valedictory mode, by the PAP today—as in Lee's speech at SUTD.

22. Teh Cheang Wan, "Public Housing," in *In Modern Singapore*, ed. J. B. Ooi and H. D. Chiang (University of Singapore Press, 1969).

23. For more on the SIT's history, see Tan and Phang, *Singapore Experience in Public Housing*.

24. Stephen H. K. Yeh and Research and Statistics Department, HDB, *Homes for the People: A Study of Tenants' Views on Public Housing in Singapore* (Singapore Government Printing Office, 1972).

25. Loh Kah Seng notes that migration was the central force behind the expansion of Singapore's population and economy from the very outset. The opening of Suez, with the tin boom in the Malay states, drew a steady source of predominantly single, male Chinese and Indian workers. Colonial authorities attempted to control the influx with the Immigration Restriction Ordinance of 1928 and again with the Aliens Ordinance of 1933, which limited male Chinese immigrants to one thousand between spring 1932 and 1933. See Loh Kah Seng, "Dangerous Migrants: The Representations and Relocation of Urban *Kampung* Dwellers in Postwar Singapore," Working Paper 140, Asia Research Centre, Murdoch University, Perth, Australia, 2007, and *Squatters into Citizens: The 1961 Bukit Ho Swee Fire and the Making of Modern Singapore* (NUS Press, 2013).

26. Tan and Phang, *Singapore Experience in Public Housing*, 2.

27. Michael Hill and Lian Kwen Fee, *The Politics of Nation Building and Citizenship in Singapore* (Taylor and Francis, 1995), 117.

28. The presence of pigs and chickens, among other animals, was something mentioned as a signal degradation by both the SIT and, later, the HDB. This is mentioned by both Chua, *Political Legitimacy and Housing*, and Loh, "Dangerous Migrants." Interestingly, however, *kampung* meat (especially chicken) is still considered a desirable food in contemporary Singapore—in contrast to the "processed" foods of commercial farms. Contemporary *kampung* chicken comes predominantly from nearby Malaysian towns such as Johor Bahru. A terrific study remains to be

written concerning the symbolic valences of the *kampung* chicken, perhaps as a fundament of Singaporean nostalgia. For the general sense of ungovernability, see Loh, "Dangerous Migrants," 2–3.

29. The name "Tiong Bahru" in fact translates to "New Cemetery" (*tiong* being Chinese for "cemetery," *bahru* being Malay for "new"). The name contrasts this burial ground from the older graveyards around Chinatown. See Lily Kong and Brenda S. A. Yeoh, "Place-Making: Collective Representations of Social Life and Built Environment in Tiong Bahru," in *Portraits of Places: History, Community and Identity in Singapore,* ed. Brenda S. A. Yeoh and Lily Kong (Times Academic Press, 1995), 89.

30. Kong and Yeoh.

31. The document is the *Report of the Committee Regarding Burial and Burial Grounds, Colony of Singapore* (Singapore Government Printing Office, 1952). The full listing of burial grounds, their religions, and their sizes is given in the appendix.

32. Janet W. Saldaff, *State and Family in Singapore: Restructuring a Developing Society* (Cornell University Press, 1992). Saldaff notes that these were, in fact, very powerful and wealthy organizations. The Hokkien *hui guan* was "a major private landowner with assets of S$100 million" (21) and founded Nanyang University in 1956. The issue of burial was one of great acrimony, as the new state wrested the responsibility of funerary practices from the *hui guan.* The PAP also closed Nanyang University in 1980; it was later subsumed into the National University of Singapore. The Hokkien *hui guan* continues to be a very rich organization and occupies a modern mid-rise building overlooking Telok Ayer and Stanley Streets in Chinatown.

33. Informal food selling, or "hawking," was a major concern. Government experts worried that this flexible, lucrative trade kept young men out of the workforce and attempted to limit the total number of hawkers through a registration program. See Government of Singapore, 1974 Budget, col. 498, per Mr. Chok Yeok Eng.

34. This was stated explicitly by Chief Minister Lim Yew Hock in a speech of 1958, as quoted in Loh, "Dangerous Migrants."

35. This was a phrase in common use and is quoted in Hill and Lian, *Politics of Nation Building,* 119. The conflagrations were described as "some help from providence" by the *Straits Times* (September 16, 1964). The possibility of fire as an inherent risk of wood shacks was continually used as a veiled threat by the PAP. Lim Yew Hock's 1958 speech, quoted earlier, includes the crepuscular statement that "fire, though accidentally begun, spreads quickly and destructively."

36. Teh, "Public Housing," 173.

37. The bracing efficiency of this machine is evident in the numbers: between 1960 and 1965, the HDB provided 55,430 new units; by 1980,

the number had grown to more than 305,000 (which, in fact, represented a significant surplus over declared goals). The PAP's culture of excess and overperformance was gathering pace. The crisis mentality is a cornerstone of PAP government, as is the tendency toward excessive and emphatic gestures and expressions, on the part of Lee Kuan Yew, Goh Chok Tong, and others. One of the first moves by the PAP was to carry over wartime emergency legislation into the independence period to suppress leftist radicalism. But overshooting goals has also become a hallmark of the state's political style.

38. Saldaff, *State and Family in Singapore,* 20.

39. Aline K. Wong and Stephen H. K. Yeh, *Housing a Nation: 25 Years of Public Housing in Singapore* (Mauzen Asia and Housing Development Board, 1985), 93.

40. Teh, "Public Housing," 175.

41. Early fears of the HDB as a "shadow state" led to the reallocation of many of its functions to separate organs. For example, its planning operations were placed in the charge of the new Urban Renewal Department (later the Urban Redevelopment Authority). For the history of this, see https://www.nlb.gov.sg/main/article-detail?cmsuuid=7a64797c-e86c -44ac-ab2f-6c82a5e213b5.

42. Sharon Siddique, "The Phenomenology of Ethnicity: A Singapore Case Study," in *Understanding Singapore Society,* ed. Ong Jin Hui, Tong Chee Kiong, and Tan Ern Ser (Times Academic Press, 2000); Hill and Lian, *Politics of Nation Building;* Lily Kong and Brenda S. A. Yeoh, *The Politics of Landscapes in Singapore: Constructions of "Nation"* (Syracuse University Press, 2003). A quota of 20 percent Malays per building, for example, was made public by the prime minister in 1987 and formalized in 1989. This racial distribution policy was justified in the guise of building community through integration. Minorities are housed amid a Chinese majority, both at home and in school—in fact, it is part of the determinist position of the PAP that "underperforming" Malay children should experience a "keener" standard of competition. Savage, "Human Environment Relations," 196. Quotas are maintained under the national Ethnic Integration Policy, and new blocks are designed to reflect "demand"—that is, the economic profile of the market. A proportional quota of rental flats for low-income families is mandated, as is (since March 2010) a 5 percent cap on permanent residents in any given block.

43. Racial conflict was also a recurrent threat of the colonial period and a preoccupation of the British. In the early 1950s, "riots" occurred around the mosque in the mostly Malay Hertogh district. More importantly, perhaps, the Malay–Chinese violence of 1964 centered on a decision by the HDB not to grant a special community concession area to a Malay housing area

that was to be resettled. Fighting broke out during a procession to commemorate the prophet Muhammad's birthday and resulted in the deaths of thirty-six people. See Hill and Lian, *Politics of Nation Building,* 115. The specter of these riots is still raised from time to time by the PAP as an example of the inherent volatility of the multiethnic society.

44. Pasi Falk and Colin Campbell, eds., *The Shopping Experience* (SAGE, 1997), 9. Anderson is quoted in Carl A. Trocki, *Singapore: Wealth, Power, and the Culture of Control* (Routledge, 2006), 7. His lack of interest is interesting, given the high incidence of invented tradition at work on the island generally.

45. These flats themselves became spaces of modern bourgeois aspiration. This was communicated very clearly in *Our Home,* a publication by HDB that was delivered to all homeowners, combining imagery of an ideal, contemporary lifestyle with lessons on good behavior and hygiene. HDB Singapore, *Our Home* (HDB, 1972–89). See also Lilian Chee, "The Public Private Interior: Constructing the Modern Domestic Interior in Singapore's Public Housing," in *The Handbook of Interior Architecture and Design,* ed. Graeme Brooker and Lois Weinthal (Bloomsbury, 2013), and Jane M. Jacobs and Stephen Cairns, "The Modern Touch: Interior Design and Modernisation in Post-Independence Singapore," *Environment and Planning A* 40 (2008): 572–95.

46. For an account of the last days in an urban *kampung,* see K. K. Seet, "Last Days at Wak Selat: The Demise of a *Kampung,*" in Yeoh and Kong, *Portraits of Places.*

47. https://urbis.com.au/insights-news/singapores-secrets-to-density -done-well/#:~:text=Singapore's%20density%20is%20among%20 the,inner%20suburbs%20has%20reached%2014%2C500.

48. https://www.nlb.gov.sg/main/article-detail?cmsuuid=7a64797c -e86c-44ac-ab2f-6c82a5e213b5.

49. Chua, *Political Legitimacy and Housing,* 52.

50. Otto Koenigsberger, Susumu Kobe, and Charles Abrams, *Growth and Urban Renewal in Singapore* (United Nations Program of Technical Assistance, Department of Economic and Social Affairs, 1963). Both Kobe and Abrams died relatively young, but not before making major contributions to global housing and development initiatives for the international organizations of the time. Their obituaries in the *New York Times* are illuminating in this regard: https://www.nytimes.com/1971/01/09/archives /susumu-kobe-67-expert-special-to-the-new-york-times.html; https:// www.nytimes.com/1970/02/23/archives/charles-abrams-worldwide -housing-expert-dies-lawyer-author-68.html.

51. https://www.nlb.gov.sg/main/article-detail?cmsuuid=fbca0654 -cd2b-4638-b1ef-c18ba06344ad.

52. As noted in chapter 1, land sales have averaged S$17 billion per year from 2013 to 2019, with another S$10 billion or so from previous investments.

53. Temasek was founded in 1974 and is primarily an equity investor. https://www.temasek.com.sg/.

54. The fairness of these is debated. See Tommy T. B. Koh, "The Law of Compulsory Land Acquisition in Singapore," *Malayan Law Journal* 35 (1967): 9–22; Bryan Chew, Vincent Hoong, Tay Lee Koon, and Manimegalai d/o Vellasamy, "Compulsory Acquisition of Land in Singapore: A Fair Regime?," *Singapore Academy of Law Journal* 22, special issue (2010): 166–88.

55. https://sso.agc.gov.sg/Act/LAA1966.

56. Eunice Seng, "People's Park Complex: The State, the Developer, the Architect, and the Conditioned Public, c.1967 to the Present," in *Southeast Asia's Modern Architecture: Questions of Translation, Epistemology, and Power*, ed. Jiat-Hwee Chang and Imran bin Tajudeen (NUS Press, 2020), 245. Seng has shown how this transpired for the creation of People's Park Complex, the first mixed-use retail and housing complex, completed in 1967 under the influence of Japanese Metabolist urban theory. Here developer Ho Kok Cheong—a local window glazing magnate—saw the role of the private firm as "gifting" a center of Chinese commerce to a modernizing public. This was built on a long-standing informal open space and market associated with migrant labor (and, in particular, a kind of Chinese urban life unpopular with the colonial administration and later the PAP). Increasingly against the vision of the architects, People's Park transformed from a naturally ventilated, regionally influenced urban market to a Western-style, air-conditioned mall. A similar partnership occurred in 1981 with Marina Square—a world-standard shopping and hotel complex on a newly reclaimed piece of land to the south of the CBD. This was to become the anchor of Marina Bay, later a showpiece of iconic architecture and home to the Sands casino and convention center. S. P. Tao, then chairman of Singapore Land Group Ltd., was tasked by Lee Kuan Yew with the construction of this new design by hospitality superstar John Portman, a household name in America and perhaps architecture's first truly global brand. By now, there was to be no talk of plein air; this space was explicitly built as a cool and luxurious atmosphere for the equally cool and brand-aware Singaporean consumer. See Joshua Comaroff, "On the Materialities of Air," *CITY* 21, no. 5 (2017): 607–13.

57. In a manner characteristic of this cyclical business, the leading developers of the day were called upon to deliver the offices from which their shares, as publicly listed companies, would be traded. Many of the daring, ultramodern works of this time are now under threat, and such

"everyday modernism" is being recorded in architectural volumes like Jiat-Hwee Chang, Justin Zhuang, and Darren Soh, *Everyday Modernism: Architecture and Society in Singapore* (NUS Press, 2023), and Ho Weng Hin, Dinesh Naidu, and Tan Kar Lin, eds., *Our Modern Past: A Visual Survey of Singapore Architecture, 1920s–1970s* (Singapore Heritage Society/Singapore Institute of Architects Press, 2015). Not least, these provide some serious consideration regarding histories of "alternate" modernism(s) in Asia. For discussion of this, see William S. W. Lim and Jiat-Hwee Chang, *Non West Modernist Past: Rethinking Modernisms and Modernities Beyond the West* (World Scientific, 2011).

58. These are central to Singapore's strategy of moving up the value chain. See Chua Hui-Ching Emily, "Survival by Technopreneurialism: Innovation, Imaginaries and the New Narrative of Nationhood in Singapore," *Science, Technology, and Society* 24, no. 3 (2019): 527–44, and Wong Kai Wen and Tim Bunnell, "'New Economy' Discourse and Spaces in Singapore: A Case Study of One-North," *Environment and Planning A* 38, no. 1 (2006): 69–83.

59. In the image market of social media and the internet, several of these have come to stand, metonymically, for the nation itself: Jewel at Changi Airport, the Flower Dome and Cloud Forest buildings at Gardens by the Bay, the Parkroyal Collection Pickering, the Oasia hotel tower, and even Singapore's national pavilion at Expo 2020 Dubai.

60. Lee Kuan Yew, *From Third World to First: The Singapore Story—1965–2000* (Harper, 2000), 188.

61. Timothy Barnard, *Nature Contained: Environmental Histories of Singapore* (NUS Press, 2014), 297.

62. Trocki, *Singapore,* 213.

63. For a more detailed account on this history, see Hill and Lian, *Politics of Nation Building,* 119; Edmund Waller, *Landscape Planning in Singapore* (Singapore University Press, 1991), 48ff.; and Timothy Auger, *Living in a Garden: The Greening of Singapore* (Singapore National Parks Board/ Editions Didier Millet, 2013).

64. Trocki, *Singapore,* 137.

65. https://www.nparks.gov.sg/who-we-are/mission-history.

66. The government also directly sought to involve the public, and still does. This began in 1971, when Tree Planting Day was initiated in the attempt to create an affective bond ("green consciousness" or "biophilia") between Singaporeans and trees.

67. R. Corlett, "The Ecological Transformation of Singapore, 1819–1990," *Journal of Biogeography* 19 (1992): 413.

68. Waller, in *Landscape Planning in Singapore,* places the development of government policy in three phases. The first takes place between 1959

and 1971, during which a "neatening" ethic, as well as the ambition toward a Garden City concept, emerged (47). A second phase is defined by the years 1971 to 1991, during which larger-scale projects and an increase of available resources led to the marriage of landscape planning, "social engineering," and the creation of themed natural environments, such as "vest pocket" parks, the Jurong Bird Park, and Singapore Zoo (53).

69. Corlett, "Ecological Transformation of Singapore," 418.

70. Clarissa Oon, "Singapore's Green Trump Card," *Straits Times,* May 7, 2009.

71. See C. J. W.-L. Wee, "Staging the Asian Modern: Cultural Fragments, the Singaporean Eunuch, and the Asian Lear," *Critical Inquiry* 30 (2004): 771–99. Also see E. Tan, "Re-engaging Chineseness: Political, Economic, and Cultural Imperatives of Nation-Building in Singapore," *China Quarterly* 175 (2003): 751–74. By an analogous process, around the same time, the Tourist Promotion Board created a new icon for the nation, the Merlion, by attaching the head of a lion onto the body of a fish; see Choon et al., *Imagining Singapore.*

72. A number of horticultural specialists are now working toward the re-nativization of the Singapore landscape, despite a lack of support from the National Parks Board. One is Professor Hugh Tan from National University of Singapore/Raffles Museum of Biodiversity Research.

73. Singapore's landscapes do have a characteristic appearance, however—driven as they are by a common compositional design logic. Plants are corralled into monospecial clumps of irregular shape, tightly abutted. These clusters express a certain informal or organicist intention, via amorphousness and curvilinearity of perimeter. The monocultural aspect is itself significant. It is a way of planting totally alien to the tropical landscape, which typically intermingles not by "stands" of species but on a specimen-by-specimen basis. Equatorial flora tend, rather, to differentiate themselves, ladder-like, into ascending "trophic" levels or tiers. Nowhere in the designed national landscape do plants mingle at the level of the individual. But nor do they appear en masse; rather, they are replicated in small, tightly bounded, homogeneous groupings.

74. Quoted in Oon, "Singapore's Green Trump Card."

75. Cited in Robert Boyers, "This Way, Not That: Nadine Gordimer Does As She Pleases," *Harper's,* February 2008, 89.

76. This recalls the famous argument of Charles Tilly that warfare has a galvanizing effect on state capacity. See Tilly, *Coercion, Capital, and European States, AD 990–1992* (Blackwell, 1990). Singapore figures the existential crisis of landscape as a state of war. Here are echoes of the United States, in the so-called wars on terror, on poverty, or on drugs—or the other politically useful conflicts ongoing in Mexico or Israel or Brazil,

where "civil" unrest has emerged as the new technology of state making. The reality of this combat can be set against the beguiling fiction of Rem Koolhaas's tabula rasa, the famous concept of Singapore as a "laboratory" in which all things are possible, because history—enshrined elsewhere in Western notions of genius loci, heritage, or context—is not an obstacle. See Koolhaas, "Singapore Songlines," in *SMLXL* (Monacelli, 1996).

77. This limits the burden of maintenance but also prevents squatting or unsanctioned activity, as happened in marginal spaces, such as the former Johor–Singapore railway corridor that runs from the north coast to the Keppel district, near Marina Bay. Singapore's accumulation of invasive species has made such a biocondensing strategy easy—in fact, largely passive. In contrast to a clear gesture of occlusion, the collapse into jungle looks simply like nature taking its course. Through simple neglect, cataracts appear in the national fabric, with spaces effectively inaccessible to the public. Overgrowth simply takes sectors off the map.

78. John S. T. Quah, "Crime Prevention Singapore Style," *Asian Journal of Public Administration* 14, no. 2 (1992): 149–85; Stella R. Quah and Jon S. T. Quah, *Friends in Blue: The Police and the Public in Singapore* (Oxford University Press, 1987).

79. I acknowledge, for what follows, that *qi* has no satisfying English equivalent. While its flows are described often in a manner like energy (I use the term energetic in these chapters), it nonetheless is also seen as a structuring condition of matter. In this sense, there is a very clear analogue to the nature of subatomic elements in quantum theory, which behave both as waves and as particles—and which constitute the matter through standing waves and other mysterious conjunctions of this bimodal behavior. See Frijtof Capra, *The Tao of Physics: An Exploration of the Parallels Between Modern Physics and Eastern Mysticism* (Shambhala, 2010). While *qi* in Singapore is subject to the same polyvocality as most cosmological and spectral discourse, I am relying on the contributions of Needham, *Biology and Biological Technology,* and Kirkland, *Taoism,* as well as on the varied depictions of my respondents.

80. The increasingly bureaucratized experience of funerals—from the timing of remembrance services to the process of collecting ashes—was of great concern to respondents. Hours were spent discussing the minutiae of these and the microtraumas attributed to them. This was a concern that crosscut religious communities and was not principally or disproportionately a complaint of those who identify as following Chinese religion or Taoism or Buddhism exclusively.

81. Kong and Yeoh, *Politics of Landscapes.* This history also engages the larger question of the changing role of clan and religious organizations vis-à-vis the state. Death was one of those realms of social existence

where these bodies maintained a great deal of authority—Marjorie Topley provides some suggestive detail. See Topley, "The Emergence and Social Function of Chinese Religious Associations in Singapore," *Comparative Studies in Society and History* 3, no. 3 (1961): 289–314.

82. Even today, large groups among the public are aligned in the fight against the ongoing exhumation of Bukit Brown and other surviving graveyards and remnants. Huang Jianli, "Resurgent Spirits of Civil Society Activism: Rediscovering the Bukit Brown Cemetery in Singapore," *Journal of the Malaysian Branch of the Royal Asiatic Society* 87, no. 2 (2014): 21–45; Natalie Pang and Liew Kai Khiun, "Mediating Community in Bukit Brown," in *The Hard State, Soft City of Singapore* (Cambridge University Press, 2020). See also *Straits Times*, "Race to Save Oldest Chinese Tombs Here," August 19, 2006.

83. This idea was expressed to me, in particular, by younger respondents like Hui Ping and Renee.

84. See Claudio Lomnitz, *Death and the Idea of Mexico* (Zone Books, 2008).

85. Mr. Kok, interview, April 2, 2009.

86. One in the Bukit Timah area proved particularly troublesome. This grave, of an early Chinese settler known as Qiu Zheng Zhi and his wife, Madam Li Ci Shu, has been the subject of petitioning by a group of private-sector heritage enthusiasts. The tomb lay in the way of plans by NParks to create new horticultural displays for the Singapore Botanic Gardens. The issue was reported in the *Straits Times*, August 19, 2006, H1.

87. Dominique Mosbergen, "Cemetery Now a Park: Next, It Will Be HDB Estate," *New Paper*, December 18, 2006, 6.

88. Mosbergen. It was reported that Bidadari contained the graves of a number of famous Singaporeans, including philanthropist Lim Boon Keng, former health minister Ahmad Ibrahim, and A. P. Williams, a sailor upon whom Joseph Conrad's *Lord Jim* was based.

89. Peggy Teo, Brenda S. A. Yeoh, Ooi Giok Ling, and Karen P. Y. Lai, *Changing Landscapes of Singapore* (McGraw-Hill, 2003), 200.

90. Tong, *Chinese Death Rituals in Singapore*, 27.

91. This was described in an article, "Gravedigging: A Dying Trade," in the *Straits Times*, Home B1, November 10, 2008. A former gravedigger (now a nurseryman) subsequently explained to me that many have reluctantly moved into the landscaping industry, where income is more stable. Interview conducted December 8, 2016.

92. Teo et al., *Changing Landscapes of Singapore*, 200.

93. Tong, *Chinese Death Rituals in Singapore*, 62.

94. For more on the question of migrant labor, see Comaroff, "Ghostly Topographies," and further discussion in chapter 6.

95. Terrence, interview, January 4, 2009. I have heard this given as the cause, also, of isolation among elderly Singaporeans and the phenomenon of dying alone in HDB flats. Desmond Ng, "When Someone Dies Alone in Singapore, This Is What Happens," CNA, March 4, 2020, https://www.channelnewsasia.com/cnainsider/when-someone-dies-alone-singapore-this-is-what-happens-seniors-769486.

96. Chua has noted, more generally, that the shift to public housing has forced modes of spatial and material accommodation with long-standing religious practices. See Chua Beng Huat, "Adjusting Religious Practices to House Forms," chapter 9 of *Political Legitimacy and Housing*.

97. Mrs. Tan herself claims to be a spiritual person, from a family all gifted with the "second sight." Interview conducted April 2, 2009.

98. This is a very interesting statement that deserves some analysis. I would point out that this statement is not a sort of "secularization theory." That is, it precisely does not mean "it is interesting that in modern Singapore we still believe all these things." It means "it is interesting that in modern Singapore we still have so many ghosts." Mrs. Tan's comment, like those of some other informants, expressed a frank wonderment at the stories that were being told.

99. Comaroff, "Coastlines of the Self." *Koro* was a form of cyclical, mass hypochondriacal panic, occurring in a series of waves in the years after 1965, when Singaporean men became convinced that their genitalia were retracting and that the completion of this process would result in their deaths. The term is taken from the Malay *kura-kura* (meaning "tortoise" and referring to the retreat of the animal's head). It overwhelmingly affected Chinese males, who showed up to emergency rooms and clinics with thread tied around their penises. Koro manifested also in a female version, where victims worried that, in the words of one journalist, "their breasts [would] retreat into their chests like the magical islands of Brigadoon." Scott Mendelson, *The Great Singapore Penis Panic and the Future of American Mass Hysteria* (pub. by author, 2010). The retraction of the penis is understood to be an indicator of low *yang jing,* and below a certain threshold, the belief is that death will result.

100. Mendelson.

101. Mr. Kok, interview, February 4, 2009.

102. Interview conducted September 10, 2007.

103. Interview conducted March 30, 2009. Jean is a Catholic who nonetheless shares many assumptions about ghosts that appear to match those of Chinese religion. The view expressed in this interview was shared by numerous Christian respondents, who see Singapore's ghosts as "unclean spirits" that are attracted to those whose faith and personal strength are at an ebb. This is one of many beliefs through which Chinese religious

traditions and those of Christianity and Catholicism are reconciled. These discourses are not nearly as opposed as one might expect. Father JP, a Singaporean parish priest, laughed when he said that many local evangelical practices are simply "Chinese religion in Christian language." And it appears true that there are many accommodations between charismatic interpretations of scripture and more traditional beliefs. This recalls other Asian examples, such as the connections between modernity, Christianity, and shamanism in contemporary Korea; see Kim, "Christianity, Shamanism." In both cases, there is a perhaps unexpected link between an upwardly mobile church going bourgeoisie and popular, traditional practices associated with "backward" populations. Although many Christian Singaporeans dismissed ghosts as "superstitious," they were perfectly comfortable with accounts of "unclean" and "evil" spirits.

104. The name of the latter was officially changed from the less cheerful Pulau Blakang Mati, or "Island of the Dead Left Behind." By contrast, *sentosa* means "peace and tranquility" in Malay.

105. While ghosts are not described to be seeking dissipation via cathexis, or resolution into nothingness, they nonetheless are understood as subject to powerful energetic drives toward disturbed memory and place. In this sense, their behavior is not so different from humans' attitude toward trouble sites; see, e.g., Kenneth Foote's analysis of negative placemaking in *Shadowed Ground: America's Landscapes of Violence and Tragedy* (University of Texas Press, 2003). As I have argued elsewhere, ghosts in this regard play their received role as a kind of collective memory. See Comaroff, "Ghostly Topographies," and Carole Faucher's "As the Wind Blows and Dew Came Down: Ghost Stories and Collective Memory in Singapore," in *Beyond Description: Singapore, Space, Historicity,* ed. Ryan Bishop, John Philips, and Wei-Wei Yeo (Routledge, 2004).

5. APPARITION AND INSECURE SPACE

1. Winnie is in her sixties and lived in Hong Kong, which also practices the seventh month. However, she felt that the rites were largely constrained to that period, as opposed to in Singapore. Interview conducted March 29, 2009.

2. Interview conducted March 15, 2009. Charles means by this statement that they do not observe Ghost Month in China. This is clarified in further discussion of his comment, later.

3. I refer here to Russell Lee's The Almost Complete Collection of True Singapore Ghost Stories series, published by Angsana Books in Singapore from 1989 onward. Volume 1 is on its twenty-third edition at the time of writing; it has sold more than 115,000 copies. The *Straits Times* and

Singapore Press Holdings have also joined this bonanza, publishing their own *Singapore Urban Legends: Myths and Mysteries* in 2005. Lee compiles stories by "a team of 'ghost writers,'" who are contributing members of the general public.

4. Although, in a manner similar to Shan's comments, some informants expressed skepticism of their peers' "encounters" with ghosts while still holding out the possibility of their existence.

5. Interview conducted February 3, 2009.

6. Interview conducted at a recently completed project, April 5, 2009.

7. The production of paper commodities follows loose conventions of representation and exchange, and continual innovation builds on Chinese ancestral traditions. A clear sense of this was communicated in an interview with Ho Yu Yin, a paper artist working in Hong Kong; see Ho Yu Yin, "Paper: The Magic Material," *IdN* (Hong Kong) 13, no. 3 (2006). There is a complex terminology that describes the relationship between the paper figures that are made and their object of representation, comprising four major categories. *Ji zhao* (direct reflection) describes the paper objects that a recently deceased person "is thought to need with him/her in heaven—everything from money and small trinkets to a house and a car" (29). Other terms, such as *shou kou* and *hua pao*, are used to describe the representation of animals, flowers, lamps, and other objects (artists who work in the paper medium also produce artworks for Lion Dances and other festivals). Ho notes change in the medium: "In the past, 'ji zhao' had less variety. Nowadays, whatever a person owned in real life can be replicated in paper for the funeral." He adds, "The key to making Chinese paper artwork is to *catch the spirit* of the objects you want to copy" (30, emphasis added).

8. I have found it interesting to note Singaporeans' continuing cognizance of the geographical specificity of former burial sites. These are remembered with a great deal of unease—one respondent was in the habit of avoiding the otherwise convenient Pan-Island Expressway because a site of disinterment of his paternal line of the Ong clan exists along its length.

9. Chan Hong Yin, "The Hungry Ghost Festival in Singapore: Getai (Songs on Stage) in the Lunar Seventh Month," *Religions* 11, no. 7 (2020): 365.

10. In part because the ghosts are logically seen to be drawn to these events. I heard from many that joss burning scents, loud noises, and bright lights attract wandering spirits. Where ancestors are said to move in orderly and intentional ways, the ghosts meander confusedly and are drawn to sources of intensity. In this respect, the discourses mimic what Chu has described of the mobility of the dead in Fujian in *Cosmologies of Credit*.

11. One should read this, also, against the stories of paranormal activities that seem to plague military installations; see later.

12. See the preface.

13. Proverbs 3:5–6.

14. *Desire line* is the term, in landscape design, for a dirt path that appears where pedestrians take shortcuts across lawns or fields. It is usually taken as a sign that a path should be placed there.

15. In *Cosmologies of Credit,* Chu offers the insight that joss paper, as money, has a particular materiality when burned (see later) that closely mirrors the assumed materiality of specter itself. And as Vivien Zhiying Su has observed, this immediately "smokes out," so to speak, the problematic nature of air as commons. Su, "Smoking in an Air-Conditioned Nation: The Politics of Air in Singapore" (capstone undergraduate thesis, Division of Social Sciences, Yale-NUS College, 2021). In Singapore, this is undoubtedly part of the disgust that people feel when they accidentally walk into someone else's bonfire—one quite literally inhales the ghost, alongside the value that is released to them. For more on the issue of value in this medium, see the next chapter.

16. Tan Tock Seng Hospital is Singapore's premier integrated public medical facility.

17. Lim, *Between Gods and Ghosts,* 53.

18. Harry, interview, March 26, 2009. There are some issues with what happens to the detritus. One common opinion is that it is no longer dangerous after the joss sticks have burned down, as these are what attracts the spirit and creates the ritual opening (hence the belief that sacrificed food can be eaten afterward). Many still confess to feeling uncomfortable with and avoiding such waste, which is fairly ubiquitous on certain days of the year. In truth, it is the army of maintenance workers on HDB estates and elsewhere—often foreign workers—that clears these items. There was a frankly racist sentiment, expressed to me on a few occasions, that this is the appropriate state of things—as the term *gui* is also used as an epithet for foreigners (and South Asian non-Chinese, Singaporean or not), there was assumed to be a certain understanding at work there. One respondent told me, "We say '*gui da gui*'—'let the Indians [*gui*] fight the ghosts [*gui*].'"

19. Stanley, an independent businessman in his thirties, recounted perhaps the most famous army ghost story, one told to me in various iterations by others as well. This concerned the Charlie Company 2, located in the second camp at Tekong until the end of the 1990s. A rectangular, hand-painted outline on the wall of the barrack was "a doorway to hell. They painted it to pacify some of the ghosts who were messing around with the soldiers. Like an exit, to invite the ghosts to leave if they were stuck inside the building." The spirit said to terrorize those in Charlie 2 was that of a soldier taken by forest ghosts. Army stories, and their discourses of the jungle, are described later.

20. Lewis Mumford, *The City in History: Its Origins, Its Transformations, and Its Prospects* (Mariner Books, 1968), 215.

21. Interview conducted October 22, 2009.

22. A similar method safeguards workplaces, as in Chinatown. Here small shrines extend from office portals and stairways to the covered "five-foot ways" at the roadside. Large burners are temporarily erected at green patches in front of the buildings, and group offerings are made here at the beginning, middle, and end of the seventh month. In other areas, such as the CBD, business parks, and construction sites, it is common to see fires in nearby liminal areas—side lanes, residual green spaces, driveways, and the like.

23. Interview conducted October 10, 2009.

24. Renee noted to me that "in peak season, people will actually just use the pavement. Sometimes they will draw a shape in chalk and burn inside. The grass nearby goes brown, and people won't step on it until it regrows." Interview conducted October 11, 2009. This practice is frowned upon, but I have personally seen it many times and have heard complaints from others. Annually, there appear editorials in the national papers and online posts decrying "lazy" residents who simply burn "on the ground." Town councils in multiple districts have warned against "mess" and "pollution," largely in response to residents' concerns that half-burned fragments blow onto nearby pavements and are easy to step on by mistake. Nadine Chua, "Bedok South Residents Advised to Use Incense Burners After 'Mess' Seen 'Flying Around': Town Council," *STOMP*, September 23, 2020, https://stomp .straitstimes.com/singapore-seen/bedok-south-residents-advised-to-use -incense-burners-after-mess-seen-flying-around; https://www.reddit.com /r/singapore/comments/1ejjz4e/incense_bins_problem/?rdt=50467.

25. See Comaroff, "On the Materialities of Air." Su has also demonstrated, in the case of cigarette smoke, how the fluid volumes of our aerial commons simply cannot be partitioned or delimited in an unambiguous manner. Su, "Smoking in an Air-Conditioned Nation."

26. This reversal of capital's typical relations and equations is discussed more extensively in the conclusion.

27. Water bodies have a doubly uncanny aspect, as these have often been sites of drowning. Ghosts during seventh month are thought to try to lure individuals near lakes and the coastline to a watery death.

28. A more extensive analysis of army ghost stories, with particular attention to the "resistant" behaviors of ghosts vis-à-vis state power, is given in Joshua Comaroff, "Vulgarity and Enchantment: Religious Movements and the Space of the State" (PhD thesis, University of California, Los Angeles, 2009).

29. Interview conducted April 6, 2009.

30. Or "Thursday night" in Malay. This term is discussed later.

31. And here, again, there is an interesting moment of either projection or syncretism. The sensitivity to ground forms—which was a topic of concern among Chinese respondents only—seems much more likely to be drawn from geomantic notions like feng shui, and from the characteristic earthworks of Chinese cemeteries, than from Malay discourses of ghosts or forest spirits.

32. Interview conducted April 6, 2009.

33. Of course, some of this has to do with the army's attitude toward gay men, or "302s" ("2" being the Ministry of Defense's code for male and "3" for female). There is certainly a notion here that the national body, as an agglomeration of individuals given over to the state, should remain pure. Many "302s" are given specific jobs considered fitting, such as roles in SAF's entertainment corps. The fact about HIV infection was told to me by informant Ming in an interview on February 30, 2009, and verified by an informant at the Ministry of Defense, March 10, 2019.

34. Interview conducted April 6, 2009.

35. Dawn, NParks employee, interview, June 8, 2018.

36. Master Goh's Singlish here translates to "people think the government has no problems [can do what it likes], but the government can't [chop the tree]."

37. Interview conducted October 2, 2009.

38. A similar account can be found in Tan Mae Lynn, "Nights of the Living 4D Pests," *New Paper on Sunday,* November 19, 2006.

39. This suggests, of course, that some Chinese court reciprocal transactions with non-Chinese ghosts. I have not been able to speak with anyone who pursues such practices, so I am unable to understand how the ghosts' needs and powers would fit within more paradisaical Islamic notions of the afterlife. When I asked Mrs. Tan about this, she merely shrugged and said that some punters "will try their luck with anything."

40. Though 4D is the most popular lottery overseen by Tote Board (the state lottery commission), there are others with a popular following. These include Toto and Singapore Sweep, as well as structured bets on football, horse racing, and the Formula 1 Grand Prix.

41. Tong, *Chinese Death Rituals in Singapore,* 83.

42. See Cook and Zhao, *Stalk Divination.* This is a type of cleromancy in which the stalks are used to compose hexagrams from the *I Ching.* It is much more complex than contemporary forms of stick-thrown divination used currently in Singapore. It should be noted, also, that other Southeast Asian cultures associate ghosts and numbers; Alan Klima has explored this association extensively in Thailand in *The Funeral Casino: Meditation, Massacre, and Exchange with the Dead in Thailand* (Princeton University Press, 2002).

43. This was sensationally, if evocatively, reported in the *New Paper,* November 19, 2006, 12–13. The article appeared to mix moralistic concern about such practices with a sense that they represent "local color" of a sort.

44. Susan Tsang and Edward Hendricks, *Discover Singapore* (Marshall Cavendish, 2007), 20.

45. Those who win using ghost-selected numbers are expected to make lavish sacrifices afterward, to avoid vengeful retaliation. https://www .hungzai.com/4-d-punters-in-choa-chu-kang-cemetery/.

46. Terrence and Edward, both architects, interview, October 23, 2008.

47. Many accounts have been circulated to explain the hauntedness of this building, which is now used as an arts and technology "incubator." There were rumors of prisoners having committed suicide in the holding cells. Another urban myth involved the suicide of a policeman. However, buildings with any association with violent crime or punishment are commonly thought to be haunted. https://remembersingapore.org/former -cid-hq/.

48. The traditional Chinese coffin is a rectangular enclosure with a vaulted lid, assembled from solid wood sections. Owing to material constraints and changes in fashion, these plain versions have been replaced with ornate plywood, veneers, and metal (often with an aperture so that they may be air conditioned during the lengthy wakes that are common in Singapore). The aged character of the coffin is one of the uncanny or ominous signifiers in Terrence's story, especially as its provenance is never explained.

49. This will have added significance for those familiar with construction procedures. The engineer's structural drawings, once completed, are "staked out" (physically delineated) by site surveyors to ensure that they are accurate. There are usually minor discrepancies between the design drawings and the physical world, but Terrence is describing an almost unheard-of variation between the documentation and the site—suggesting that something highly abnormal was occurring.

50. https://www.nirvanasingapore.sg/en/niche-relocation-grave -exhumation/ or https://www.facebook.com/exhumationsingapore/.

51. This might sound like the setup to a joke, but in Singapore such an interfaith team is considered "best practice," as the dead are presumed to be more responsive to appeals from their coreligionists. *Ghost-busting* is a common term in Singapore for this activity, including by those who perform this service. In official language, it is a "blessings team" dispatched from an interreligious organization (IRO) that does a range of interfaith work.

52. Interview conducted December 11, 2017. I spoke, also, to the priest, who remembered the story differently. He said that there was no single

site but an "uneasy sensation" throughout the building. According to this account, blessings were performed throughout.

53. Interview conducted May 13, 2008.

54. Interview conducted September 30, 2009.

55. Mrs. Tan is a Chinese homemaker in her eighties. Interview conducted July 4, 2009.

56. Benson Ang, "Places in Singapore with a dark past," *Straits Times,* January 10, 2016, https://www.straitstimes.com/lifestyle/entertainment /places-in-singapore-with-a-dark-past.

57. Meizi, interview, May 5, 2009; Ann, interview, August 6, 2008.

58. Harry, email communication, April 4, 2010.

59. For example, carrying or rolling a pineapple across the threshold. *Pineapple* in Hokkien is *ong lai,* which is an almost-homonym for "luck coming your way." The bag of rice is more straightforward and symbolizes ongoing prosperity in a particular location.

60. Emily, member of New Creation Church (aka the "Rock"), interview, September 26, 2009.

61. In particular, the damming of the mouth of the Singapore River with the Marina Barrage project created a reservoir in Marina Bay. This was seen as dangerously interrupting the in- and outflows of the river from the Singapore Straits. As is often the case, concerns based in feng shui were echoed by others in the ecologically aware community: there was a prevalent rumor that the Barrage had exacerbated the flooding in parts of the city in years after completion.

6. UNREAL ESTATE

1. Their consolidation expresses the economic logic of development, in which it is far more profitable to build large projects than small ones, especially where the base cost of land is high.

2. This is reminiscent of the account given by Marshall Berman in *All That Is Solid Melts into Air: The Experience of Modernity* (Simon and Schuster, 1982).

3. See Rogers, *Speculation,* and Banner, *Speculation.*

4. Marble and large-paned glass effectively increase the liquidity of the flat as an asset.

5. By this scheme, the developer avoids the "development charge" (DC) levied by the government on gross floor area. They can still add this to the per-square-foot cost that is chargeable to the family that buys the flat. While the construction is paid for, this is typically a minor premium compared the additive cost of the same area in DC.

6. The maximum allowable size of units is often determined by, for example, "running distances" to fire egress. An error in code interpretation by the architect can thus result in units that must be smaller than expected—in order to reduce this distance to escape—and a lower chargeable price as measured in per-square-foot costing. Such a minor, and common, mishap will ramify across repeated units, and the collective losses may wreak havoc upon the profitability of a development model that had assumed larger salable areas. The interpretation of such fire code measures is notoriously subjective, and the documentation of the regulations is both contradictory and open to interpretation. The dreaded Fire Safety and Shelter Department (FSSD) submission is thus always a breathless moment in the design process, as it is subject to what Max Weber called "khadi-justice" on the part of the FSSD officer reviewing the plans. Each of the nation's regulations—over fire safety, construction quality, traffic and environmental impact, and many others—is assigned to a different statutory organ, and these operate largely as their own fiefdoms. This is often seen with some incredulity by the uninitiated, who would expect that this sector would follow the larger nation in its heavily centralized organizational model. It most certainly does not.

7. Locations next to hospitals, police stations, or places of *sha qi* (intensified or traumatic energy) are well-known violations of good feng shui practice, a fact that would be obvious to most raised in the contemporary Taoist tradition.

8. Charlene Chin, "Unit at 8 Napier Incurs $969,000 Loss," EdgeProp, June 23, 2019, https://www.edgeprop.sg/property-news/unit-8-napier -incurs-969000-loss.

9. For example, 8 Nassim Hill, by the architect Chan Sau Yan, went on sale only a few months later. Nassim Hill Road, which sits directly behind Napier Road, has four similar completed projects.

10. Certainly there are cases of claims being dismissed—chiefly by Christian development executives or managers—as mumbo jumbo. This typically results in subterfuge, such as hidden shrines or rituals conducted in the wee hours of the morning. Even Christian senior managers at construction firms are typically sympathetic, as they see this as a major issue of worker morale. I do not know of a single case in which no propitiating action (overt or covert) was taken.

11. Interview conducted October 10, 2009.

12. I have witnessed this pattern repeatedly in my work as an architect in Singapore. The timing of incidents is only, in fact, truly random when accidents are involved—and even then, they are typically ascribed meaning by proximity to some near event (ground breaking, completion of a construction stage, Zhong Yuan arriving or just past, etc.). Allegations of

haunting without accident are very rarely reported during the "normal" course of works.

13. In this latter period, the architectural and interior works are substantially completed, and all parties wait anxiously for a temporary occupation permit (TOP), allowing occupants to move in. During this phase, the architect, clients, and purchasers will make periodic checks to identify defects in construction, which are rectified by the contractors. Defect rectification typically lasts from six months to a year, depending on the contract and extent of works.

14. In fact, Singapore law is very precise about when certain sums are due and when the purchaser can no longer exit the sale without substantial penalty. These dates are typically tied to "stages" of completion by the contractor, such as acquisition of permits and TOP.

15. "Upgrading" is a powerful concept in Singapore's political lexicon. It is commonly deployed to describe both physical and human capital; an HDB block or estate can be upgraded (through improvement of physical structures or amenities), but so may a worker or retiree. The term captures a key component of PAP ideology, which is the notion of the state and the self as undergoing a continual process of incremental improvement. Robbie Goh, "Ideologies of 'Upgrading' in Singapore Public Housing: Post-Modern Style, Globalisation, and Class Construction in the Built Environment," *Urban Studies* 38, no. 9 (2001): 1589–1604; Tiffany Ho, "The HDB's Upgrading Programme: Its Political and Social Implications," Department of Political Science, National University of Singapore, 1997.

16. The continuing appeal of such a populism is hardly unexpected in a community still rankled by the PAP's seizure of wealth and power from civil organizations of clan and dialect, remanding them to new elites. See chapter 4.

17. In this sense, it appears very much as a *wayang* (a local term meaning "shadow play" or political theater) of the PAP's strategy for producing wealth and national fabric.

18. However, a more recent challenge is fixing a date when most of the client's consultants' representatives can attend.

19. Such services are now predominantly online, for example, at https://www.yourchineseastrology.com/calendar/.

20. The name is part of the branding; Nassim Road remains Singapore's most high-end housing enclave.

21. Using exchange rates at time of writing, this sum is equivalent to US$7,852,000.

22. For example, this was reported in "Unfair Scare Tactics at Farrar Court," *New Paper on Sunday,* March 18, 2007, 6. This tactic has been rather

overused, and such rumors now are almost immediately met with counter-rumors alleging skulduggery.

23. This is the Hokkien translation. The term is *hong bao* in Mandarin, also meaning "red packet." A notable fact of mediumship is how much of its terminology remains in the nation's major dialects (Hokkien, Teo Chew, Cantonese) despite the general drift toward Mandarin as pushed by the PAP.

24. Resident engineer.

25. Interview conducted January 11, 2009.

26. Interview conducted February 20, 2009.

27. Or in the case of a government building, the "blessings team" of an IRO will be called in to maintain a kind of secular equivalence (see the previous chapter).

28. Master Goh claims to be very strict about certain Buddhist prohibitions. He believes, for example, that a monk should follow very strict codes of nonaggression, and when we met, he spoke disparagingly about "rioting monks" in Tibet prior to the Beijing Olympics. In other ways, however, he is very liberal—he smokes a great deal and also enjoys black coffee.

29. This is not straightforward, as most urban sites are not oriented to cardinal directions. This means that a north "corner" (for example) may not be a corner at all. Also, the vast majority of sites are geometrically irregular to some degree, so locating the center involves interpretation on the part of the medium.

30. Conceptions of *qi* hold that it moves both within and above the ground, and the connection from soil to air is extremely important to the health of a site. The center of the site, in the older "Form School" of feng shui, is identified as an aperture where the various energies, in various phases, converge.

31. When asked why this should be the case, Goh pointed out that "money wants to move." See the discussion of "stagnant" elements and landscape aesthetics, later.

32. These five phases *(wuxing)* are not literal substances but periods of instantiation through which *qi* passes. These are linked with a great array of phenomena, which they determine through complex interrelationships of influence, such as bolstering, tempering, and hindering.

33. In fact, traditional feng shui practitioners are quick to point out that their art is not "about" ghosts. Many concede, however, that the energies that they do work on affect ghosts as well as living beings and natural forces. There is, by contrast, a very large swath of contemporary geomantic practices that deal very specifically with *gui* and their potentials for wealth.

34. "Bungalow" or "good class bungalow" refers to a single-family, freestanding residential building with a land area of a given, minimum size.

It does not refer specifically to a single-level dwelling, as in other contexts. The "GCB" connotes a large house. These are rare in Singapore and are extremely expensive.

35. Whether or not special ceremonies are held on a particular job, nearly all will conduct some sort of propitiation during Zhong Yuan. These have somewhat different formats, and Choo's contained elements of both.

36. *Ngoh hiang* is a Southeast Asian Hokkien and Teo Chew spring roll of fried bean curd filled with pork and water chestnut and (depending on provenance) onions and yam. Its appearance and consistency are perhaps more like sausage than like the fried spring rolls familiar in the West.

37. Poison arrow *qi* is a mode of intensified *sha qi* (negatively agitating energy) radiating from sharp points and acute angles oriented toward a person or place.

38. The architect was standing nearby.

39. For more on the division of labor among the gods, see Fabian Graham, *Voices from the Underworld: Chinese Hell Deity Worship in Contemporary Singapore and Malaysia* (Manchester University Press, 2020).

40. Meaning "shrine."

41. This translates to a 38.7 percent chance that the work will conclude. However, if the toss fails, the representative will simply redo it. This means that there is, in fact, an absolute certainty that the deity will deem the works concluded.

42. Anxieties at this stage are further fueled by the government's 2011 Qualifying Certificate scheme, which added key additional stipulations to the Residential Property Act. In this case, developers may be subject to heavy financial penalties for any units that remain unsold two years after TOP is granted (meaning that buyers can move in). This hit developers with foreign ownership in particular, and thus by nature any publicly listed company. At the time of writing, developers are given a typical period of five years to design and build a project to TOP and a further two to clear the units, to prevent land banking by private concerns.

43. It is worth briefly noting that there exist parallel Christian practices of site blessings. These are employed by developers with a more evangelical bent, such as the Lippo Group, which substitutes prayer meetings for offering ceremonies, and their message focuses on glorifying Christ. Despite the shift in faith, these are also very much concerned with "locating" sites, their longer histories, into a narrative about renewal; predictably, the metaphor here shifts to rebirth and conversion. As the faithful have been born again, so might the site and its finances.

44. This evocative phrase is borrowed from Nancy Munn's analysis of urban demolition and the construction of Central Park in nineteenth-century Manhattan. Munn, "The Becoming-Past of Places: Spacetime and

Memory in Mid-19th Century New York," manuscript chapter, provided by the author.

45. Hilda, Chinese and in her late fifties, works for a leading multinational hotel chain. Interview conducted December 10, 2009.

46. Max Gluckman, "Ethnographic Data in British Anthropology," in *The Manchester School: Praxis and Ethnographic Practice in Social Anthropology,* ed. T. M. S. Evens and Don Handelman (Berghahn Books, 2006).

47. See, e.g., Laura Antona, "Geographies of Bodily (Dis)possession: Domestic Work, Unfreedom, and Spirit Possessions in Singapore," *Annals of the Association of American Geographers* 114, no. 5 (2023): 943–57. It is beyond the scope of the present work to explore the relationships between ghosts and migrants or "guest" laborers. Antona has undertaken an insightful ethnography of this in the case of spirit possession among Singapore's foreign domestic workers in their dormitories, and this has likewise been a matter of some pop-cultural exploration in horror films like Kelvin Tong's *The Maid* (2005). As mentioned earlier, the word *gui* is used as an epithet for non-Chinese and for foreigners, as *gwai lo* is in Hong Kong, and the migrant (especially in their nonlinear peregrinations) is often associated with ghostlike behaviors and terrors. For a discussion of Tong's film, see Sophia Siddique Harvey, "Mapping Spectral Tropicality in *The Maid* and *Return to Pontianak*," *Tropical Geography* 29, no. 1 (2008): 24–33.

48. At one project site where I conducted extensive observation throughout the course of 2010, a well-intended foreman tried to convince a reluctant Muslim worker to join a ceremony by comparing ghosts to jinn. The worker, of course, understood the ghost perfectly well—and, in fact, was a big fan of videos in the horror genre. There is a constant work of intercultural and interreligious accommodation in this area that is not without its ironies.

49. Of course, nonspeculative buildings (especially government ones, as in the CID and early HDB examples) are also haunted during construction. Overwhelmingly, these are said to experience incidents during the demolition of existing structures. Here the narrative seems to be rather unequivocally about the destruction of existing environments and about transformative violence.

50. Certainly Singapore grows and fells trees, but it no longer has the large-scale productive capacity to turn these into wood. At the same time, the lack of a forestry industry means that such timber is in inadequate supply to satisfy the building trades' (admittedly limited) appetite for solid wood.

51. Here they have much in common with urban homeowners worldwide.

CONCLUSION

1. The comments in the chapter's epigraph were delivered at a tea party on Gurgadhi Day, in the People's Association at Kallang, October 31, 1965. https://www.nas.gov.sg/archivesonline/data/pdfdoc/lky19651031.pdf. I am indebted to Singaporean artist Ila Ila, who brought this quote to my attention in the context of her own writing on nature in the *Portside Review*: https://www.portsidereview.com/5y2b-ila-ila#_ftn1.

2. I use the term *utopian* loosely here—and not in any formal, ideological, or political sense. While Chinese religion does not articulate any sense of civic collective, it is nonetheless holistic and social in nature. Persons are subject to complex relations of reciprocity and risk, both with each other and with the broader spatial-ecological environment.

3. See Friedrich Nietzsche, *Human, All Too Human: A Book for Free Spirits* (Cambridge University Press, 1996), introduction.

4. Of course, it can be objected that Singaporean discourses of the ghost still posit a being dependent on living humans and thus on "society" in some sense. Although this is true to a degree, it is an essential aspect of *gui* that they have already slipped beyond that order through neglect or tragic event. They are thus anonymous figures, dependent on collective charity and not on specific care by their descendants. This anonymity is the source of their power and what distinguishes them from ancestors, deities, and other spiritual beings.

5. See, e.g., Anna Tsing, Heather Swanson, Elaine Gan, and Nils Bubandt, *Arts of Living on a Damaged Planet: Ghosts and Monsters of the Anthropocene.* (University of Minnesota Press, 2017), or David Wallace-Wells, *The Uninhabitable Earth: A Story of the Future* (Allen Lane, 2019).

6. See Mbembe, *Necropolitics*; also see John Gray, *Black Mass: Apocalyptic Religion and the Death of Utopia* (Farrar, Straus, and Giroux, 2008).

7. Derrida, *Specters of Marx,* 111.

8. This is the central theme of the essays in Fisher, *Ghosts of My Life.*

9. This view is neither ahistorical nor reactionary, though it tends to stress repetition and other universal principles. There is certainly enough of the Buddhist influence to value the present, and we can see that much of the expectation for radically improved life—for prosperity, health, and luck—is immanent.

10. This is not exclusive to Chinese religion and is evident in the liturgical transformations of Singapore's megachurches, for example, which have progressively deemphasized discourses of heaven in favor of discourses of this-worldly happiness and prosperity that, as local priest Father JP points out, are nothing more than those of Taoism cloaked in Christian raiment. In

interviews with megachurch youth groups, excited expectation was directed less toward the afterlife and more at the imminent context of contemporary Asia. Singapore was repeatedly described as the "new Antioch"—that is, as a stage from which China (and, eventually, Islamic neighbors) might be evangelized. While the Messianic endgame was not in any way disavowed, it was largely deemphasized in favor of discourses of a victorious Christian contemporary (a kind of heaven on earth).

11. In this sense, it resembles a spiritually turbocharged form of bourgeois-populist ideology, as embodied by Dale Carnegie and other advocates. In a similar manner, and in direct contrast to left-wing critique, capitalist economy is not imagined as "zero sum."

12. This principle is outlined in the following post on the Feng Shui Nexus website: https://fengshuinexus.com/feng-shui-rules/feng-shui-rules-related-to-supernatural/.

13. Differences of method and emphasis among these approaches are well summarized in Anna Tsing, "A Multispecies Ontological Turn?," in *The World Multiple: The Quotidian Politics of Knowing and Generating Entangled Worlds,* ed. Keiichi Omura et al. (Routledge, 2018).

14. Marcuse argues that the forms of gratification repressed by social and economic reality operate as ghosts. See Herbert Marcuse, *Eros and Civilization* (Routledge, 2024), 14.

Index

Joshua Comaroff is an architectural designer, urban geographer, and assistant professor in the Department of Architecture at National University of Singapore. He is coauthor of *Horror in Architecture: The Reanimated Edition* (Minnesota, 2024).